T0321220

Dynamically Enabled
Cyber
Defense

Dynamically Enabled
Cyber Defense

Lin Yang

Quan Yu

World Scientific

NEW JERSEY · LONDON · SINGAPORE · BEIJING · SHANGHAI · HONG KONG · TAIPEI · CHENNAI · TOKYO

Published by

World Scientific Publishing Co. Pte. Ltd.
5 Toh Tuck Link, Singapore 596224
USA office: 27 Warren Street, Suite 401-402, Hackensack, NJ 07601
UK office: 57 Shelton Street, Covent Garden, London WC2H 9HE

Library of Congress Cataloging-in-Publication Data
Names: Yang, Lin (Writer on computer security), author. | Yu, Quan (Engineer), author.
Title: Dynamically enabled cyber defense / Lin Yang, Sun Yat-sen University, China,
    Quan Yu, Peng Cheng Laboratory, China.
Description: Singapore ; Hackensack, NJ ; London : World Scientific, [2021] |
    Includes bibliographical references and index.
Identifiers: LCCN 2021003540 | ISBN 9789811234330 (hardcover) |
    ISBN 9789811234347 (ebook for institutions) | ISBN 9789811234354 (ebook for individuals)
Subjects: LCSH: Computer security. | Internet of things--Security measures. |
    Electronic apparatus and appliances--Security measures.
Classification: LCC QA76.9.A25 Y3635 2021 | DDC 005.8--dc23
LC record available at https://lccn.loc.gov/2021003540

British Library Cataloguing-in-Publication Data
A catalogue record for this book is available from the British Library.

动态赋能网络空间防御
Originally published in Chinese by Posts & Telecom Press
Copyright © Posts & Telecom Press 2016

Copyright © 2021 by World Scientific Publishing Co. Pte. Ltd.

For any available supplementary material, please visit
https://www.worldscientific.com/worldscibooks/10.1142/12210#t=suppl

Desk Editors: Aanand Jayaraman/Amanda Yun

Typeset by Stallion Press
Email: enquiries@stallionpress.com

Printed in Singapore

Preface

The Internet is one of the greatest technical inventions of mankind in the 20th century. Since its birth, after half a century of development, the Internet has become an important infrastructure driving global economic and social development and profoundly changed people's production and life styles. However, benefits and risks always coexist. Cyber attacks accompany the process of informatization like nightmares and cannot be got rid of. Cyber security has become a global problem that affects the development of human society.

Vulnerabilities are prerequisites for cyber attacks and defenses. They are the root cause of cyber insecurity, and the strategic resources that both attackers and defenders scramble for. Information systems are designed and implemented by people. Due to people's inherent inertia and cognitive limitations, vulnerabilities cannot be avoided. As the complexity of the system increases, the vulnerability problem will become more severe. In cyber attacks and defenses activities, attackers find and exploit vulnerabilities, while defenders find and mitigate vulnerabilities to reduce the chance of being exploited. However, in the face of vulnerabilities, both sides are asymmetric. Using an undisclosed vulnerability, attackers may drive straight into the attack target. While no matter how many vulnerabilities defenders already have, they still dare not rest easy. The longer attackers have known and analyzed the system, the more vulnerabilities they will find, and the system will become more dangerous. Therefore, there is a serious asymmetry between attackers and defenders, i.e. a big defense against a small attack, and an overall defense against point attack.

Advanced Persistent Threat (APT) is a major threat to cyber security. Advanced means high-level, up-to-date, and heavily invested, emphasizing the organizational and national behaviors with background. Persistent means long-lasting, so it is the most terrible. Opponents have been persistently watching, studying, and analyzing us for a long time. Attackers may know more about the protected system than we do. They discover problems and develop weapons against us continuously. Have we ever studied our own system like the attackers, and continuously paid attention to the security vulnerabilities of the protected system? We are continuously developing informatization, launching new projects, and building new systems, but we have not continuously paid attention to the security of these information systems. Opponents continue to discover problems, while we continue to accumulate problems.

From the perspective of security, there are still many problems in the construction of information systems. Many systems are still solving the problem of functions availability, and have no time to consider the security vulnerabilities of the system itself, let alone the supervision and inspection of security vulnerabilities. We have no awareness and energy to focus on the vulnerabilities and security, let alone continuous security concerns. In the process of information system construction, we are used to equate security system construction with general system construction, and consider security system construction as the static stacking of security products. "Connectivity is good" is often a sign of security readiness. There is a process of state solidification in the opening of the information system. Once the state is solidified, the capabilities are solidified accordingly. The information system emphasizes "three inters" — internetworking, interconnection, interoperability — which require the unification of technologies and systems. In engineering practice, we often replace the intangible systems with the tangible products, and unify the systems with the same products. The capabilities become unitary once such systems are unified. The staticity, similarity, and certainty of information system architectures, as well as the homology, isomorphism, and homogeneity of information products, provide great convenience for attackers to spy on network characteristics, discover system vulnerabilities, and implement attack penetration, resulting in information systems always in a passive situation. Once a single attack method takes effect locally, it can often spread quickly, causing a large-scale impact on the entire network.

Traditional protection methods based on prior knowledge and accurate identification are difficult to deal with unknown vulnerabilities and threats. For the information systems built on static, similarity, and certainty, it is difficult to deal with dynamic, professional, and continuous high-intensity attacks. Vulnerabilities are the root cause of security problems, but mining and fixing vulnerabilities cannot solve security problems completely. In terms of vulnerability attack and defense, the rules of the game are inherently not equal. No matter how many vulnerabilities defenders discover and mitigate, it can not stop an unknown vulnerability attack from the attackers. If defenders want to break away from this passive situation, they must change the unequal game rules, from defenders following attackers to attackers following defenders. Dynamic cyber defense is a good way to build the asymmetric defense systems that are easy to defend and difficult to attack.

In the military field, the idea of dynamic defense has a long history. *Master Sun's Art of War* says: "War is a kaleidoscopic and unexpected art that uses ever-changing and surprising ways to fight the enemies." Moving target defense technology applies the idea of "change" to cyber defense. Its innovation lies in the unusual change from positional defense to mobile or guerrilla warfare. In deployment and running of the information system, we can build a continuously changing, dissimilar, and uncertain information system by effectively reducing its certainty, similarity, and static, and increasing its randomness and unpredictability. This makes the information system present an unpredictable state of change, and it is difficult for attackers to have enough time to find or use the security vulnerabilities of the information system, let alone allow them to continue to detect and repeatedly attack, thus greatly increasing the difficulty and cost of attack. Obviously, this is a big shift in defense strategy and a big shift in the rules of the game, changing the asymmetric situation that the network easy to attack and difficult to defend.

Based on the dynamic target defense, this book puts forward the concept of dynamic enabled cyber space defense, applying the idea of "change" to all aspects of cyberspace, and subverting traditional protection with the systematic dynamic defense idea. The dynamic security concept is fully implemented throughout the entire life cycle of the information system, which requires that the information system not only completes its own functions during the development, deployment, running phrases, but also changes its security-related feature attributes at all levels such as the hardware platforms, software services, information data, and network communication, etc. This change involves two dimensions of time and space. It may be an attribute change alone or multiple attributes change at the same time. With these changes, the endogenous security of the information system can be enhanced. In addition, the defense system guided by this dynamic enablement idea not only implements protection in the foreground, but also intensively schedules the professional resources and forces gathered in the background to output new security capabilities dynamically to the foreground in a continuous manner, thereby providing the new vitality of global enablement. From the perspective of the system, dynamic enablement transforms the statically defensive "dead" equipment into the dynamically enabled "live" system, forming a dynamic and active cyber defense system with front-end protection and back-end enablement.

Dynamically Enabled Cyber Defense is an exploration of cyber security defense technology and systems, and an assumption that security capability is regarded as a standard attribute of information system itself. The future cyber defense must be a security system guided by the idea of dynamic enablement. Therefore, this book mainly focuses on various system dynamization and randomization technologies and methods, their relationship and compatibility with existing protection methods, their contribution and evolution, as well as challenges and problems they brought to the next generation of protection products and even information products.

At present, the theoretical research on dynamic defense has made some progress, and the development of some key technologies has also made the engineering application of dynamic defense possible. Because the research on dynamically enabled defense involves wide-ranging fields and has a great many challenges, the current research results are relatively fragmentary and not systematic. In an attempt to facilitate readers to understand the technologies involved in dynamically enabled defense more systematically, this book summarizes the current basic development status of the dynamic defense technology. Based on the physical hierarchy of the information system, the book studies the dynamic defense technology from system platforms, software services, information data, and network communication, respectively. It explores the possible evolution route of the dynamic defense technology, ascertains its relationship with existing security technologies, analyzes and discusses security gains and the overall system efficiency of these technologies. The book is designed to present readers with the relevant ideas, technologies, and achievements of dynamically enabled cyber defense, implement the advanced ideas, technologies, and methods, provide support for capability-oriented cyber security, and provide a reference for the future information system structure design and software/hardware product development with endogenous security capabilities.

It is hoped that the publication of this book will help the researchers in the field of cyberspace security accurately grasp the technical development direction of cyberspace security and provide ideas for the development of next-generation IT infrastructure. It is also helpful to promote the construction of the future active defense system in cyberspace, so that security is no longer an obstacle to the development of information systems, instead one of its endogenous capacities.

Given the wide scope, technical difficulty and immaturity of dynamically enabled cyber defense, there may be gaps in the book, despite our best efforts. Your suggestions would be appreciated.

Lin Yang
Quan Yu

About the Authors

Lin Yang received his Ph.D. degree from National University of Defense Technology, China, in 1998. He is currently a research fellow and Ph.D. supervisor at Network Information Institute, Beijing, China. His main research interests include information system and cyber security. He is a national candidate for the Millions of Talents Project, a winner of the Qiu Shi Youth Award of China Association for Science and Technology and the National Young and Middle-aged Expert with Outstanding Contributions award.

Quan Yu received his B.S. degree in radio physics from Nanjing University, China, in 1986; his M.S. degree in radio wave propagation from Xidian University, China, in 1988; and his Ph.D. degree in fiber optics from the University of Limoges, France, in 1992. He is currently a research professor at Peng Cheng Laboratory, China. His main research interests include network architecture and cognitive radio. He is an academician of the Chinese Academy of Engineering and the founding Editor-in-Chief of the *Journal of Communications and Information Networks*.

Contents

Chapter 1

Introduction

1.1 Development and Crisis of Information Age

Since its advent, Internet technology had been first used in military, education and scientific research departments, and then rapidly penetrated into various fields such as politics, economy, society and culture. The Internet has brought people from the industrial age to the information age, and its development speed has been beyond people's expectations. In just a few decades, the Internet has completely changed aspects of human society and ways of our life and production.

1.1.1 *Rapid Development of Informatization*

At present, general development trend of information technology is focusing on development and application of Internet technology, from a typical technology-driven development mode to a combination of technology-driven and application-driven modes. On the one hand, domestic appliances and personal mobile terminals are developing into network terminal equipments, which has lead to diversification and personalization of network terminal equipments, and gradually changed the situation that computer network dominated the world more than ever before. On the other hand, technologies such as e-government, tele-education, and e-commerce are becoming more and more mature, and the Internet has increasing impact on personal lifestyle, from personalized applications based on information acquisition and communication & entertainment needs, even to people's livelihood services that are deeply integrated with public services such as medical care, education, and transportation. Meanwhile, with the launch of the "Internet Plus" initiative plan, the Internet will drive changes and innovations in traditional industries. In the future, driven by application of the technologies such as Internet of Things, cloud computing, and big data, the Internet will accelerate transformation and upgrading of agriculture, modern manufacturing, and production service industries, forming a new economic development mode with the Internet as its infrastructure and implementation tool.

China today has become a major network power. Just taking the Internet as an example, since it was officially introduced into China in 1994, it has developed rapidly in just over 20 years. Its penetration rate has exceeded the global average level, and it has become an important social infrastructure in China. According to the statistics from China Internet Network Information Center (CNNIC), as of June 2015, the number of Chinese Internet users had reached 668 million, and the number of mobile Internet users had reached 594 million. The total number of domain names in China was 22.31 million, of which the number of CN domain names was 12.25 million and the number of websites was 3.37 million. Statistics showed that people took very active part in various network applications, and the average online time of Internet users was 25.6 hours per week and 3.7 hours per day. The number of search engine users had reached 536 million, the number of Netnews users had reached 555 million, and the number of online shopping users had reached 374 million, of which the number of group-buying users was up to 176 million, online payment users up to 359 million, users who used the Internet to book air tickets, train tickets, hotel or travel and resort products were up to 229 million, Internet wealth management users up to 78.49 million, instant messenger users up to 606 million, and microblog users up to 204 million.

With the rapid development of the mobile Internet, the scale of mobile Internet users continues to grow, and the Internet devices are gradually concentrated on mobile phones. With large screen of the mobile terminal and continuous improvement of mobile phone application experience, the trend of mobile phone as the main Internet terminal of netizens is further obvious. Mobile commerce applications are developing rapidly, which boosts consumption-driven economy development. With development of mobile Internet technology and the popularity of smart phones, consumption behavior of netizens has gradually migrated and penetrated to mobile terminals. With the rapid growth of mobile Internet users, mobile commerce applications have become a new engine driving the growth of network economy because of the instant and convenient characteristics of mobile terminals that better fit the business consumption needs of Internet users.

Concept of the Internet of Things is becoming a key foundation and engine for green, smart, and sustainable development of the economy and society. Application of the Internet of Things is still in the early phase of development. It will be gradually applied into some fields extensively, for example, it is beginning to emerge in public market. Machine to Machine (M2M) communication, Internet of vehicles, and smart grid have become the key application fields that have developed rapidly around the world in the past two years. M2M application takes the lead in shaping a complete industrial chain and internal driving force. The Internet of vehicles is one of the application fields with the greatest market prospects, and the application of the global smart grid has gradually entered into its peak period of development. In the near future, we will also move from today's Internet of Things (IOT) era to the Internet of Everything (IoE) era, where everything will gain contextual awareness, enhanced processing capabilities, and better sensing ability, so creating endless possibilities.

1.1.2 *Fantastic Experience of Informatization*

Development of information technology constantly brings all kinds of surprises to us. In today's information age, numerous novel information products, like blossoming bud, give an infinite sense of beauty to people, and bring new and excellent experiences to every aspect of personal life and work. They are convenient, instant, diverse, or fashionable.

Online shopping allows you to buy satisfactory goods without leaving home. Is there anything you cannot buy online? I'm afraid there are very few things. Now, when you move to a new house, only through the computer or mobile phone, you can go into a home page of a home appliances e-commerce platform, search for required favorite appliances, place an order, then wait for the goods to be delivered to your home. E-commerce vendors will send technical staff to your house to install and debug. In contrast, a few years ago, you might have had to take wads of cash to a distant appliance mall, go from one shop to another to compare performance and price of various appliances, select them, and get a van to take them home.

WeChat makes communication zero distance. Somehow, one day you no longer communicate with your relatives and friends via QQ. You become used to WeChat to send messages, share something on your moments, and view your friends' shared messages at any time. Suddenly one day, a chat group with many familiar names may pop up on your WeChat. It is your university classmates who have not contacted for many years after graduation. They are scattered all over the country or abroad, but at the moment when the group is established, the distance between you becomes a distance of a few clicks on the phone screen. One day when you go back home from work, you find your elderly mother has also learned to play with WeChat. She holds a tablet and excitedly video chats with her distant relatives. Over the next few days, she resumes to contact all the relatives and friends she hadn't heard from for a long time.

Car-hailing apps make it easier for you to go out. Living in a metropolitan city like Beijing, you cannot buy a car without a plate that has been got through license-plate lottery, and it's not easy for you to take a taxi, so Didi Dache and Kuaidi Dache appear. They can quickly inform hundreds of taxi drivers around you, and soon a driver will contact you. A minute later, a taxi comes up to you.

Internet finance facilitates wealth management and entrepreneurship. In the past two years, Alibaba, Baidu, Tencent, and other Internet companies have launched financial services and products, making inroads into traditional financial fields such as payment, lending, foreign exchange, and wealth management. Some signs suggest that the Internet is accelerating its entry into financial fields. In fact, Internet finance is penetrating into traditional financial business fields such as transfer and remittance, cross-border settlement, micro-credit, cash management, asset management, and supply chain finance from a pure payment business. Consider micro-credit as an example, statistics show that the total volume of China's e-commerce small loan has reached 230 billion yuan in 2014. It can be expected that in the future, more loan businesses involved with small and micro firms will be completed on e-commerce platforms such as Alibaba for small loans.

Today, a little bracelet brings you a healthy lifestyle. It can record your sleep, exercise, and other data so that you can keep track of your physical condition. It has become a little health secretary. You can set goals for yourself. For example, if you want to walk 8,000 steps a day, you can set reminders to ensure that you reach your goal every day. The bracelet can do professional statistics, telling you how many kilometers you have walked and how many kilocalories you have burned during which time period, estimating that the energy consumed is equivalent to that of a bottle of coke or a fried egg. It's a good news for dieters. The bracelet compares your exercise data with that of other users from the cloud and tells that your step counts exceed by what percentage of other users. The bracelet also tells you how many hours you slept and how many hours you slept deeply last night, allowing you to evaluate your sleep quality.

You may be upset by not getting a train ticket for traveling, but you do not want to wait in front of the computer for a long time for the ticket to refund, so ticket-snatching software appears. You only need to enter the number of train you want, and it will help you snatch the ticket.

When your children reach school age, and you feel anxious that they will walk away from your sight, an online children's watch appears. With the location function, you can always know where he is, and he can call you if he needs to.

There are many other surprises like these. The examples mentioned above may be just the beginning. Greater marvels await in the future.

1.1.3 *Crisis Caused by Informatization*

The Internet is both a "window of opportunity", bringing people a lot of conveniences and benefits, but also a "window of vulnerability", which has huge hidden risks. The more strongly the society depends on the Internet, the more important network information security becomes, and the more serious the threat from cyber attacks becomes. With Internet penetrating into various fields of society, communication networks, power grids, financial industries, transportation systems in most countries are combined into an enormous network, which brings huge security risks to many countries. The network has no boundaries, but for a sovereign state, it is a huge challenge for protecting critical national infrastructure and civil networks involving national economy and people's livelihood. Almost all countries around the world agree that the current cyberspace is very fragile and vulnerable, and cyber security makes us really concerned.

Rapid development of informatization will inevitably pose security threats to the Internet. There are many vulnerability risks in China's basic network, and cloud services have become an increasingly important target for cyber attacks. The domain name system is faced with severe denial of service attacks. Important websites are frequently attacked by DNS tampering attacks. Network attack threats are increasingly penetrating into the industrial Internet field. Some of China's network addresses are infected with malicious program viruses specifically aimed at industrial control systems. Distributed reflective denial of service attacks are getting more rampant. A large number of counterfeit attack data packets come from foreign networks. Attacks and exploits against important information systems, basic applications, and common software/hardware vulnerabilities are thriving, and vulnerability risks are evolving toward the traditional industry field and intelligent terminal field. Website data and personal information leakage is still serious, and mobile applications have become the new subject of data leakage. Mobile malwares continue to evolve and thrive, and network environmental governance still faces challenges.

Construction of various new facilities, application of new technologies, and emergence of new products have made it impossible for people to ignore dark clouds hanging over their heads while enjoying conveniences and benefits from them. If no effective measures are taken, all kinds of unpredictable consequences will occur.

(1) Industrial control system threat: Putting the country at risk

Industrial control system has been commonly used in almost all industrial fields and critical infrastructures, involving a wide range of aspects. Therefore, security problems of industrial control systems pose a great threat to normal operation of national economy and national security. Stuxnet virus [1], which appeared in 2010, was targeted at SIMATIC WinCC system of Siemens, which is a Supervisory Control And Data Acquisition (SCADA) system running on Windows platform and is widely used in industrial systems such as steel, automobile, electric power, transportation, water utility, chemical industry, and petroleum, etc. Stuxnet is able to control physical system parameters and use PLC Rootkit to modify control system parameters and hide PLC alterations, thus causing physical damage to real physical equipment and systems. Iranian government later confirmed that its first nuclear plant, Bushehr, had been attacked by the Stuxnet virus, which disabled a fifth of its centrifuges.

(2) Cloud computing platform: Data security concerns

In-depth development of cloud platform technology and refactoring of service model make services ubiquitous. Cloud platform service is a mixed service model, which may incur both traditional and new cyber threats. Cloud platforms differ from traditional system platforms in their deployment patterns and are more vulnerable to threats. For example, in 2011, Sony's PlayStation network and Sony online entertainment suffered a series of attacks, causing online game cloud platform crash, and making user account data security threatened [2].

(3) Mobile intelligent terminals: Know their danger but addicted to them

Nowadays, mobile intelligent terminals have infiltrated into almost every user's daily life. These devices can not only connect to the Internet through base stations or wireless networks, but also make phone calls, send short messages and MMS, take photos, take recording, navigation, orientation, Bluetooth transmission and Near Field Communication (NFC). A rich set of functions not only improve terminal applicability, but also bring more forms of loopholes. Taking text messaging as an example, in 2012, French hacker pod2g discovered a text spoofing vulnerability [3] in all versions of Apple's smartphone (iPhone). Anyone can send a text message to any iPhone user with a fake number, and direct victim's reply to the forged number. In July 2015, Israel Zimperium mobile security company researcher Joshua Drake discovered serious security vulnerabilities in an Android core component named Stagefright Framework, allowing hackers to execute remote malicious programs. Once a user received and opened up an MMS, downloaded a specific video file, or opened a Web page embedded with multimedia content via a browser, hackers could hack into the mobile phone. The vulnerability is arguably the most dangerous on Android, affecting 95 percent of Android users.

The mobile intelligent terminal represented by smart phone carries a lot of high-value user information. Therefore, rapid increase in the number of users has attracted attention of many manufacturers, including developers of malicious programs. There emerged many programs that attempted to collect user information, especially their private information.

(4) Smart bracelet: User's bracelet has been controlled even before it is unpacked

As a new high-tech wearable smart device, popularity rate of smart bracelet is quite high. At present, there are many diversified bracelet brands on the market from which users can freely choose, as shown in Figure 1.1. The bracelet generally records user's information in detail. Many users wear their smart products as soon as they go out, allowing hackers to easily find out where they live, what they do and even their favorite restaurants. There was a presentation [4] in CCTV program, in which a software enforced to make a pair with a new bracelet unopened in the box and let it perform actions. A technical staff with smart bracelet moved around in one room, while another staff hacked into the bracelet in another room, as shown in Figure 1.2. The computer screen showed that every movement of the

Figure 1.1.   Diverse Smart Bracelet Products

wearer could be monitored in real time and displayed in the form of dot jittering. Wearer's movement behavior could even be identified based on the extent of dot jittering.

Wei Lin, an Internet security expert, explained: "When you withdraw money from an ATM, the attacker can analyze and restore the password you have entered according to movement of the bracelet, or even completely record your daily routine, including when you sleep more soundly, at which time a burglar can sneak into your home, when you are totally unprepared."

(5) Quick Pass card: Personal privacy is completely disclosed with one swipe

Quick Pass is a contactless payment product application developed by Unionpay, which can provide quick small amount payment. Users choose and buy goods or services, confirm the corresponding amount, and pay it by the bank card with the quick pass function. On the contactless payment terminal with Unionpay quick pass, payment can be completed quickly with a simple wave. In addition to bank cards, some mobile terminals, such as smart phones, also support quick pass. Quick pass mobile products authenticated by Unionpay include some models of Samsung, HTC and other mobile phone brands. Quick pass uses NFC technology, a short-range high frequency wireless communication technology, which can be used to identify electronic identities or transmit data within a distance of 10 cm. In attack presentation [4] broadcasted in the CCTV program, a

Figure 1.2. Monitor User Through Smart Bracelet

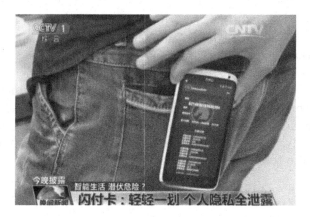

Figure 1.3.   Quick Pass Card Reveals Personal Information

technical staff put a bank card with the quick pass function into his wallet which was enclosed in his pocket. With a swipe of a smartphone next to his pocket, another technical staff could immediately reads a number of personal information, including bank card number, card usage information, cardholder's name and ID number, and recent transaction records, as shown in Figure 1.3. Insufficient security protection of the quick pass card will lead to a large amount of user privacy leakage.

Now please take out your wallet and see if there is a quick pass logo on the right side of your bank card. If so, you should be careful.

(6) Tesla: More fans doesn't mean safety

Intelligent transportation system is the development direction of transportation in the future, bringing more efficient and fast experience. As an important part of intelligent transportation, an intelligent vehicle is a comprehensive system that integrates environmental perception, planning and decision-making, multi-level driving assistance and other functions. Tesla, an electric car, is known as the "Apple" of the automotive industry, as shown in Figure 1.4. Many bigwigs of IT technology companies are Tesla's followers, such as Google CEO Larry Page. In July 2014, 360 company claimed there was a design flaw in the Tesla app that could allow an attacker to remotely control the vehicle, such as unlocking the lock, honking the horn, flashing the lights and opening the skylight while the vehicle is

Figure 1.4.   Electric Car Tesla

Figure 1.5.   Security Experts Showed How to Crack a Tesla Car

running. In response to vulnerabilities pointed out by 360 company, Tesla said it was willing to cooperate with security researchers to deal with and fix vulnerabilities. In August 2015, at the 23rd DEF-CON Digital Security Conference as shown in Figure 1.5, security experts Kevin Mahaffey and Marc Rogers showed how to exploit vulnerabilities of Model S to open the door, start, and drive the car away. In addition, they could also send "suicide" order to Model S which suddenly closed system engine to stop the car during normal driving.

(7) Medical devices: They can also claim your life

At present, many medical systems use Internet of Things devices to control the connection between the doctor's computer and the treatment equipment carried by the patient. Once this connection is exploited by attackers, it is easy to cause huge damage to patient's body. In December 2011, security researcher of McAfee company Barnaby Jack announced vulnerability [5] in the insulin pump at the Black Hat conference in Dubai. The insulin pump, a device implanted into the diabetic patient, is used to inject insulin into the patient at regular intervals. The device uses a wireless network to communicate. The vulnerability allows an attacker to manipulate injection dosage of the insulin pump, which causes a patient to fall into a coma if given a large dosage in a single injection. In 2012, Barnaby Jack announced that he would make cardiac pacemakers produced by several manufacturers stop working, and only a laptop more than ten meters away he could make it emit 830 V voltage, enough to kill people.

(8) Smart home: Property security is delivered to the unknown world

Smart home systems generally support remote control of home operation through mobile smart terminals, such as smart phones and tablets. Therefore, security risks of mobile terminals may cause a chain reaction, leading serious consequences. Figure 1.6 is a diagram of a smart home, in which home network is the most likely to be attacked and harmed seriously. At present, most smart home systems adopt Wi-Fi wireless communication technology. Therefore, Wi-Fi signals will be exposed to the public environment. The attacker can gain control of the whole smart home by attacking the wireless route, and then operate and manipulate all kinds of smart home appliances in the system and threaten safety of users' property. At the 2013 Black Hat conference, two researchers demonstrated an example [6] of controlling various home network connection devices remotely, further controlling various household devices.

Today, we have been attracted and surrounded by a variety of new information products. We have felt their infinite glamour, and our lives is indeed better because of these information products. People and various devices are connected into a vast network. We are bathed in this huge network which runs on the track of the Internet of everything like a high-speed train. National infrastructures,

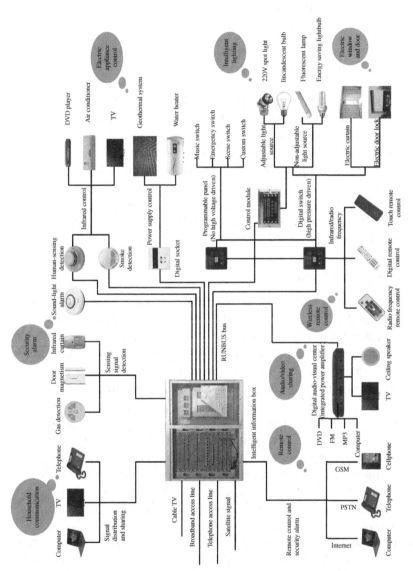

Figure 1.6.   Diagram of A Smart Home

data and business of enterprises, and all kinds of personal valuable information are bundled with the network. Perhaps you do not realize that countries, businesses, and individuals have already been at great risk, you just do not know when, where, or how risk will turn into reality, or you still may not perceive it when it becomes a reality.

1.2   Omnipotent Cyber Attacks

Informatization process is accompanied by cyber attacks, like nightmares we cannot get rid of. Targets of attacks are seen everywhere, any terminal connected to the network may become a target. The perpetrator behind a cyber attack could be an individual, an organization, or a sovereign state. A cyber attack may take the form of a joke, a cyber crime, or a cyber war. A joke may be innocuous, but a cyber crime may result in loss of life and property of the victim, while a cyber war could lead to more tragic consequences though without smoke of gunpowder.

1.2.1   *Cyber Crime*

Cyber attacks are usually initiated by hackers. As we know, a coin has two sides, and there are also good and bad hackers. In IT industry, hackers are usually distinguished by the color of their hats. White hats are those who are proficient in security technology but do anti-hacking work and protect users' security. Black hats, on the contrary, are groups that use hacking technologies to cause damage or even commit cyber crimes.

Cyber crime refers to perpetrators using computer technology to attack, destroy, or commit crimes on other systems or information through the network. Network fraud crime is another form of network crime, which emphasizes application of social network knowledge rather than that of pure technology. There is a difference between network fraud crime and technology crime. This book focuses on the use of technology to commit cyber crimes.

With arrival of era of big data, big network, and intelligent manufacturing, a large number of security vulnerabilities may be put into various information systems and information products in the process of research, development, and operation. Some people study a large number of penetration testing and exploitation techniques to exploit

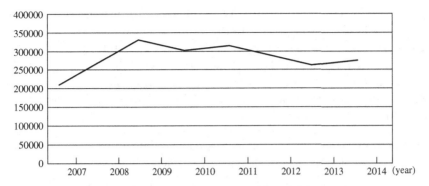

Figure 1.7. Number of Reported Cyber Crime Cases

these vulnerabilities every day, while others use these technologies to achieve various ulterior motives.

Although the network monitoring measures are becoming more and more complete, and the cyber security legislation is also being constantly evolved and refined, statistics show that the number of cyber crimes has not been effectively controlled. Figure 1.7 is a statistical chart from U.S. Department of Homeland Security and Internet Crime Complaint Center (IC3), which shows that the total number of cases registered by various channels still stays at a high level.

Although the security researchers mentioned above are also called hackers, they are actually white hats. They spare no effort to find various vulnerabilities, inform the corresponding manufacturers to fix them, and tell people of the various network risks. Cyber criminals, on the other hand, can be a bottomless, unscrupulous group of people who exploit various vulnerabilities to achieve different demands.

Cyber criminals have done a lot of bad things over the years, inflicting others and possibly themselves.

(1) Li Jun tragedy: Panda Burn Incense virus is actually sleazy

In 2007, a young man named Li Jun from Hubei province, China, wrote a worm variant called Panda Burn Incense, which wreaked havoc on the Internet through large-scale infection, and almost all mainstream anti-virus software was defeated. It caused blue screen, frequent restart, and corrupted data files on the system's hard drive when the user's computer was infected. Meanwhile, some variants of the virus spread through Local Area Network (LAN), and then infected all the computers in LAN, eventually resulting in enterprise LAN crash. According to statistics, Panda Burn Incense had hundreds of variants which infected millions of computers. It used a PE program infection method and exploited known vulnerabilities, which is not difficult for people with basic programming skills to do. Li Jun obstinately tried to prove the value of his existence in a destructive way, but this brought him two years in prison.

(2) Sexy photos of Hollywood actresses were leaked. Hackers claimed that they exploited vulnerabilities in Apple's cloud service

In August 2014, private photos of many Hollywood actresses, including Oscar winners Jennifer Lawrence and "Spider Woman" Kirsten Dunst, spread online wildly. It was reported that the photos were first made public on 4chan forum, and publishers claimed that hackers had obtained them by attacking Apple's iCloud accounts. It was later confirmed that photos posted by hackers were authentic. Several years have passed, criminals are still at large.

(3) Check-in information of Home Inns and other hotel chains was leaked

20 million hotel check-in records were leaked, allowing unrelated people to view these records. In 2013, customer's check-in records of a large number of economic chain hotels and star hotels, such as Home Inns, Hanting Inns, and JinJiang Hotels, were attacked and leaked. Perpetrators opened an online query website, you could get personal check-in information when entering names and ID numbers. Later, domestic third-party vulnerability monitoring platform released a report, indicating that the wireless portal authentication system provided by Hui Da Yi Zhan company for a large number of domestic hotels had potential security vulnerability. By exploiting the vulnerability, sensitive information such as hotel customers' names, ID cards and dates of room openings was exposed to public.

As can be seen from the above examples of cybercrimes, the motives of cybercrimes may be diverse, and the attack methods are also diverse, but success of these cyber attacks cannot be attained without successful exploitation of various vulnerabilities. As the saying goes, a fly does not bite a seamless egg. Due to various known or unknown vulnerabilities in information products and information systems, criminals can seize the opportunity to commit cyber crimes.

1.2.2 *APT*

In January 2010, a Google employee clicked on a malicious link in an instant message, setting off a chain of events that led to the search engine giant's network being hacked for months and caused data from various systems to be stolen. The famous attack was called the Google Aurora attack. In July 2010, Stuxnet virus attacked Iran's nuclear facilities and disabled a fifth of its centrifuges, shocking the rest of the world. The attack mainly used five vulnerabilities in Microsoft's operating system, four of which were brand new 0-day vulnerabilities. Through a complete set of intrusion and propagation processes, it broke through physical restrictions of dedicated LAN for industrial control, forged digital signatures of drivers, and launched a destructive attack on a system by exploiting two vulnerabilities of WinCC system. It was the first malicious code to directly destroy industrial infrastructure in the real world. Since then, Advanced Persistent Threat (APT) has become a well-known buzzword in the circle of information security.

(1) APT history review

The timeline of network attack events related to APT is shown in Figure 1.8. Some case names represent a series of attacks or intrusion attempts that affect a wide range of objects. The earliest disclosed APT attack can be traced back to the Moonlight Maze attack that started in 1998. According to the incident report, the attack focused on the computers at the Pentagon, NASA, U.S. Department

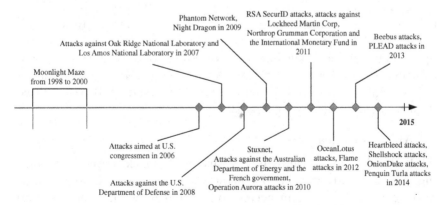

Figure 1.8. APT Development History

of Energy, National Laboratory, and private universities, and attackers successfully obtained thousands of files. Since 2006, APT attacks have shown continuous growth, and APT has become gradually well known to people. Among them, notorious attacks include Stuxnet, RSA SecurID, Operation Aurora, and more.

At present, APT has become a major security threat to all kinds of networks. It makes the network threat change from a random attack to a targeted, organized, and premeditated group attack.

It is difficult to define APT accurately. According to Wikipedia, APT is a long-term, complex, and organized cyber attack against specific targets such as governments and enterprises, which is usually supported by a government or a specific organization. The National Institute of Standards and Technology (NIST) defines it as: attackers who are proficient in complex technologies exploit multiple attack vectors (such as network, physics, and fraud) and rich resources to create opportunities to achieve their own goals. These goals typically include tampering with the information technology architecture of the target enterprise to steal data (for example, transmitting data from the Intranet to the extranet), executing or preventing a task, procedure, or infiltrating into the other enterprise's architecture to steal data.

As stated, an APT is a complex, multi-dimensional cyber attack against a specific organization. Its mechanism is highly advanced from technologies used by attackers to their knowledge about the environment inside the target. APT can use a variety of methods, such as malware, vulnerability scanning, targeted intrusion, or make use of malicious insiders to undermine security protection. APT is a long-term and multi-phase attack. Its early phase may focus on collecting detailed information about network settings and server operating systems, then install a rootkit or other malware to gain control, or establish a connection to the control server by command. Subsequent attacks may focus on copying confidential or sensitive data to steal intellectual property.

(2) APT attack features

APT attacks take advantage of a variety of attack methods, including the most advanced cyber attack technologies and social engineering methods, to gain access to internal networks step by step. APT attacks often use network's internal operators as an attack springboard. In order to carry out targeted attack, APT attackers usually write special attack programs against targets, rather than using some public and common attack code. In addition, APT attacks are persistent, even lasting for several years, which is reflected in attackers' continuous attempts at various attack means, long-term dormant after infiltrating into the network, and continuous collection of various important confidential data and information, even achieving the purpose of paralyzing the entire attacked system.

APT attack has the following features:

(a) APT attack is an organized attack. Early attacks were often implemented by perpetrators independently, while APT attack is complex, with clear organizers and leader, and a certain collaborative process is formed.

(b) It attacks targets out of political or economic interests. Early attacks usually scanned a segment of addresses randomly and started attack after finding a vulnerable host. The attacks had strong randomness. But APT attack is launched to gain some political or economic benefits, and has certain research and attack abilities. Stuxnet attackers did not spread the virus extensively, but launched an infection attack on the computers connected to the Internet, such as home computers and personal computers of the nuclear power plant related staff. They used this as the first springboard and further infected mobile devices of relevant personnel. The virus entered inside the attacked fort through mobile devices, then lurked in it. The virus spread around slowly and patiently and destroyed the target little by little. The example mentioned above is a very successful APT attack. The scariest thing lies in tactfully taking control of the attack range. The target is very clear, and the attack is very precise.

(c) It is a long-term consecutive attack. In an attempt to achieve a specific purpose, the attacker will constantly monitor the network and collect information, which can even last for up to one year. If the Trojan program loses contact with the control center, the attacker will try to connect again and never give up.

(d) APT attack is more hidden. Traditional attacks typically cause the network to slowdown or crash, leaving victims with visible clues of damage. However, APT attack attempts to evade "capture" without leaving any trace, and tries not to cause obvious damage to the user's system caused by their intrusion behavior. When the attack is successful, the important information obtained will be quietly transferred through secret channels.

(e) It exploits 0-day vulnerability. Exploitation of 0-day vulnerability is a significant characteristic of APT attacks. Traditional antivirus software, intrusion detection and prevention systems (IDS/IPS), and firewalls are all defense systems based on signatures. If there is no attack signature of 0-day vulnerability in the signatures, they are unable to resist the attack from tools that exploit 0-day vulnerability. Security protection software and security protection equipment themselves may also have 0-day vulnerabilities, which can be used by attackers to avoid detection or as a fast and hidden attack channel.

(3) APT protection

The core work mechanism of APT is that malicious attackers, through careful observation and analysis, elaborate design, and various means, quietly invade and lurk for a long time, search for and find confidential data and high value data, steal data without triggering any alert, leaving users unaware of their data loss. This makes it difficult for traditional rule-based, knowledge-based firewalls and IDS/IPS to trigger, and passive defense methods cannot detect invasion threats of APT in a timely and effective manner. To cope with threats of APT, we must adopt a new way of thinking. Namely, we can achieve in-depth cyber security defense by deploying hierarchical control from 4 levels to deal with APT threats and challenges.

(a) Strengthen macro-security management. This includes improvement of enterprise security management system, and implementation of cyber security assessment to find out vulnerability or possible deficiencies in the enterprise network and the weakest links in the whole network, so as to be aware of them and take rectification and improvement steps in a timely manner.

(b) Enhance end-user security literacy. Improve security awareness of end users, because the weakest link in the whole security process is the people. A general rule is that you cannot stop stupid behavior, but you can control it. Improve security understanding of end users so that they can master the basic security knowledge.

(c) Abnormal behavior detection. No matter what kind of attack, it may cause abnormal behavior in the host and network. The corresponding system abnormal behavior detection can be divided into two aspects: host behavior detection and network behavior analysis. Through the analysis and correlation of abnormal host behavior and abnormal network behavior, the clues of APT could be found.

(d) Study big data analysis technology to cope with challenges of APT. Compared with traditional attacks, APT brings two major challenges: One is A challenge, caused by advanced invasion methods, the other is P challenge, caused by persistent attacks. This makes it difficult to implement border defense technology based on feature matching and real-time detection technology based on a single time point. Therefore, it is necessary to continuously monitor access behavior of all nodes in the whole network, comprehensively analyze and integrate security incidents from multiple perspectives, and conduct an in-depth analysis of long-term and full-flow data.

With development and disclosure of APT attacks in recent years, we can see that attackers have been focusing on targets, continuously discovering security problems, developing attack weapons, while network and information technologies are continuously accumulating problems in the process of sustainable development. Certainty, similarity, quiescence, and continuity of vulnerabilities are fatal security defects of the existing network information systems. These defects lead to the passive situation where current network information systems are always attacked. There are endless security vulnerabilities and endless security patches, so we have to blindly pursue strength of the defense system. However, the fact has proved again that no matter how advanced the protection technology and mechanism are, and how meticulous the protection software and system are, they cannot withstand attackers' long-term observation, analysis, and repeated attacks.

1.3   Unavoidable Security Vulnerabilities

In practice, people gradually realize that vulnerabilities are the source of security problems. In the face of vulnerabilities, the attacker side and the defender side are not equal. As long as there is one vulnerability, the malicious attacker will be likely to reach his

Table 1.1. Exploit Number of Specific Operating System

Operating System	Exploit Number
Linux	73
Windows	239
Mac OSX	5

Table 1.2. Annual Number of Vulnerabilities Published by China's National Vulnerability Database

Year	Number of New Vulnerabilities
2014	8,623
2013	7,025
2012	7,198
2011	5,353
2010	4,649
2009	5,736
2008	5,622

purpose easily. No matter how many vulnerabilities defenders have found and eliminated, they dare not rest easy.

1.3.1 *Endless 0-day Vulnerabilities*

Every year security researchers, enthusiasts, hackers, and others find a huge number of vulnerabilities in a variety of platforms and software. According to data retrieved from the exploit databases, Table 1.1 shows the number of exploits for a specific operating system in 2014. According to data released by China's National Vulnerability Database, the number of newly added vulnerabilities every year since 2008 has been shown in Table 1.2.

The above is data about vulnerabilities that have been discovered and made public. But there are still various security vulnerabilities on platforms and software that are undiscovered or undisclosed, or are not released after they were found. For the vulnerabilities that have been discovered and made public, the manufacturer can take corresponding protection measures, while for the unknown vulnerabilities, protection work are out of the question.

1.3.2 *Insecurity of Top Manufacturers' Products*

In recent years, domestic and international cyber security sectors have been flourishing, security protection technology has also made great progress. The major manufacturers, such as Microsoft, are constantly introducing various new security protection mechanisms, means, methods, and concepts. These new technologies and methods have really made great contributions to cyber security but has the Internet become more secure?

(1) Pwn2Own and browser security

Pwn2Own is the most famous and bountiful reward hacking competition in the world. It is organized by the project team Zero Day Initiative (ZDI), a U.S. Pentagon cyber security service provider and is affiliated to HP's TippingPoint company. Internet and software giants such as Google, Microsoft, Apple, and Adobe all provide support for the competition to improve security of their own products through hacker challenge.

The 2015 Pwn2Own was described as the most challenging competition in history. All manufacturers have applied the latest and the most comprehensive security defense technologies and mechanisms in their products. Internet and software giants were full of confidence, claiming that security of their products had reached the strongest level in history. What was competition result? Were the products as secure as the manufacturers claimed? Let's look back at the competition held in Vancouver, Canada.

First, take a look at IE11 known as the Unicorn level protection in the 64-bit Win8.1 operating system. Before the competition, IE was generally recognized as "no cracked golden body." Technically speaking, to hack IE browser at Pwn2Own 2015, hackers must break through the following five major challenges.

(a) Microsoft vulnerability defense software EMET.
(b) IE enabled Enhanced Protected Mode (EPM).
(c) IE enabled Enable 64-bit Processes for Enhanced Protected Mode option.

(d) New Microsoft security mechanisms, such as isolation heap, delay release, and CFG.

(e) Disable system restart and logoff.

The team from China chose to take the bull by the horns and challenged IE Unicorn level protection. In the pre-competition draw order, 360 Vulcan Team was ranked in the sixth group and was also the first team to challenge IE. According to rules of the competition, 360 Vulcan Team launched attack on a brand new 64-bit Win8.1 operating system computer without any third party preinstalled. They used multiple combinations of 0-day vulnerabilities to break through all IE's defenses and gain control of the system. So far, IE 11 was hacked completely.

Now let's see the other browsers' fates: Mozilla Firefox browser was hacked by security expert ilxu1a in less than a second; Safari browser was crashed by South Korean hacker Jung Hoon Lee who exploited an uninitialized stack pointer vulnerability on the opening day of the competition, stable versions and Beta versions of Google Chrome browser were also cracked on the same day by Jung Hoon Lee who used buffer overflow race condition. The final results of Pwn2Own 2015: in a two-day competition, five vulnerabilities were found in Windows, four in IE 11, three in Firefox, three in Adobe Reader and Flash, respectively, two in Safari, and one in Chrome. The numbers say it all.

Attack and defense always move forward together in an ebb and flow and in each other's antagonism. After a new attack technology appears, there will always be a corresponding protection technology or mechanism to protect or mitigate. Similarly, after the mitigation technology or defense mechanism against a new attack appears, there will always be a corresponding technology or method to find the flaws in logic or implementation, break through or bypass its limitations, making protection ineffective. In other words, software vulnerabilities are inevitable, security defense mechanisms are also not omnipotent.

(2) Vulnerabilities in security provider's products

When a security problem occurs in our software or system, we usually hope that security providers can offer effective solutions to help us solve the problem or trouble as soon as possible. Security providers have objectively played the role of the immune system in the Internet ecosystem, which requires security providers themselves to be healthy and secure. So how secure are security providers themselves? First, let's take a look at the recent media-hyped FireEye vulnerability incident.

FireEye was founded in 2004. It is a U.S. cyber security company that provides protection products for enterprises and is best known for solving 0-day attacks. Its working mechanism is to observe all network behaviors by loading a virtual machine on the customer's system. In 2012, the order value of FireEye, founded for only 8 years, was worth more than $100 million, with an order growth rate over 100%. It had more than 1,000 partners and customers, and is used by a quarter of Fortune 100 companies.

FireEye claims to be able to solve two real security challenges – prevent cyber attacks which companies could not stop before, namely, 0-day attack and APT attack. But 0-day solution of FireEye did not seem to work this time.

Let's go back to this incident, researcher Kristian Erik Hermansen discovered a 0-day vulnerability in the FireEye core product that could lead to unauthorized file leakage. He also provided a brief example of vulnerability trigger and a copy of a user database file. "The FireEye device allows unauthorized remote access to the root file system, and web server runs as root," Hermansen wrote in disclosing the vulnerability. "Now that the security company has presented a perfect security paradigm, why do you believe that these people will run their security products on your network? This is just one of many 0-day vulnerabilities in FireEye/Mandiant products. FireEye's security experts did nothing to fix it over the past 18 months. It's sure that Mandiant employees have encoded this vulnerability and other flaws into their product. More sadly, FireEye has no external security researchers to report this problem." So how secure is FireEye itself?

Soon after the incident, media CSOonline emailed Hermansen asked for details. Hermansen replied that another researcher Ron Perris and he had identified 30 vulnerabilities in FireEye products when they worked together, including multiple remote root permission vulnerabilities. In an email to *Salted Hash*, Hermansen said that he had tried to contact FireEye through a responsible channel to solve the problem in the past year and a half, but they are all talk and no deed. Hermansen thought that the incident should be disclosed, and everyone should know about the vulnerabilities, especially Gov-approved Safe Harbor devices with remote root permission vulnerabilities.

Was FireEye the only security vendor to have vulnerabilities exposed? The answer was no. Among well-known antivirus manufacturers, whether it's Kaspersky, McAfee, Norton, or Trend Micro, they all had serious vulnerabilities exposed. The facts have proved once again that security providers cannot eliminate software vulnerabilities. If security providers with a large number of professional security researchers cannot guarantee security of their products, who can guarantee security of users and the Internet?

(3) Apple XcodeGhost virus incident and its extension

We generally assume that legitimate software downloaded from reputable application markets with strict censorship such as App Store have no security issues such as backdoors. But Apple XcodeGhost incident gave a loud slap on the credibility and censorship of application markets such as App Store.

This dates back to September 12, 2015, when Tencent Security Response Center (TSRC) was tracing a bug. They found that an app sent abnormal encrypted traffic to a domain name through the network when it started and exited. They thought the behavior was very suspicious, so the terminal security team immediately followed it up. After a weekend of overtime analysis and tracing, they have basically restored its infection mode, virus behavior and influence surface. At present, the backdoor has infected thousands of Apple Store apps, including well-known apps such as WeChat, Netease Cloud Music, Didi, 12306, and Gaode Map.

XcodeGhost can cause the following damages.

(a) When the infected app starts, stays in the background, recovers, and exits, its information will be reported to the server controlled by hackers.
(b) Hackers can issue pseudo-protocol commands to be executed on infected iPhones.
(c) Hackers can pop up a dialog window with content controlled by the server on an infected iPhone.
(d) The remote control module protocol is vulnerable to man-in-the-middle attack.

In the process of analysis, they found that all the apps with abnormal traffic were well-known products from large companies, which were all downloaded from App Store and had official digital signatures. Therefore, there was no possibility that the apps could be maliciously tampered with. Subsequently, Tencent security team focused their efforts on developers and related compiling environments. They quickly got the answer from the developer's Xcode as expected.

They found that developer's Xcode installation package was implanted with a remote control module by someone with bad intentions. By modifying Xcode compiling parameters, the malicious module was automatically deployed to any Apple app (iOS/Mac) compiled by Xcode. Therefore, the fall out of this incident was that developers downloaded Xcode development environment from non-official Apple channels.

(4) Extension of XcodeGhost incident – UnityGhost

Before the XcodeGhost incident was over, one of the most mainstream mobile game engines in China – Unity – was exposed to vulnerabilities. On September 21, 2015 (23:21), Baidu security lab member @evil_xi4oyu revealed that unofficial versions of Unity 4.x had been confirmed to be tampered with and added with malicious backdoors. WooYun Knowledge Base author Zhengmi analyzed Unity's malicious backdoor sample UnityGhost and found that the sample behavior was very similar to XcodeGhost. It could collect basic information from the phone and upload it to init.icloud-diagnostics.com with remote control ability. After receiving server instructions, UnityGhost can perform the following malicious behaviors.

(1) Download and install the App with enterprise certificate.
(2) Pop up App Store for application promotion.
(3) Pop up phishing pages to further steal user information.
(4) If there is a URL Scheme vulnerability in the user's mobile phone, it can launch a URL Scheme attack.

Apple XcodeGhost and the subsequent UnityGhost incidents are not only the public crises of manufacturers, but also need our ordinary users to think about security issues. Even in Apple's closed system, security and privacy issues of software downloaded from reputable app markets, such as App Store, are facing severe challenges. Such security issues are likely to become more prominent on more open source systems like Android, and will become more acute as smart devices become more prevalent.

The security incidents above tell us that those manufacturers who are usually considered to have strong technical force and high security awareness, such as Microsoft and Apple, are not performing well in practice, and FireEye, Kaspersky, and other big-name security vendors could not completely reassure users.

1.3.3   *SDL Cannot Eradicate Vulnerabilities*

Security Development Lifecycle (SDL) is the method proposed initially by Microsoft company, which is embedded in software engineering to help solve software security problems. SDL is a security assurance process that focuses on software development and introduces principles of security and privacy in all phases of development. Since 2004, SDL has been a mandatory, company-wide strategy for Microsoft. SDL process is shown in Figure 1.9.

Security development lifecycle can help companies improve product security at minimal cost.

SDL has positive significance for reducing the number of vulnerabilities. According to data of U.S. National Vulnerability Database and China National Vulnerability Database, thousands of security vulnerabilities are discovered and published every year, most of which are less complex. These vulnerabilities mostly appear in all kinds of applications, and most of them are easy to be exploited.

Microsoft SDL is suitable for manufacturers that develop software based on the traditional waterfall model, but not for teams like Internet companies that use agile development technology. Agile development adopts Small and Quick Steps method to constantly

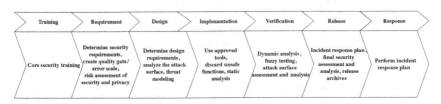

Figure 1.9.   SDL Process

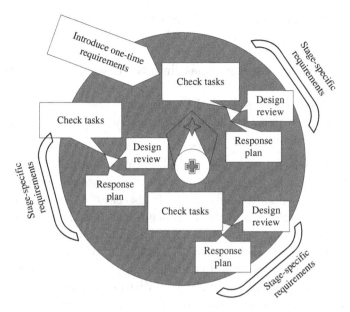

Figure 1.10. The Process of Agile SDL

improve the product. It usually does not require standardized process and high-level documentation. It helps to release products and meet customer needs quickly, but flaws of this development model are that there are no clear requirements at the beginning of development, and the security design will change as the requirements change in the process of development.

Microsoft has designed a dedicated agile SDL for agile development, as shown in Figure 1.10. The idea behind agile SDL is to implement secure work from a changing point of view. Requirements and functions may change over time, so the code may also change with them. This requires updating the threat model and privacy policy in each phase of implementation of SDL, and Iterative fuzzing and code security analysis at the necessary nodes.

In the process of implementing SDL, enterprises summarize the following guidelines from their own experiences.

(a) Leave enough time to communicate with the project manager fully.
(b) Regulate the company's project approval process to ensure that all projects can be notified to the security team.

(c) Establish authority of the security department, and all the projects must be reviewed by the security department prior to releasing.
(d) Add the security testing phase into the development and testing workbook.
(e) Provide security design and development training for engineers.
(f) Record all security vulnerabilities and motivate programmers to write secure code.

SDL requires enterprises to drive its implementation from the top to down. Success of SDL implementation ultimately depends on the people who implement it, meanwhile, it also closely relates to support of senior management and the technical level of SDL implementers.

After Microsoft implemented SDL, the code quality has been significantly improved. But due to the expansion of software code and emergence of new vulnerability mining methods, Microsoft is still exposed to a large number of vulnerabilities every year. From the perspective of actual effects, SDL has a positive significance for improving security of products, but it has always been unable to eradicate software vulnerabilities, and software manufacturers cannot get away from harassment of vulnerabilities.

1.3.4 *Passivity of Existing Defense Solutions*

In the fierce struggle with malicious code, security vendors have successively introduced a variety of security protection mechanisms, means, and methods. Application of these technologies and methods has really made great contributions to users and Internet security, but confrontation between malicious code and security software is actually a topic of spear and shield. No matter what kind of attack or defense technology, it's restricted to its time and conditions, and a technology is generally only effective for a particular scenario in a certain time period.

(1) Signature killing and bypass

Signature killing is an antivirus technology based on analysis and killing of known viruses. It is the most widely used and basic killing method in antivirus software. The basic principle is to compare with the program files one by one according to the virus signature extracted from the virus body. Signature is a series of binary strings determined by the antivirus company that may be specific to a virus when the company analyzes the virus. The virus can be distinguished from other viruses or normal programs by the signature. Upgrading of antivirus software refers to updating the virus signature database of the software so that it can detect new known viruses.

Among all kinds of virus detection methods, the signature method is the fastest, simplest, most widely applied and effective. But due to its own flaws, it is merely applied to known viruses. In addition, to capture a virus' signature, it is necessary to obtain the virus samples. Due to different descriptions of the signature by different antivirus companies, it is difficult to obtain extensive support in the international community. The main technical defects of signature virus detection are large false detection and false alarm.

Since signature killing has the above limitations, it is just a palliative method rather than a permanent method. Attackers can easily bypass it through a variety of methods, such as instruction replacement and junk code addition, invalidating the protection.

(2) Active defense and bypass

If signature scanning is a passive and static method, active defense is a technical attempt of active, real-time malicious code detection and interception that makes automated analysis and judgment based on program behaviors. It judges a virus directly based on program behaviors rather than virus signature from the most original definition of the virus. Active defense uses software to automatically perform virus analysis and judgment process in place of anti-virus engineers, thus solving the problem that traditional security software cannot defend against unknown malware.

Active defense technology mainly includes the following technologies and ideas: (a) a dynamic judgment method based on virus identification rule base. It can realize automatic recognition of new viruses through automatic monitoring of various program behaviors, automatic analysis of logical relationship between program behaviors, and comprehensive application of virus recognition rule knowledge. (b) a dynamic behavior analysis technology based on system hooks. It can dynamically monitor behaviors of the program calling various Application Programming Interfaces (API), automatically analyze logical relationship between program behaviors and determine legitimacy of program behaviors, thus realizing automatic diagnosis of a new virus and providing definitive diagnosis results. (c) an active interception technology. It can automatically analyze program behaviors while fully monitoring operation of the program, it can automatically prevent virus behaviors and terminate operation of the virus program after discovering new viruses, clearing viruses, and fixing registry errors.

Active defense technology is a kind of protection method which is complementary to static signature scanning, significantly improving protection capability of security software. However, it has been plagued by various bypass methods since its release. For example, these methods include bypassing functions hooked by active defense systems; copying the code into data segment of the program and jumping to execute; blurring the entry point such as Inline Hook.

(3) Heuristic protection, killing and bypass

Differences between a virus and a normal program can be seen in many ways. For example, usually initial instructions of an application are to check the command line input for parameter items, clear the screen, and save the original screen display, etc. But the virus program does not do that. Its initial instructions are to execute a sequence of instructions of related operation, such as direct writing disk operation decoding instructions or searching for the executable program under a specific path. These significant differences can be seen at a glance by a skilled programmer in debugging mode. Heuristic code scanning technology is actually a specific embodiment that transplants this experience and knowledge into an antivirus software.

Heuristic killing can be divided into static and dynamic killing. The static heuristic killing fully considers differences between the virus and the normal program, that is to say, determines whether the file is infected by analyzing the order or combination of instructions. By setting a security threshold, when cumulative weight of a potentially malicious code fragments or their combinations in the program exceed a certain limit value, the program is determined to be malicious, and the killing is initiated. Dynamic heuristic killing is also known as virtual killing. Its basic principle is to create a virtual environment, let the program fully execute for a while, then scan and compare behavior and features of the virus during the execution. Virtual killing is mainly for viruses in shells or Trojans. Applying virtualization technology to program protection is the sandbox technology we will elaborate in what follows.

Heuristic killing looks good in theory, but in practice it is easy to produce false reports, thus affecting normal use of programs by users. In addition, to deal with current heuristic killing technology, attackers have also developed many bypass technologies which can invalidate it. For example, virtual killing bypass technology based on timeout, that is, adding a large number of meaningless confusing instructions before the real function segment to make runtime of the program exceed depth of virtual execution, thereby bypassing the heuristic killing. Another example is a bypass method exploiting exception handling mechanism. It puts malicious API calls into exception handling, then manually triggering an exception to indirectly call API to achieve bypass by exploiting vulnerability where heuristic killing cannot fully virtualize exception handling.

(4) Sandbox protection and its bypass

Sandbox technology, as the name suggests, is a protection technology that allows modifying something freely and then restoring it to the original state. If you still do not know what a sandbox is, imagine this: In a box filled with smooth and fine sand, we can draw pictures or scribble something freely, no matter how well or bad they are drawn. Finally, with a touch of dabbing off, the sandbox restores to its original smooth state. Charisma of the sandbox lies in allowing you to make mistakes and giving you a chance to correct them.

The principle of sandbox technology is very different from that of active defense technology. Active defense is to immediately intercept and stop the program upon detection of its suspicious behaviors, while sandbox technology lets the program continue to run when suspicious behavior is detected, and only terminates when it is found that it is indeed a virus. The practical application process of sandbox technology is as follows: make suspicious behavior of the suspected virus file be fully performed in the virtual sandbox, which will record every action of it. When the suspicious virus has fully exposed its virus attributes, the sandbox will perform a rollback mechanism to erase traces and actions of the virus and restore the system to its normal state.

Using sandbox technology to protect applications is to direct files generated and modified by a program to its own folder through the redirection technology. These data changes include registry, files, and other core system data. Sandbox technology, also known as driver-level kernel protection, can protect the underlying data by loading its own drivers. By design, sandbox technology protects applications by means of isolation, so is there any way to break through or bypass it? The answer is yes.

Sandbox escape is a general term for bypassing sandbox methods, and usually has different bypass methods according to different scenarios and applications. For example, CVE-2015-1427 is a typical vulnerability that bypasses the sandbox through reflection method. Since the sandbox code blacklist for dangerous methods in Java are incomplete, malicious users can still use reflection method to execute Java code. Another example is three sandboxes escape vulnerabilities in IE Enhanced Protected Mode (EPM) fixed in MS14-065. These three vulnerabilities are caused by the permission problem of IE proxy process under Enhanced Protected Mode because access check in App Container ignores all resources below intermediate level. If a resource passes DACL check, it will be granted permission regardless of IL, leading to bypassing the sandbox.

For many years, security vendors have gained rich experience in coping with malicious code, malicious programs, and vulnerability detection, etc. They have also adopted a lot of new technologies and means, but any kind of new protection technology, in the face of various researches and tests by a large number of attackers, will sooner or later be found to have vulnerabilities or methods that attackers can exploit to break through or bypass the system protection mechanism.

1.4 Dynamically Enabled of Pre-Enemy Changes

By exploring the nature of security vulnerabilities, it can be found that vulnerabilities are pervasive and inevitable throughout the entire life cycle of R&D and application of information technology. First of all, defects of Von Neumann architecture itself and insecurity of the Internet system based on the TCP/IP protocol stack lead to inevitability of security vulnerabilities. Secondly, rapid growth in the scale of computer software systems, introduction of new technologies and new applications, and improvement of software system complexity increase probability of vulnerabilities. Finally, software and systems are designed and implemented by people. Due to inherent inertia and cognitive limitations of people, vulnerabilities cannot be avoided.

The existing protection methods are mainly passive protection. In addition to encryption and authentication, they are mainly based on prior knowledge. Once state of the security protection system is solidified, capabilities will also be solidified. Likewise, once the security protection equipment is finalized, capabilities are also finalized. This static, closed, and passive protection method cannot deal with unknown vulnerability attacks. As mentioned in the previous examples, the intrusion detection system based on prior features cannot cope with unknown attacks; behavior-based host protection software can be deliberately bypassed; there are a variety of bypass methods against sandbox-based malicious behavior analysis technology, according to different scenarios and applications.

Objective existence of vulnerabilities and passivity of the existing protection make the network attack and defense present an asymmetric situation that is easy to attack but difficult to defend. In order to reverse this passive situation, it is necessary to break through the traditional thinking mode, develop and innovate technologies and systems that can change "rules of the game". As shown in Figure 1.11, *Master Sun's Art of War* says: "War is a kaleidoscopic and unexpected art that uses ever-changing and surprising ways to fight enemies." This "changing" way of thinking applies to battlefields as well as cyberspace. In the battlefield, it can achieve unexpected victory through changes of the array and formation; in cyberspace, it also achieves the goal of "the enemy does not know where to attack" through dynamic changes of the structure of software, networks, and platforms.

1.4.1 *"Changing with Enemy Situations" in the Art of War*

In the traditional Chinese culture, "a flexible approach is adapted to practical needs" is seen as the highest ideal, and Confucianism, Buddhism, and Taoism all think so. In *Wen Zi Morality*, there is

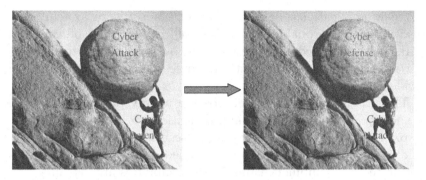

Figure 1.11.   Change Rules

a saying that "The sage should use different ways in response to various occasions." In *Zhuang Zi Great Master*, Zhuang Zi replied to his disciples, "Those who understand Taoism must be good at coping with things, and those who are good at coping with things must understand how to be flexible to deal with changes, and those who understand how to be flexible to deal with changes will not be harmed by external things." Confucius also said, "To know that adversity is fate, and prosperity is fortune."

Compared with Confucianism and Taoism, military strategists especially advocated the fundamental thinking way of "flexibility". Sun Tzu, in his article *Nine Changes*, explained the truth that to lead troops to defeat enemies needed to play it by ear. The general should think problems comprehensively and dialectically, think of harms behind benefits, think of benefits when seeing harms, try to make the best of advantages and avoid disadvantages to remain in an invincible position. Flexibility in technology needs integration of motion and stillness, and needs to know how to manipulate opponents to change the situation. "Make enemies do things against themselves, find something to torment them and make them tired, and lure enemies into traps. So the general rule of war is: Do not expect enemies not to come to us, instead get everything ready to wait for the enemy to come at any time; do not expect enemies not to attack us, instead build our own strong military power to prevent enemies from attacking us." The general is required to know how to be flexible, in addition to making the tactics change, but also know military arrays in the art of war, which are the most intuitive embodiment of changing with the enemy situations. The most famous and mysterious ancient military array is probably Zhuge Liang's "the Eight Battle Arrays Plot". We will delve into the mysterious "Wuhou eight battle arrays" in the following.

(1) The origin and characteristics of the Eight Battle Arrays Plot

"With his exploits, history is crowned; For his eight battle arrays plot, he's renowned. The river flows, but stones still stand; Though he'd not taken back lost land." Anyone who has read the book *Romance of the Three Kingdoms* knows the unpredictable and infinitely powerful Eight Battle Arrays Plot created by Zhuge Liang, prime minister of Shu kingdom, which made the strong Wei kingdom frightened. By virtue of the unique military advantage of his eight battle arrays, he was able to launch several wars against Wei kingdom with the weak force of Shu kingdom and attempted to take back the central plains. Although these wars did not achieve the expected goal, for Shu kingdom in a weak position among the three kingdoms of Wei, Shu, and Wu, this flexible tactic of taking the offensive played a defensive role for a time period.

So, does the mysterious Eight Battle Arrays Plot exist? If so, what does it look like? In fact, the military array was a deployment of the battle formation in ancient times of cold weapons. It was produced under close distance battles in ancient wars, in order to meet the unified command and cooperative combat requirements of the battlefield. Ancient China was very particular about battle arrays and the related books have been handed down. Sun Tzu used eight battle arrays, and Sun Bin also wrote the chapter *Eight Battle Arrays* in his book *Sun Bin's Art of War*. Eight battle arrays were widely used in the combat training in the Eastern Han dynasty. Zhuge Liang created the Eight Battle Arrays Plot based on the original ancient eight battle arrays from the reality that Shu kingdom took the infantry as the main force. It took many years to be mapped.

On the whole, Zhuge Liangs eight battle arrays are a defensive formation, and its main idea is to combine dynamic operations with static operations, change with enemy situations and manipulate opponents. Its main characteristic is that there are no weaknesses in the deployment, and it is unnecessary to make a fundamental change in the overall large battle array when it is attacked in any direction. When one area is attacked, adjacent battle arrays of its two wings can automatically change into two wings to protect and support the attacked array.

(2) The structure and variations of the Eight Battle Arrays Plot

To figure out unpredictability of the eight battle arrays, we must have a basic understanding of their component structure. Text of the Eight Battle Arrays Plot is brief and its meaning is vague, but according to the textual research and interpretation by many scholars in past dynasties, its general structures and arrangements are clear. Zhu Xi said in the 136th volume of *Zhu Zi Language Category*, "Every army is useful in eight battle arrays, which respectively represent sky impact, earth axis, dragon fly, tiger wing, snake, bird, wind, and cloud. Some battle arrays are dedicated to fighting, some to causing conflicts or some to entangling with enemies, but we do not know how to use them." He briefly described names and characteristics of the eight battle arrays. The eight battle arrays were also described in *Wo Qi Scripture*, "four battle arrays represented by sky, earth, wind, and cloud are called the positive battle arrays, and four battle arrays represented by dragon, tiger, bird, and snake are called the odd battle arrays. The four positive battle arrays and the four odd battle arrays constitute the total eight battle arrays." The general mastering mobile forces (so-called "Yu Qi" soldiers) are in the center of the eight battle arrays, known as "Wo Qi". The chapter also described steps of the formation and methods of dealing with enemies: when arranging battle arrays, guerrilla troops would first guard both flanks in front of the battle arrays; after arranging the battle arrays, they withdrew to the rear of the battle arrays to await orders; when fighting, soldiers of four positive battle arrays and four odd battle arrays engaged in a confrontation with enemies. The guerrilla troops attacked enemies from the rear of the battle arrays in coordination with the eight battle arrays. The general commanded in the center of the eight battle arrays and cooperated with the main forces. The eight battle arrays are shown in Figure 1.12.

This has been described in more detail in *Combination and Transformation of the Eight Battle Arrays Plot*, written by Long Zheng in the Ming dynasty. In the book, structures and variations of the Eight Battle Arrays Plot were described in detail. All the changes were based on the structural elements defined in the book, which included sky balance, earth axis, wind, cloud, front impact and back

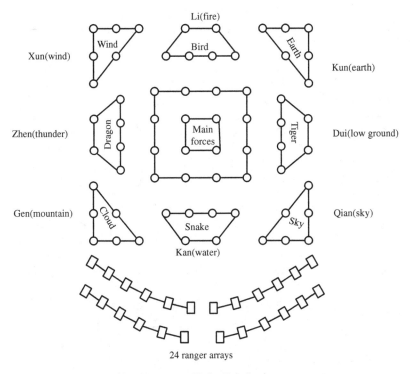

Figure 1.12. Eight Battle Arrays

impact, etc. To understand how eight battle arrays change, we need a basic understanding of structural elements. There are 64 small battle arrays in the entire big square battle array, and there may be 24 small battle arrays formed by rangers after the big square battle array, constituting a total of 88 small battle arrays. As shown in Figure 1.13, each small circle in the figure represents a small battle array.

It can be seen that this structural element map basically corresponds to the general eight battle arrays, including both 64 small battle arrays plus 24 ranger battle arrays. With this plot, we can describe variations of the eight battle arrays (sky covering, ground supporting, wind blowing, cloud drooping, dragon flying, tiger wing, bird flying, snake coiling). Each of the eight battle arrays is formed by changing the part extracted from the overall battle array structure. They are interrelated and changing with each other depending

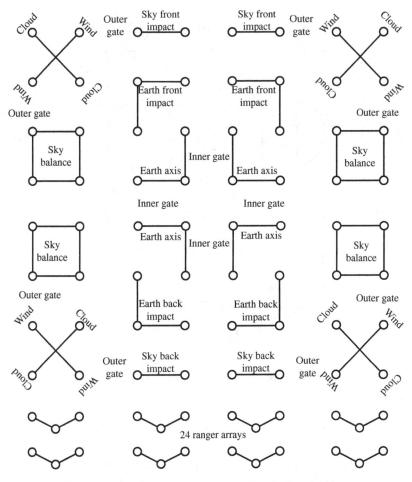

Figure 1.13. Structural Elements of Eight Battle Arrays

on situations. This section gives a brief description of four basic variations of the Eight Battle Arrays Plot by means of intuitive graphics.

(a) The first variation: Inside and outside division

When we are on the defensive, and enemies are on the offensive in battle, eight battle arrays can be changed into a circular sky covering array to strengthen the defense. If the offensive and defensive stalemate, it can be changed into the ground supporting array with combination of attack and defense to improve flexibility and adaptability, as shown in Figure 1.14.

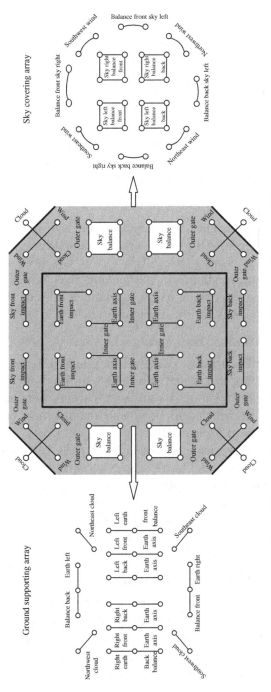

Figure 1.14. First Variation of the Eight Battle Arrays Plot

(b) The second variation: Left and right division

The left and right sides are changed into cloud drooping array and wind blowing array. At the beginning, the cloud array has no fixed shape, which can be used to confuse enemies. As the situation changes, the cloud drooping array can be quickly changed into bird flying array. At this time, the defensive state is transformed into the attack state, and a sharp attack is launched on enemies. The wind blowing array itself is majestic and arrogant, but as the situation changes, it can be quickly changed into a snake coiling array to obstruct and entwine enemies, as shown in Figure 1.15.

(c) The third variation: Front and back division

The second half of the eight battle arrays becomes dragon flying array and the first half becomes tiger wing array. Dragon flying array "lurks unfathomably and moves powerfully", and it can both attack and defend, changing unpredictably. "Crouching tiger will fight, showing its power", the tiger wing array can launch all-out attack when enemies are trapped, as shown in Figure 1.16.

(d) The fourth variation: Four corners division

The northeast and southwest corners can change into an extremely aggressive bird flying array, and "one man can hold out against ten thousand"; the northwest and southeast corners can change into snake coiling array, which can bend and extend, and enclose and surround, as shown in Figure 1.17.

The four kinds of variations above are only the basic battle array transformations, in practical battle, the general can also adjust battle arrays at any time as the situation evolves.

We can envisage that when a battle array with such a dynamic variation fights against an unchanged battle array after deployment, it's easily apparent who wins or who loses.

1.4.2 *Principle of Unpredictability*

In fact, the "variation" way of thinking in *Master Sun's Art of War* has already been applied in the field of cyber security. The random factor introduced in the security protection mechanism can effectively resist various attacks, such as buffer overflow attack based on fixed memory address, data packet tampering and forgery attack, and

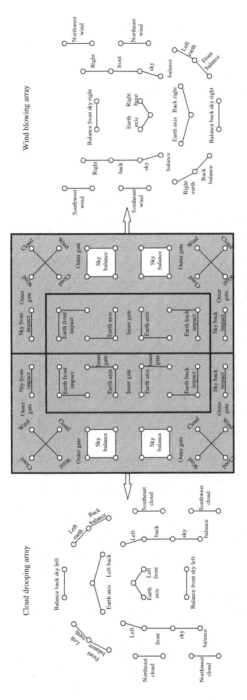

Figure 1.15. Second Variation of the Eight Battle Arrays Plot

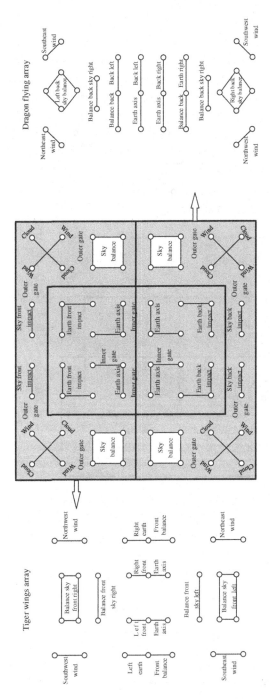

Figure 1.16.   Third Variation of the Eight Battle Arrays Plot

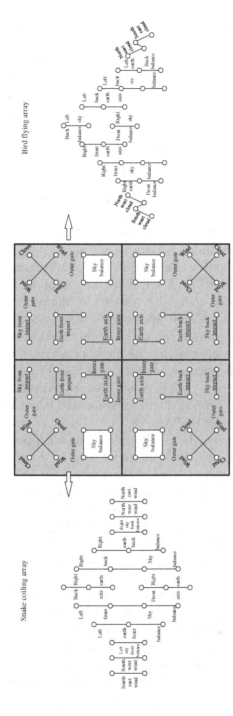

Figure 1.17. Fourth Variation of the Eight Battle Arrays Plot

authentication bypass attack. This can increase difficulty of attacks, and significantly improve security of systems or software.

Microsoft's Windows operating system has always been an important target for hackers. For years, confrontation on buffer overflow between hackers and Microsoft has never stopped. Users of Microsoft Windows operating system have long been threatened by buffer overflow attacks and suffered heavy losses. Microsoft has also been adding new security mechanisms in new versions to combat buffer overflow attacks. Microsoft cannot guarantee that the system itself or the software running on the system is free of vulnerabilities. While taking measures such as SDL to mitigate vulnerabilities, it endeavors to adopt new methods to invalidate vulnerability attacks. "Dare not provoke them, but can avoid them." Microsoft started playing hide-and-seek with Windows Vista operating system and deployed Address Space Layout Randomization (ASLR) to increase difficulty of attacks. Implementation of ASLR requires support from both the program itself and the operating system, so Microsoft added ASLR switches starting with Visual Studio 2005 SP1. ASLR makes stack base addresses of the process change randomly, so that the attack programs cannot accurately predict the memory address, which greatly raises the threshold of attack. In fact, the idea of address randomization was not created by Microsoft. Before Windows Vista, this technology had been proposed and implemented in some open source systems, such as FreeBSD, PAX, etc.

ASLR technology used by Microsoft is also supported in newer versions of Linux kernel, Android version 4.0 or higher, and Apple iOS version 4.3 or higher. Under the control of ASLR, when the program starts, stack base addresses of its process are different, which is random and is unpredictable for attackers to some extent.

Unpredictability can also effectively defend against attacks based on tampering and forgery. Assume that the user uploads attachments in ascending order of id numbers in an office system, such as id = 123, id = 124, id = 125, etc.

It allows attackers to easily traverse id numbers of all attachments in the system, including id numbers of attachments uploaded by other users. The attacker can delete an attachment as long as he modifies the corresponding number in the attachment deletion request. If the attacker wants to delete all attachments, he can do batch deletion by writing a simple script. If developers of the office system have a sense of security, they will assign the numbers randomly to make the id value unpredictable. For example, these ids such as id = 094e5c24 − a2d4 − 92adcbad0932, id = ec13bc26 − a39c − 34d457aa826e, and id = 9f68801b − a3ee − 68c37e27ea67 are completely unpredictable, so attackers cannot use previous methods to traverse and delete other attachments, thus increasing the threshold of attack.

Unpredictability can also be used to combat authentication bypass attacks. Authentication is a behavior of verifying a person's identity. Interactions between the browser and the Web server are managed through session, and information from each session is used to identify whether the user has been authenticated. Thus, if the session is predictable, a malicious user can use a variety of rules to guess a valid session and then modify the session in the request to a session that is predicted to be valid. For example, using the system time to generate a session = 20151010151313, which is an id including date and time accurate to the second and can be easily predicted by attackers. Once the attacker can calculate the session in real time, he can hijack the session, pretend to be the real owner of the session, and bypass the authentication process. Similarly, with the idea of unpredictability, if you can make the date and time accurate to milliseconds, difficulty of attack will increase significantly. If a random number is added, difficulty of attack will reach a higher level.

1.4.3 *Dynamically Enabled Cyber Defense Idea*

This book applies the idea of "change" to the cyber defense system and proposes the idea of dynamic enablement. Application of the unpredictability principle mentioned above in security protection is mainly about transformation of some mechanisms. On this basis, dynamic enablement applies the idea of "change" systematically. Through the dynamically changing technical mechanism and system, it creates the "mist" of cyberspace so that attackers cannot find attack targets, access paths and system vulnerabilities, thereby completely changing the long-term passive situation of security protection.

The concept of enablement derives from the word "enable". Enablement is usually used in the computer field, and is often used in conjunction with a system or technology to form a compound adjective, indicating that it has (endows) a certain capability.

Dynamic enablement is a basic security concept which needs to be strictly implemented in the design process of cyber information system throughout its lifecycle. Its purpose is to try all possible means to make all participating subjects, communication protocols, and information data in the whole lifecycle operation process of information system actively or passively, individually or simultaneously change all possible signature attributes or capabilities of attributes presenting information to the outside world both in time and space field when maintaining information system availability in cyberspace. So achieving part or all of the following effects when attackers attack the information system: (a) difficult to find a target; (b) find a wrong target; (c) find a target and cannot take attacks; (d) carry out an attack that is unsustainable; (e) carry out an attack but it can be quickly detected. Any technology that fits into the above categories can be categorized as dynamically enabled cyber security defense technology.

There are three main meanings of dynamic enablement in this book: linkage enablement, change enablement, and system enablement. Linkage enablement mainly gives a system dynamic enhancement capabilities in the time dimension through linkage between security elements. A typical example of linkage enablement is the security life cycle (PDRR). Change enablement represents changes of system structure and technical mechanism. It mainly gives a system dynamic security protection capabilities in the space dimension so as to increase cost and difficulty of attackers exploiting system security vulnerabilities, thus increasing protection strength of the system. System enablement is about making full use of the dynamic connection between system elements to change a static, fixed, and dead protection system into a dynamically enabled, live system from the perspective of cyber security systems. This saves limited resources and power, and provides new vitality of global enablement. According to the idea of "consolidating the front end and strengthening the back end", system enablement is to build a service-oriented dynamically enabled security defense system based on front-end prevention and detection facilities, supported by the back-end attack analysis and support service facilities, and with professional security forces as the core.

References

[1] Langner, R. Stuxnet: Dissecting a cyberwarfare weapon. *IEEE Security & Privacy*, 2011, 9.3: 49–51.

[2] Empson, R. Hack attack: Sony confirms play station network outage caused by external intrusion. http://techcrunch.com/2011/04/23/hack-attack-sony-confirms-playstation-network-outage-caused-by-external-intrusion, 2011.

[3] PCMeg UK, iOS Flaw Facilitates iPhone SMS Spoofing. https://uk.pcmag.com/mobile-phones/61142/ios-flaw-facilitates-iphone-sms-spoofing, 2012.

[4] 360 Security Guard. Have You Been Violated at the Internet of Things Era?. http://www.aiweibang.com/m/detail/49666997.html, 2015.

[5] Parmar, A. Hacker shows off vulnerabilities of wireless insulin pumps. http://medcitynews.com/2012/03/hacker-shows-off-vulnerabilities-of-wireless-insulin-pumps, 2012.

[6] Black hat 2013. https://www.blackhat.com/us-13, 2014.

Chapter 2

Overview of Dynamically Enabled Defense

Rapid development of informatization has brought great changes to human society. Around the world, whether food, clothing, housing, transportation, and social communication related to people's daily lives or more socialized politics, economy, culture and scientific research, all aspects have been influenced or changed by the Internet age. High-tech products such as cloud computing, big data, search engines, smart phones, online shopping, and online social networking have entered into millions of homes. It allows us to see splendour and marvel never seen before in human history but that the Internet age has brought us in just a few decades. However, in the context of the prevalence of cyber attacks discussed in the previous chapter, benefits and risks always coexist, and constantly evolving cyber attacks are like the "Sword of Damocles" hanging over global cyberspace, or worse. The Sword of Damocles was at least visible, but cyber attacks are not only unpredictable, they further increase the extent of damage due to convenience of the network. How to curb spread of this vicious trend, how to get rid of the fear, and how to find the "penicillin" to curb network viruses are issues that we must think about today.

This chapter will comprehensively introduce research status and technical classification of dynamically enabled cyber defense technology, and discuss the effectiveness and rationality of dynamic enablement technology from the perspectives of kill chain and attack surface respectively.

2.1   Overview of Dynamically Enabled Cyber Defense

2.1.1   *Basic Status of Cyber Defense*

The existing cyber security defense system comprehensively uses a variety of methods such as firewalls, intrusion detection, host monitoring, identity authentication, antivirus software, and vulnerability patching to build a fortress-type rigid defense system to block or segregate outside invasion. This static-layered, deep defense system is based on prior knowledge and possesses advantages of quick response and effective protection in the face of known attacks, but has insufficient capability to counter against unknown attackers, therefore being at risk of being attacked. In this defense system, since the basic security protection facilities usually adopt fixed deployment patterns, related protocols, services, applications, and operation parameters are also generally lacking changes in deployment. Thus, attackers can make a long-term analysis on fixed deployment, find and exploit system vulnerabilities, and take control of compromised systems for a long time after successful attacks. They can continuously jeopardize system security. Once a single attack takes effect locally, it is easy to spread and cause a large-scale impact on the whole network.

In today's society, with rapid development of informatization, cyber security has drawn great attention from countries around the world. The United States formally promoted cyber security to strategic heights of national security in 2003. In 2005, cyberspace was listed as a battle field with equal importance as land, sea, and air battle fields. In 2009, it proposed that "the control of network in the 21st century is as decisive as the control of sea in the 19th century and the control of air in the 20th century". Russia compared network information warfare to the future "sixth generation war", defined cyber attacks as military weapons of mass destruction, and elevated network information warfare to an important position second only to nuclear war. The UK, France, Germany, Japan, and other countries have also increased their investment in cyber security construction and set up professional forces. They have frequently conducted attack and defense drills such as "Cyber Europe", "Cyber Piracy", and "Baltic Cyber Shield", and stepped up efforts to improve their cyber attack and defense capabilities. In October 2012, NATO Center of Excellence issued the *National Cyber Security Framework Manual*, which regulated and planned protection mechanisms and policies from the perspective of national strategic security.

As the cradle of information technology and Internet technology, the United States attaches particular importance to cyber security. It has not only issued a large number of directive and strategic policies, but also invested heavily in research and development of cyber security defense technologies. It is actively seeking breakthrough technologies for cyber security protection. After American Internet specialists made an in-depth study on the national cyber security defense, they found that traditional network protection methods could hardly resist new network threats and urgently needed revolutionary changes, which spawned a new idea of "game-changing" cyber security defense. This idea could be traced back to *The National Comprehensive Cybersecurity* Initiative [1] released by the United States in January 2008, which required establishment and development of "pioneering" technologies, policies, and plans. Obama administration further promoted cyber security work after he took office, and released the *Cyberspace Policy* Review [2] in May 2009, which proclaimed that the American government should implement the idea of the game-changing cyber security research and development. At the same time, the American government launched the National Cyber Leap Year, and began to explore the idea of changing game rules of future cyber security. In December 2011, the National Science and Technology Council (NSTC) released *Trustworthy Cyberspace: Federal cybersecurity research and development strategic plan*. The core is to develop game-changing revolutionary technologies in dealing with real and potential cyber threats. Four "game-changing" research and development themes including built-in security, moving target defense, customized trustworthy space, and cyber economy stimulus were identified as key fields of the White House's strategic plan for cyber security research and development. Among them, Moving Target Defense (MTD) [3–10] technology is regarded by the academia and the industry as the most promising research direction for practical application.

2.1.2   Research Status of Dynamic Cyber Defense Technology

MTD technology represents the latest concept and technology of cyber security game rules. This technology aims to dramatically increase cost of attacks and change the passive situation of network defense by deploying and operating uncertain, random, and dynamic networks and systems. After the direction of MTD was established, relevant researches were carried out rapidly. The U.S. government, the Army, Navy, and Air Force have successively conducted MTD research and development projects, which have achieved preliminary results in both theoretical research and technical realization.

In terms of theoretical model, the related research constructed an attack and defense game model based on the attack surface, mainly from the perspective of strategic confrontation between attackers and defenders, and the mechanism and effectiveness of moving target defense and effectiveness. The typical representatives engaged in related research include scholars such as Pratyusa K. Manadhata from HP Lab, Jeannette M. Wing from the computer science department at Carnegie Mellon University [11]. Pratyusa K. Manadhata and Jeannette M. Wing proposed the formulaic model of system attack surface and introduced the measurement method of system attack surface as an indicator of system security. Then, Pratyusa K. Manadhata defined the concept of attack surface shifting [12] and proposed a two-person stochastic game model based on game theory to determine the optimal moving target defense policy. Jain *et al.* [13], funded by the Center for Risk and Economic Analysis of Terrorism Events under U.S. Department of Homeland Security, applied game theory to challenging realistic problems in the security field, and elaborated ideas and algorithms for resolving large-scale realistic security game conflicts. With the support of the U.S. Department of Defense, Bilar *et al.* [14] studied the collaborative evolution of Conficker worm viruses and relevant defense measures, and established the corresponding quantitative model. With the support of the U.S. Army Research Office, Gonzalez [15] studied cyber security and behavioral game theory based on Instance-Based Learning Theory (IBLT).

In terms of technology implementation, moving target defense technology covers all aspects of information system from network, platform, operating environment to software and data.

By comprehensively using the existing moving target defense technology, American research institutions have successively developed prototype systems such as Helix Metamorphic Shield (HMS) [10], chameleon software system, and MTD command and control framework. HMS is a moving target defense system developed by Claire Le Goues *et al.* [10] under the support of U.S. Army and Air Force research projects. The system is capable of constantly shifting the program attack surface in both time and space dimensions. At the same time, it can use evolutionary algorithms to automatically fix vulnerabilities and reduce the program attack surface. The experimental results have shown that the system can be applied to multiple layers of the software stack. Mohamed Azab from Virginia Tech developed the chameleon software system, which is based on a new type of Cell-Oriented Architecture (COA). It encrypts the software execution behavior by applying multi-dimensional spatiotemporal polymorphism and variable obfuscation technologies, and adopts system change and recovery policy to realize continuous change of operating environment at runtime, thereby effectively resisting malicious code attacks. MTD command and control framework, a joint project held by the Florida Institute of Technology and the Florida Institute of Human and Machine Cognition, addresses the problem of moving target defense system in the process of change being visible and predictable to managers and users.

In addition, mutable networks, adaptive computer networks, and self-cleaning networks developed based on moving target defense technology have made a series of prototype technology achievements. Among them, the mutable network facility (MORPHINATOR) project that restricts enemy reconnaissance was developed by Raytheon Company with a grant from the U.S. Army in 2012. The total investment was $3.1 million, and its purpose was to develop a computer network prototype with "mutable" capability to enable administrators to dynamically tune and configure networks, hosts, and applications in a way that opponents cannot detect and predict, thereby achieving the goal of preventing, delaying, or stopping cyber attacks. Adaptive computer network was a project researched by the University of Kansas with a grant from the U.S. Air Force Research Office in May 2012. It focused on study and quantification of impact of moving target defense on computer networks. The project studied whether computer networks could automatically change their settings and structures to counter online attacks, and developed effective analysis models to determine effectiveness of the moving target defense system. These achievements have been preliminarily applied in the U.S. army, colleges and other institutions.

Importance of moving target defense technology has attracted more attention from the academic community. Sushil Jajodia and Anup K. Ghosh *et al.* from Virginia, USA., published two books about moving target defense for the first time, namely, *Moving Target Defense — Creating Asymmetric Uncertainty for Cyber Threats* [5] and *Moving Target Defense — Application of Game Theory and Adversarial Modeling* [6]. H. Okhravi and M. A. Rabe *et al.* from the Massachusetts Institute of Technology published a technical report *Survey for Cyber Moving Targets* based on development of moving defense technology. The Association for Computing Machinery (ACM), the most famous computer organization in the world, has held a series of seminars on moving target defense [7, 9, 16–18] to discuss further development direction of this technology.

2.1.3 *Definition of Dynamically Enabled Cyber Defense*

We previously discussed attitude and basic research situation from the international community on the dynamic cyber defense technology. It can be seen that there are a variety of technical branches and names for this technical topic, and more influential technologies mainly include: moving target defense [5, 6], mutable network [3], adaptive computer network [19, 20], and self-cleaning network [21].

In addition, a lot of specific field-oriented change technologies are used to defend against cyber attacks, such as communication spectrum transformation technology for communication security.

In the process of informatization, security capabilities are often mentioned and seem to be taken seriously, but serious asymmetry in security attack and defense today shows precisely that people still have some deviations in certification of security capabilities. Some people think that security capabilities are "nice-to-have"; some people think that "Since big companies were attacked, it's normal for small companies to be attacked," "America was attacked, so it does not matter if we were attacked"; some people think that "security is important, but less important than availability." In their eyes, security technology is just an auxiliary tool used for logistical support, a derivative of information systems and, at best, icing on the cake. But damage caused by cyber attacks becomes more serious, which affects not only individuals and companies, but also armies, societies, countries, and the whole world. We think that security should be regarded not only as a common attribute of cyberspace, but also a main metric of cyberspace external functions. Security should not be the opposite of availability, instead a part of availability. Therefore, we hope to use the word "enablement" to express importance of security. The core technology of dynamic enablement is based on a variety of dynamic technologies. But it is not just a technology, it should become a basic capability of information systems, and it is a standard attribute of an information system itself when presenting its capability to the external world. This book proposes dynamically enabled cyber defense technology and the majority of the book will discuss how dynamic technology supports cyber security defense. However, we should call it dynamically enabled cyberspace, as dynamic technology is not only a kind of external factor of protecting cyberspace, but also a kind of basic prerequisite capability of any cyber operation. Only with this level of cognition can we put security into practice, so that dynamic security defense technology can be effectively implemented in the whole life cycle of information system design, generation, operation, and maintenance. Dynamic defense technology must not be an antivirus software or intrusion detection system installed on the large operating system — cyberspace, but should be a kernel part of the large operating system.

Based on this understanding, we proposed the definition of dynamically enabled cyber defense.

Dynamic enablement is a basic security concept that needs to be implemented in the design process of a cyber information system throughout its life cycle. Its purpose is to use all possible means to enable all participating subjects, communication protocols, and information data in the whole life cycle of the information system to have capabilities to actively or passively, individually or simultaneously transform all of its possible characteristic attributes or information presented by attributes in two fields of time and space while maintaining availability of cyber information system, so as to achieve all or part of the following effects: (a) It is difficult for the attacker to discover a target; (b) the attacker discovers a wrong target; (c) the attacker discovers a target but is unable to launch an attack; (d) the attacker can launch attacks but cannot sustain them; (e) the attacker can launch attacks but they are quickly detected. Any technology that conforms to the above characteristics can be categorized into dynamically enabled cyber security defense technology.

This concept has a wider scope than the moving target defense and mutable network mentioned above. The key point is that it not only describes a security technology, but also describes an internal security capability formed by changes in the information system itself. Specifically, the concept of dynamically enabled cyber defense covers security technologies or concepts based on the dynamic ideas, such as moving target defense and mutable network, meanwhile, it also provides a larger changing space for all entities of the information system. The specific space of this concept includes both the dynamic defense technologies we have known so far and security enhancement methods based on dynamic change capability of entities that we need to further discover.

2.2 Dynamically Enabled Defense Technology

Each technology of dynamically enabled defense is designed to protect an entity in the information system. As shown in Figure 2.1, generally speaking, entities in the information system mainly include

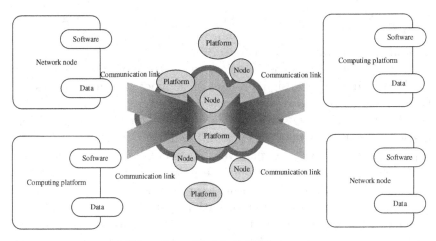

Figure 2.1. Entities in Cyberspace

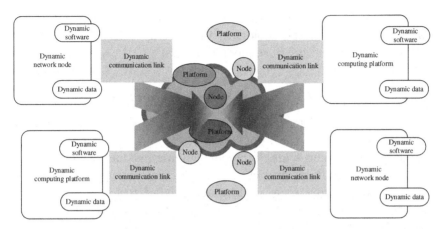

Figure 2.2. Dynamic Entities in Cyberspace

software, network nodes, computing platforms, and data. So, we propose four categories of dynamically-enabled defense technologies: dynamic software defense technology, dynamic network defense technology, dynamic platform defense technology, and dynamic data defense technology, as shown in Figure 2.2.

The technology classification here is dominated by entity objects and mainly illustrates the role of dynamically enabled defense technology in ensuring security of entity operation process. Some dynamically enabled technologies are only useful for some entities, but there are also situations in which the concept of a technology is adopted by various entity protection measures, such as classical randomization technology and N-variant technology, which are applied to different degrees in protection of multiple entities. Taking randomization technology as an example, in the dynamic software defense, the technology can be concretized into instruction set randomization technology and address space randomization technology, etc.; in dynamic network defense, it can be concretized into IP address randomization technology; in dynamic data defense, it can be concretized into data randomization technology. Although the above dynamically enabled defense technologies for different entities are all derived from the concept of randomization technology, in the actual operation process, there exist specific improvements and environmental adaptations for different entities. Therefore, it is necessary to further elaborate and analyze these technologies in a fine-grained way.

This section will provide an overview of four categories of dynamically enabled defense technologies, and specific technical details will be further discussed in subsequent chapters.

2.2.1 *Dynamic Software Defense Technology*

Dynamic software defense technology refers to the technology that dynamically changes the application itself and its execution environment. Such changes may include changing instruction sets, memory space distribution, and changing program instructions or their execution order, grouping, or format. Related technologies mainly include Address Space Layout Randomization (ASLR) technology, instruction set randomization technology, in-place code randomization technology, software polymorphism technology, and multivariant execution technology.

(1) ASLR technology

Address space randomization or ASLR [22–26] is the most successful and widely used diversification technology. The basic idea is very simple: randomizing the location of objects in memory to prevent attacks based on addresses of these objects. In 2000, address space randomization was first implemented in Linux kernel PaX patch [27]. After that, most of the major operating systems used this technology, including Windows (first used for Windows Vista in 2007, later used for Windows Server 2008, and Windows 7), Linux (after 2005, partial implementation in Linux kernel, and more complete implementation in most Linux-enhanced versions), and Mac OS (limited implementation since OSX 10.5).

The easiest way to implement ASLR is to randomize base addresses of large memory areas. For example, PaX randomizes base addresses [27] so that the executable area contains program codes and static data structures, the stack area contains execution stacks, and the mapped storage area contains heaps, shared memory, and dynamic load libraries. By adding a randomly generated offset to the address, the address of each area can be randomized. However, the layout remains the same within each area. The advantage of this approach is that it can be implemented by the program loader without any modifications to the executable program. The other implementation method of ASLR is to randomize the address layout more comprehensively. For example, address obfuscation is randomization of absolute and relative locations of data and code. Specifically, it randomly changes the order of variables in the stack or structure and fills some data between objects. However, unlike the segment base address randomization, making this change requires an in-depth analysis of the target program.

(2) Instruction set randomization technology

Instruction set randomization is a common technology to prevent code injection attacks by blurring target instruction sets [28–30]. Using instruction set randomization technology, although the attacker knows that he can inject the malicious code into the target application through a vulnerability, he cannot build the code with expected behavior without knowing the target instruction set.

Randomized Instruction Set Emulator (RISE) proposed by Barrante *et al.* [29] is a typical instance of instruction randomization. In this system, the method of instruction set randomization is to generate random bit sequence when the code is loaded, and xor operation is performed on each instruction in the program according to the corresponding random bit. Then, the program is run in the emulator and xor operation is performed on the instruction with random bit to obtain the original instruction. This will cause the instruction injected by the attacker to be xored with the random bit before it runs, but the attacker does not know the random key, so the injected code will not produce the expected behavior.

Another implementation method of instruction set randomization is block encryption. For example, Hu Wei *et al.* [30] used Advanced Encryption Standard (AES) to encrypt the program code and realized instruction set randomization. Higher-level instruction sets can also be randomized. For example, by adding random numbers to SQL instructions, SQL injection attacks can be prevented; by randomizing Perl language components, Perl injection attacks can be prevented.

(3) In-place code randomization technology

Based on randomization of binary executable file code segments, in-place code randomization technology uses a binary code conversion technology to disrupt the exploit code that implements ROP (Return-Oriented Programming) attacks, so as to defend against

ROP attacks [31]. Common in-place code randomization technologies mainly include atomic instruction replacement, instruction rearrangement, and register redistribution.

The basic idea of atomic instruction replacement technology is to use different instruction combinations to achieve the same calculations. In code randomization applications, the original instructions are replaced by instructions with equivalent functions but different sequences. It can break ROP link, although the program produces the same result.

The core idea of instruction rearrangement is that, for a binary file, its internal instruction sequence is fixed, which is determined by the compiler according to the specific input conditions. If different conditions are selected, differentiated target files with the same functions but different internal instruction sequences can be generated. Based on this discovery, instruction sequence in the basic block of binary file can be rearranged to achieve the purpose of disrupting the ROP attack.

The core idea of register redistribution is that, during compilation of binary file code, the compiler randomly assigns many variables of a high-level program to smaller register groups. That is, at some program points, a variable should be stored in the register. Such program points are selected by complex allocation algorithms. At this time, if a new variable needs to be mapped to a register, the compiler can select any available register at that point to save the new variable. Therefore, the actual register allocation is only one of many possible register allocations. Based on this observation, the name of register operand can be redistributed in existing code by different but equivalent register allocations, without affecting semantics of the original code. Therefore, this can also disrupt ROP attacks.

(4) Software polymorphism technology

In order to break the huge security risk caused by the static nature of software, software polymorphism technology arises at the right moment. This technology generates a large number of software entities with the same functions and different internal structures for the same source code based on the compiler, and distributes them to different users, making the same software used by each user have different internal structures, thus effectively increasing cost of attack. In the process of generating polymorphic software, it is possible to comprehensively apply the related technologies based on memory address space randomization, and other various technologies such as variable rearrangement and function adjustment.

(5) Multi-variant execution technology

Multi-variant execution is a technology that prevents execution of malicious codes at runtime. By running multiple semantically equivalent variants at the same time and comparing their behaviors at synchronization point, once different behaviors are found at the premise of the same input, it can determine whether there is an attack behavior by the monitor. Compared with software polymorphism technology, polymorphic software only runs one entity at runtime, and software used by different users is different. However, multi-variant software used by the same user runs multiple semantically equivalent variants simultaneously.

The design by Cox *et al.* implemented N-variant system framework [32] and modified the system kernel to make the monitor run at the core layer. Todd Jackson *et al.* [31] from the University of California designed and implemented Multi-Variant Execution Environment (MVEE) by using multi-variant execution technology. Multi-variant execution is completed jointly by the compiler and MVEE: compilation instructions generated by multiple variants are added to the core algorithm or key control process of the program that needs to be heavily protected in the source code, so as to generate diversified code variants at compile time. Multiple variants in the MVEE are run, so as to synchronize and monitor behaviors of each variant on system call. When finding a variant exceptional compared with other variants, it can be determined that the variant is attacked, then execution of the variant can be stopped, and execution of other variants can be selected as the result of program execution.

2.2.2 *Dynamic Network Defense Technology*

Dynamic network defense technology refers to implementing dynamic defense at the network level. Specifically, it uses dynamization, virtualization, and randomization methods to break staticity, certainty, and similarity defects of network elements such as network topology, network configuration, network resources, network nodes, and network business, resist malicious attacks against target networks, and increase difficulty of attackers' network detection and intranet node penetration. The related technologies mainly include dynamic network address translation (DyNAT) technology, allocation of network address space randomization, end information hopping protection technology, and relevant dynamic protection technology based on overlay network.

(1) DyNAT technology

On the basis of traditional Network Address Translation (NAT) technology, Dorene Kewley *et al.* [33] further expanded scope and mechanism of network node identification changes, and proposed DyNAT technology, which is used to prevent attackers from gathering information on intranets and nodes by attackers. The core idea of this technology is to provide corresponding mechanisms and methods to constantly change identification of the terminal node by changing fixed addressing of the terminal node. That is, perform scrambling processing such as encryption on the information related to host identification in the network data packet header, dynamically update the key by time or network attributes, start transformation before the data packet enters into the network, and restore change before it enters into the host. This method of periodically changing communication protocol fields can be used to prevent attackers from attacking individual terminal hosts, disrupt effect of man-in-the-middle sniffing, prevent attackers from scanning the intranets, and hinder attackers from collecting information on terminal nodes.

(2) Network address space randomization technology

Network Address Space Randomization (NASR) refers to technologies and methods by which hosts on the network can get network addresses randomly. NASR technology implemented based on DHCP protocol [34] is a method to prevent worm propagation and attack based on IP address list. Like other worm defense methods, NASR is only a partial solution for worm attacks. This approach requires modifying DHCP server to frequently change the host IP address, which is essentially an IP address-hopping technology. This technology contains speed of worm virus propagation by invalidating blacklist of IP address lists that worm attacks before the virus launches and spreads. This technology cannot actually prevent any specific attacks, but helps to reduce effectiveness of scanning attacks.

(3) End information-hopping protection technology

End information-hopping technology refers to that in the end-to-end data transmission, both parties or one party of communication change port, address, time slot, encryption algorithm, and even protocol in a pseudo-random manner according to a certain protocol, so as to destroy enemy attacks and interference and realize active network protection. According to categories of hopping participants, end information hopping can be one-end information hopping of the server or both-end information hopping of peer hosts. Because implementation of both-end information-hopping system is very complicated, most of current research and prototype system implementation are focused on one-end information-hopping research on the server side.

End information-hopping can be used in both attack and defense. As early as 2003, U.S. Army proposed a hybrid hopping defense policy based on port and address hopping in APOD (Applications that Participate in their Own Defense) project. This policy presents a network protection method against port scanning and DoS attack through false port address hopping. In this method, address and port of the server do not hop, but only use false address and port to implement address/port replacement in data transmission communication, in order to confuse external attackers. Both parties of truly legal communication know real address information through cooperation, negotiation, and authorization.

(4) Related dynamic protection technology based on overlay network

The core idea of the related dynamic protection technology based on overlay network is to build a dynamically generated network in the application layer, which is composed of a central distribution center as the root of network and several nodes that receive content from the distribution center. It also sets up a set of specific specifications to manage addition of trusted nodes, transmission of trust mechanisms between nodes, and delivery of information. This trusted network can change path of content distribution, reconfigure nodes, and respond to dynamic changes of links or nodes timely. It is an application-level dynamic network application mode, which can be used to prevent resource attacks such as denial of service and manipulation of Web content. Using this technology, due to distributed characteristics and good connectivity of the overlay network, the attacker needs to flood thousands of machines at the same time to achieve effect of the denial of service attack; on the other hand, by digitally signing distributed content, each node in the network can verify integrity of content by checking the signature, thus preventing content manipulation.

2.2.3 *Dynamic Platform Defense Technology*

Traditional platform systems are designed with a single architecture and remain unchanged for a long time after delivery, which provides enough time for attackers to spy on and attempt to attack. Once system vulnerabilities are discovered and successfully exploited by malicious attackers, the system will face serious hazards such as service exception, information theft, and data tampering. Dynamic platform defense technology is an effective way to solve this inherent defect. Platform defense technology is designated to build a diversified operating platform, dynamically change the operating environment of the application to make the system present uncertainty and dynamics, thus shortening time of application exposed on a platform and creating the reconnaissance fog for attackers. So, attackers cannot launch attacks effectively since they do not know the exact structure of the system. Related technologies mainly include platform dynamization based on dynamic reconfiguration, application live migration based on heterogeneous platforms, diversification of Web services, and platform dynamization based on intrusion tolerance.

(1) Platform dynamization technology based on dynamic reconfiguration

A dynamically reconfigurable system is a heterogeneous computing environment, usually including general processors, programmable logic devices, and so on. The programmable logic device can dynamically load different configuration data under the control of the processor, carry out runtime reconfiguration, and achieve uninterrupted tasks processing during reconfiguration process to ensure continuity of task execution.

By using the characteristic that a dynamically reconfigurable system supports dynamic reconfiguration, we can design multiple executable files and configuration data which meet requirement of a certain application task and run in general processors and programmable logic devices through diversified software/hardware task partition and differential logic circuit design. Also, in the process of system operation, executable files and corresponding configuration data files loaded in the system can be randomly changed. Since configuration data change of the programmable logic device will change its circuit logic structure, dynamization of application operating platform can be realized by randomly changing the configuration data file of the system. These dynamic changes make it difficult for attackers to carry out effective reconnaissance and detection on the system, so as to effectively resist code injection attacks against the platform and attacks against defective hardware components, and improve defense capabilities of the system.

(2) Application live migration technology based on heterogeneous platform

Application live migration technology based on heterogeneous platforms achieves diversity and randomness of operating platforms by changing application operating environments (including hardware platforms and operating systems) in a random and dynamic manner [35]. Specifically, the technology uses operating system level virtualization and checkpoint compilation to create a virtual execution environment, and migrate between different platforms while saving application states (including execution state, file state, and network connection, etc.). By changing the platform in a random and dynamic manner, platform information collected by attackers in the reconnaissance phase becomes invalid during the attack. To a certain extent, this increases difficulty for the attacker to attack the system.

(3) Web services diversification technology

This technology improves its defense capabilities by realizing diversification of Web services [36]. The basic idea is to create multiple virtual servers with different software architectures, make some virtual servers change between offline and online state dynamically, and finally use the scheduler to select which virtual server will handle received requests. It mainly includes two implementation ways: First, the virtual server has a diversified software architecture, and randomly selects an online virtual server to provide service for service requests at different times. Second, some virtual servers are switched to online or offline state at the fixed intervals or based on events.

When the virtual server is switched to offline state, it should be restored to initial security state.

(4) Platform dynamization technology based on intrusion tolerance

Platform dynamization technology based on intrusion tolerance uses technical principle of intrusion tolerance [37], adopts heterogeneous multiple service systems and dynamic change mechanism to process service requests from users, and for response result of each online service system, determines correct processing result returned to users through voting. This technology largely avoids the situation where different redundant components have the same security vulnerability, thereby preventing intruders from using the same approach to intrude multiple redundant components.

2.2.4   *Dynamic Data Defense Technology*

Dynamic data defense mainly refers to dynamically changing format, syntax, coding, or representation of relevant data according to system defense requirements, so as to increase attack surface of the attacker and achieve the effect of increasing difficulty of attacks. In current known researches, data dynamization technology mainly refers to memory data-oriented randomization and diversification technology, but diversification technology of protocol syntax and configuration data in applications is also categorized into the data dynamization technology in some researches. Related technologies mainly include data randomization technology [38], N-variant data diversification technology [39], fault-tolerant N-copy data diversification technology [40], and data diversification technology for Web application security [41].

(1) Data randomization

The main idea of this technology [38] is to encrypt the data written into memory in the program by category, so as to avoid the problem that one type of data can overflow into address space of another type of data, thus tampering with original assignment of variables. Any function that attempts to perform write operations writes randomized data in memory; any function that attempts to perform read operations also reads encrypted randomized data. As long as the overflow attack is processed in different types of data, the data that is processed randomly by this type of key cannot be correctly decrypted in another type. Data randomization is a classic case of data dynamization, which can be used to prevent non-control-data attacks that cannot be solved by dynamic technologies such as ALSR and ISR [42].

(2) N-variant data diversification technology

This technology is mainly the evolution of N-variant technology idea in the field of data confrontation [39]. By diversifying a specific type of data, it can build variant programs that are semantically consistent with the original program. In envisaged effect of data diversification, it is impossible for an attacker to successfully attack two variants simultaneously with one input. Therefore, the system manager can set a monitor to compare behaviors of the input value which is implemented by various variants, so as to judge rationality of the input value. If the behavior is abnormal, the manager will decide that the attack behavior is detected.

(3) N-Copy data diversification technology for fault-tolerance

N-Copy data diversification technology for fault-tolerance mainly provides an automatic fault-tolerant processing capability for key data application processing programs [40], such as missile launch programs and aircraft flight path planning programs. Its core idea is to assume that some form of input data may cause the system to malfunction, but it is possible to change expression form of input data and take changed data as a new system input under the premise of essential content of input data being unchanged. Therefore, system defects can be avoided and system failures can be bypassed, thereby improving system reliability.

(4) Data diversification technology for Web application security

Data diversification technologies for Web application security [41] mainly include SQL instruction set randomization, script API randomization, stored data reference name randomization, code component randomization, etc. By using one or a combination of these technologies, high-level code injection attacks (such as SQL injection attack, cross-site scripting attack) and low-level code injection attacks against internal applications can be prevented.

2.2.5   *Essence of Dynamically Enabled Defense Technology — Temporal and Spatial Dynamization*

Various possible dynamic technologies for software, network, platform, and data are introduced in the previous sections, which provide an important basis for the research of dynamically enabled cyber defense technologies. In the process of implementing predictable dynamic systems, information systems may adopt defense technologies which are based on these technologies themselves, or based on their combination or improvement, but dynamically enabled cyber defense technologies are by no means limited to above technologies. In addition to these technologies, researchers also need to choose appropriate dynamic policies according to the game model of information system development and the cost of attack and defense. However, these technologies give a hint that their application practices also stimulate us to choose dynamic technologies appropriately when facing different information system entities. This information includes the following aspects.

(a) Principle 1: The best and most common method for hiding entity feature information is the information randomization method based on encryption/decryption. Software randomization technology and instruction set randomization technology are produced when the concept is applied to software entity dynamization; network feature randomization technologies such as IP address randomization and port randomization are produced when the concept is applied to network entity dynamization. Randomization of special type of data or classified data randomization comes into being when the concept is applied to data entity dynamization. The characteristic of randomization technologies is not to detect attacks, but to try to directly prevent attacks in nature.

(b) Principle 2: Polymorphism technology (more specifically, multi-variant technology) is also a common dynamization method, and its core is to make entities exist in multiple forms simultaneously. The core idea of its counterattack is that it is difficult for the attacker to invade multiple variants simultaneously through one attack pattern. Although the attacker may still break through one of them, this technology can quickly lock onto the attack and then counter it as long as multiple variants show differentiated behavior. This dynamic concept is also embodied in dynamic technologies related to multiple entities, such as software diversification, platform diversification, and data diversification.

(c) An in-depth analysis of dynamic technologies mentioned in Principles 1 and 2 reveals the following aspects more fundamentally.

Randomization technology is more presented as dynamic change of an entity at the timeline. Taking software randomization as an example, the encryption key used by a software at time point T_1 will change over time, and the software at time point T_2 may generate different instruction sets, different memory address space distributions, or differentiated software entities themselves due to change of encryption key.

Multi-variant technology is more presented as dynamic change of an entity in space. Taking platform multi-variant technology as an example, the backend providing the same Web page service may be multiple servers with different architectures. For example, it uses two completely different architectures at the same time, Linux+Apache and Windows+IIS, to provide completely consistent Web page services.

In general, most dynamic technologies are essentially implementing regular or driving changes in space or time or space and time for some component of the entity or the entity representation.

The rules summarized above not only make it easier for us to distinguish and classify these existing dynamic technologies, but also allow us to think about more feasible dynamic defense technologies in the future, guiding us to make faster and smarter judgments.

2.3 Dynamic Enablement and Cyber Kill Chain

Value of each dynamic enablement technology lies in its capability to disrupt one or more phases of the attack. For example, instruction set randomization technology may be committed to reducing possibility of launching an attack, while dynamic network defense technology focuses on increasing difficulty for the attacker to gather information on the target machine. Therefore, by discussing relationship between the dynamically enabled defense technology and the cyber kill chain, we can intuitively see direct effects and influences of these technologies in defending against cyber attacks.

There are multiple divisions of Cyber Kill Chain in different literature, and different divisions are based on different purposes. For example, cyber warfare kill chain (including various phases such as reconnaissance, weapon development, delivery, exploit, installation, command and control, operation on the target system), behavior-oriented kill chain (including phases such as damage, protection, detection, response, and survival), and detection kill chain (including phases such as defense, disturbance, and destruction). However, these different divisions can be roughly summarized as: gathering intelligence, finding targets, taking out weapons, launching attacks, and remaining multiple states of the attack in sequence or cross-execution. Here is a description of the cyber kill chain proposed by scholars from the Massachusetts Institute of Technology [8], including five steps.

(a) Reconnoiter: The attacker collects information about the target.
(b) Access: The attacker tries to connect to the target system to get its properties (version, vulnerability, configuration, etc.).
(c) Write attack code: The attacker writes code against the system vulnerability in order to gain or increase permissions.
(d) Launch an attack: The attacker sends the attack code to the target system. It may be implemented by phishing attacks through network connection or through more complex supply chains or leapfrog attacks (such as using a USB disk containing the attack code).
(e) Attack continuously: The attacker installs more backdoors or sets path to access the target system.

2.3.1 *Dynamic Software Defense and Kill Chain*

All the network services we encounter use software as the interactive interface to exchange data and perceive information based on some hardware entity. For example, we use browser software to browse Web pages on a laptop, use weather app to view the weather on a smartphone, and use a browser or Taobao app to shop online. These facts show that software security protection is the most direct protective means of protection. There are many kinds of software, from the underlying operating system software, database software, middleware software, Web service software to browser software and mobile apps that provide front-end user interface. But all in all, compared with network, platform and data, software is mainly the user-oriented and front-end oriented entities. Therefore, when the attacker launches an attack on software, he has already completed phases such as reconnaissance and access connection. That is to say, dynamic software defense technology cannot resist attacker's detection and access to the information system, but it can destroy phases of writing attack code and launching attack in the cyber kill chain.

For example, a hacker needs to calculate return address of overflow point precisely to launch an effective buffer overflow attack. Because only when overflowed data overwrites the original return address, the attack code can achieve its goal. However, if the address space randomization technology is adopted, address space of the vulnerability detected by the hacker is different from that of the vulnerability attacked. This makes it impossible for the attacker to write the attack code with accurate overflow address, that is, the phase of writing attack code in the kill chain is broken.

At the same time, instruction set randomization technology can invalidate some attack codes against specific instruction sets. The idea is useful in dealing with attacks because hackers cannot launch attacks at will. Let's take the buffer overflow attack as an example. Even if shell code has been implanted into the target machine, its effectiveness depends on the instruction set environment in the current software environment. If core instructions (such as MOV, POP, PUSH) in the instruction set of the current operating system x86 are transformed, it is impossible for the shell code encoded with standard x86 instruction set to run correctly on the operating system with the instruction set changed. This means that the phase of launching attack in the kill chain is blocked.

2.3.2 *Dynamic Network Defense and Kill Chain*

Importance of network entities in cyberspace is self-evident, but networks we discuss here focus more on network protocols, network switching devices, and network information presented by software applications. Unlike software, which interact more with users directly, the network is an unknown underlying entity that keeps cyberspace running. Interactions between ordinary users and network entities happen mainly in the process of installing routers, configuring IP addresses, and entering Wi-Fi passwords. But for the hacker, the network entity is a bridgehead for carrying out network attacks and is the first challenge to overcome. It can be said that if the network environment is not clear to hackers, most hackers basically give up attacks on the target entity. Every remote attack by a hacker relies heavily on his knowledge of victim's network information, such as IP address and port, which are indispensable and necessary information. Therefore, the effective dynamic network defense technology will directly hinder attackers from reconnoitering and accessing the information system, and reconnaissance and access are initial steps of the attack kill chain. Without these steps, subsequent steps of the kill chain cannot be effectively implemented.

For example, when the hacker attacks a network entity, he often starts with monitoring network traffic, detects the target information by analyzing sensitive information in the traffic, such as operating system type, compiler type, and Web server type, etc. However, if the network information randomization technology is adopted, the hacker could get incorrect randomization results even if they have detected the information. This achieves the capability to destroy the reconnaissance phase in the kill chain.

Furthermore, when the hacker attacks any network entity, the target address must be determined, either by knowing the IP address or by obtaining domain name information. But if the appropriate IP address randomization technology is used, it is difficult for the hacker to lock onto the target remotely when he conducts reconnaissance and attack, since the network entity has different "house number". This effectively blocks access steps in the kill chain.

2.3.3 *Dynamic Platform Defense and Kill Chain*

The platforms here mainly refer to the computing platforms that provide network interconnection capacity and the basic network service platforms running on computing platforms. These platforms not only provide connection entities for underlying networks, but also provide operating environments for upper software applications. In the network confrontation, the platforms are not direct attack objects by hackers, but they are big backstage supporters behind defenders. Because the platforms provide software operating environments, in terms of destroying kill chain, they mainly prevent attackers from writing attack code for a particular platform, or undermine persistence of attacks.

For example, when a hacker attacks a Web service, if vulnerability code of IIS is used and Web service background attacked is built on IIS, the attack may be successful. But if the appropriate diversification platform technology is adopted, and there is also an Apache Web application server providing the same Web services, then the defender can quickly lock onto attacks by IIS server and Apache server performing the same request to send different responses (one was attacked successfully and another not). In this sense, this dynamic technology can inhibit hackers to write attack code for specific platforms and then launch attacks. At the same time, if dynamic change of this platform is not spatial change (both IIS server and Apache server are provided), instead temporal change, this platform will change to a different Web application server platform over time (for example, changing from IIS to Apache after an hour), then the originally effective attack becomes unsustainable so as to destroy persistency of the attack.

2.3.4   *Dynamic Data Defense and Kill Chain*

Data is blood and vein in the network space information system. It's everywhere on platforms, software, and networks. It is an entity itself and survives on other entities. The data here is mainly focused on the "operand" data relative to instructions in software execution environment. According to introduction of the previous dynamic data defense technologies, it can be seen that software entities generated by adopting data randomization technology and data diversification technology can also break phases of writing attack code and launching attack in the cyber kill chain.

For example, in the uncontrolled data attack [42], hackers normally overflow malicious permission ID to ordinary user ID (UserID). But if data randomization is performed, overflowed data will not be parsed correctly, and hackers cannot tamper with execution permissions and launch attacks effectively. Because decryption key of the overlay area is unknown, hackers cannot write the correct attack data. Therefore, to a certain extent, this achieves the capability to prevent the hackers from writing correct attack code in the kill chain.

2.4   Dynamic Enablement and Dynamic Attack Surfaces

In the description of effectiveness of the dynamic enablement technology, we can intuitively see effectiveness of this security technology from the perspective of breaking the cyber kill chain. But in more scientific theoretical researches, the attack surface theory is more used to verify the effectiveness of dynamically enabled defense technology. Unlike the cyber kill chain, the attack surface theory can not only qualitatively analyze capability of security technology, but also quantitatively measure defense capability of security technology more rigorously. It also helps us understand how the dynamic enablement technology improves security protection effectiveness.

This section will first introduce origin and definition of attack surfaces, then give establishment method of attack surface metrics, and finally introduce the concept of moving attack surfaces [11, 12] and their relationship with dynamically enabled defense technology.

2.4.1   *Attack Surfaces*

Many attacks against the system (such as those based on buffer overflow vulnerabilities) occur in the process of sending data from its operating environment to the system. Similarly, many other attacks against the system (such as symbolic link attack) occur because the system sends data to its environment. In both types of attacks, attackers use the system channel (such as a socket) to connect to the system, invoke the system program (such as API), and send data items (such as input strings) to the system or receive them from the system. Attackers could also use persistent data items (such as files) to indirectly send data to the system. Attackers can send data to the system by writing data in the files that the system will read. Similarly, attackers can use shared persistent data items to indirectly receive data from the system. So, attackers can attack the system through system programs, channels, and data items that appear in the system environment. Therefore, system programs, channels, and data items are collectively called system resources which are used to define attack surface [11] of the system, as shown in Figure 2.3.

However, not all resources are part of the attack surface. Only when the attacker uses a resource to attack the system, that resource

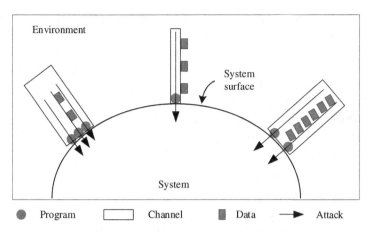

Figure 2.3.   System Attack Surfaces

is part of the attack surface. So the entry point and the exit point frameworks are introduced to identify relevant resources.

(1) Entry point

The system code base includes a series of functions, such as API function. Each function takes an input variable and outputs the result. System functions that receive system environment data items are entry points of the system. For example, functions that receive user data or read configuration files are all the entry points. In terms of system s, if function m has any of following characteristics, it is a direct entry point of the system: (a) The user or system in s environment calls m and sends input data items to m; (b) m reads persistent data items; (c) m calls system API of s environment and receives data items as return results. The indirect entry point refers to the function that can receive data items from the direct entry point.

(2) Exit point

System functions that send data items to the system environment are exit points of the system. For example, the function that writes the log is an exit point. In terms of system s, if its function m has following characteristics, it is a direct exit point of the system: (a) The user or system in s environment calls m and receives data items returned by m; (b) m writes a persistent data item; (c) m calls system API of s environment and sends input data items to API.

The indirect exit point refers to the function that can send data to the direct exit point.

(3) Channel

Each system has a set of channels that are ways for users or other systems to interact with the system, such as TCP/UDP sockets, RPC endpoints, and named pipes. Attackers use the system channel to connect to the system and call system functions. Thus, channels are another basic way to attack the system.

(4) Untrusted data items

Attackers can use persistent data items, indirectly send data to the system, or indirectly receive data issued by the system. Types of persistent data items include various files, cookies, database records, and registry entries. After attackers write to the file, the system can read it. Similarly, attackers can read the file after the system writes to it. Therefore, persistent data items are the third fundamental way to attack the system.

(5) Definition of the attack surface

The system attack surface refers to subsets of system resources that the attacker can use to launch an attack. According to this definition, the attacker can send data to or get data from the system to attack it by using set M of entry points and exit points, channel set C, and set I of untrusted data items. Therefore, M, C, and I are subsets of attack surface-related resources. For given system s and its environment, the attack surface of s can be defined as a triplet $\langle M, C, I \rangle$.

2.4.2   *Attack Surface Measurement*

Calculating the amount of attack surface resources is the most general way to measure the system attack surface. This method assigns the same weight to all resources. But since possibility of attackers using these resources to launch attacks is not equal, this method has some defects. The ratio of damage potential to attack cost can be used to estimate impact of resources on the system attack surface. Damage potential refers to degree of damage caused by the attacker using resources to attack the system, and attack cost refers to efforts made by the attacker to obtain necessary access permissions to use resources to launch an attack.

Table 2.1. Evaluation Criteria of Damage Potential and Attack Cost of Different Resources

Evaluation Object	Damage Potential	Attack Cost
Method	Permission. For example, if a method runs as root, you can get root permission by implementing buffer overflow against the method. Therefore, if this method runs as root, its damage potential is greater.	Permission required to access. For example, in order to use these resources, you need access permissions. Different access permissions represent different effort degrees required. If you want root permission, you need to make greater effort, and so on.
Channel	Protocol. For example, TCP socket allows raw data to be received, but RPC does not. As a result, TCP socket may restrict the data exchange, thereby affecting damage potential. Therefore, the attack surface of TCP protocol is a bit larger than that of RPC.	Permission required to access.
Data	Data type. For example, the file can contain executable code, but the registry entry cannot. Therefore, from the perspective of data types, the attack surface of a file is larger than that of a registry entry.	Permission required to access.

In practice, damage potential and attack cost can be estimated based on resource properties, as shown in Table 2.1. For example, damage potential of a method is estimated based on its permission. By using a method in an attack, the attacker can gain the same permission as that method. For example, the attacker uses the root method buffer overflow to get root permission. The attacker uses the system channel to connect to the system and sends data to the system or receives data sent by the system. The channel protocol restricts the data exchange using channels. For example, TCP socket allows exchange raw bytes, while RPC Endpoint does not allow. Therefore, damage potential of the channel can be estimated based on the channel protocol. The attacker can use persistent data items to indirectly send data to the system, or indirectly receive data from the system. But types of persistent data limit data exchange. For example, a file may contain executable code, but the registry entry does not. The attacker can use files to send executable code to attack the system, but cannot use registry entries to send executable code. Therefore, the damage potential of the data items can be estimated based on their types.

After the attacker obtains access permissions, he can use resources to launch attacks. But to obtain these permissions, the attacker usually needs to make certain efforts. Therefore, for three resources of method, channel, and data, we can estimate attack cost of using these resources to launch an attack based on resource access permissions.

In practice, we usually assign different values to resource properties to calculate ratio of damage potential to attack cost. For example, we can calculate the ratio of damage potential of the method to attack cost based on assigned value for access permission of the method. You can sort all the properties according to their characteristics, and then assign value to each property based on sorting result. For example, compared with a method with non-root permission, if the attacker uses a method with root permission to cause greater damage to the system, then the method with root permission should be assigned a higher value than the method with non-root permission. The actual value chosen is a little bit subjective and needs to depend on the specific system and its environment.

According to three aspects of method, channel, and data, we can quantify metric value of the system attack surface and estimate total effect of the method, channel, and data items on the attack surface, respectively. Suppose that mapping relationship between resource and the ratio of its damage potential to attack cost is method DER, and the attack surface of system s is $\langle M, C, I \rangle$, then the attack surface metric value of s is a triplet $\langle \sum_{m \in M} der(m), \sum_{c \in C} der(c), \sum_{d \in I} der(d) \rangle$.

2.4.3 Dynamic Attack Surface

This section explores application of attack surface measurement in moving target defense. Moving target defense is a protection method that requires system defender to constantly shift the system attack surface. Intuitively speaking, the defender realizes the attack surface shifting by constantly changing resources of the attack surface or changing role of various resources. However, not all changes can shift the attack surface. The defender can shift the attack surface by reducing at least one resource on the attack surface, or by reducing ratio of at least one resource's damage potential to power consumption. With other conditions remaining unchanged, if resources used by the original attack have disappeared (changed), the attack is no longer effective. However, new resources may appear on the attack surface after its shifting, which may make the system suffer from new attacks. As a result, attackers will have to increase cost to maintain original attacks or find new ones.

About research on the attack surface, Yih Huang [36] from Center for Security Information Systems of George Mason University in the United States believed that it is generally assumed that a small attack surface can increase the security when he explained the security of Moving Attack Surfaces (MAS). The common goal of many such studies is to define some indicators that measure area of a given system attack surface. These results can help administrators to identify unwanted components or insecure configurations in the system, thus reducing system attack surfaces. However, with more attack surfaces, moving attack surfaces seem to increase the overall attack surface area. Therefore, it is necessary to discuss whether the moving attack surface method weakens security of the whole system. Yih Huang also proposed that existing metrics of the attack surface area were not completely suitable for evaluating moving attack surfaces. There are two reasons: The first reason is that changing properties of the moving attack surface broke a basic assumption of existing indicators that the attack surface remained unchanged; the second reason is uncertainty of accessibility, namely, an attacker could not control over which virtual server the attack packet would be directed to. This broke another previous assumption that target attack surfaces were always accessible to attackers. Therefore, Yih Huang proposed two points based on above reasons.

(a) Because packets from the client/attacker may be sent to any one of several different virtual servers, current set of online attack surfaces can be viewed as a single hybrid surface. However, the sum of these surfaces may not be very accurate, as the detection and attack packets will be randomly assigned among M online surfaces. Similarly, uncertainty means that it seems inaccurate to evaluate security or probability of successful attack with a single attack surface. In the context of moving targets, it is more appropriate to evaluate recovery capability of the entire system after being invaded, but it is also very challenging.

(b) Unpredictable and constantly changing properties of moving attack surfaces involve some probabilistic/random models. The result cannot be represented as a single number or array, similar to attack surface indicators used previously. Selectivity probability is used to determine the possibility that a virtual server instance will be listed as a request/attack target, which may be lower limit of attack success rate.

Yih Huang, believes that although research in this field is still inconclusive, enhanced recovery capability of the invaded moving attack surface can be preliminarily evaluated. The experimental results show that attackers will have to face many changes and unpredictable attack surfaces. While it is impossible to give an accurate probability of attack success, there is no doubt that successful attacks will be more difficult and damage will be limited.

P. K. Manadhata [12] obviously recognized this problem. After proposing concept of attack surface and attack surface measurement methods, he also published a paper explaining concept of attack surface shifting (moving attack surface), and established an I/O automata model about the system and its environment to quantify the attack surface shifting.

Given a system s and its environment E, attack surface of s is a triplet $\langle M, C, I \rangle$, where M is set of entry and exit points, C is channel set, and I is untrusted data item set of s. The attack surface resource set belonging to s is denoted as $R_s = M \cup C \cup I$. Given two resources of s are r_1 and r_2, $r_1 > r_2$ represents that damage effect of r_1 on attack surfaces is greater than r_2. If attack surface R_o of s is shifted to a new attack surface R_n, then damage·effect of a resource r on R_o can be represented as r_o and its effect on R_n as r_n. From this, the attack surface shifting can be defined as follows.

Definition 2.1: Given a system s and its environment E, original attack surface of s is R_o, and new attack surface is R_n. If at least one resource r is represented as $r \in (R_o \backslash R_n)$ or $(r \in R_o \cap R_n) \wedge (r_o \succ r_n)$, then attack surface of s has been shifted.

After attack surface of s has been shifted, an effective attack against original attack surface of s may no longer be effective on its new attack surface. In I/O automata model, interaction between s and its environment can be modeled to obtain parallel combination $s \Vert E$. As the attacker generally attacks the system by sending data to or obtaining data from the system, any scheduling of combination $s \Vert E$ of input actions or output actions containing s may become an attack against s. Various possible attacks against s are represented as set *attacks* (s, R), where R is attack surface of s. In I/O automata model, if attack surface of s is shifted from R_o to R_n, some possible attacks on R_o will fail on R_n in the case where the attacker and the environment are the same. Intuitively, s containing r is not executed on a new attack surface if resource r on the attack surface is removed or effect of r on the attack surface is reduced during the attack surface shifting. Therefore, scheduling based on these execution results will not attack s on the new attack surface (see Figure 2.4).

Theorem 2.1: *Given a system s and its environment E, if attack surface R_o of s is shifted to a new attack surface R_n, then* **attacks** $(s, R_o) \backslash$ **attacks** $(s, R_n) \neq \emptyset$.

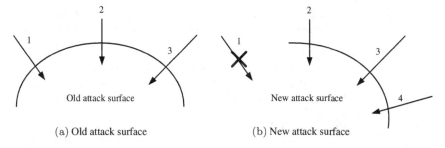

(a) Old attack surface   (b) New attack surface

Figure 2.4.   Attack Surface Shifting

Definition 2.2: Given a system s and its environment E, if original attack surface of s is R_o, the new attack surface is R_n, then the amount of attack surface shifting of s is $\Delta AS |R_o \backslash R_n| + |\{r: (r \in R_o \cap R_n) \wedge (r_o \succ r_n)\}|$.

In Definition 2.2, $|R_o \backslash R_n|$ item represents the number of resources that belong to the original attack surface of s but have been removed from the new attack surface of s. Similarly, $|\{r: (r \in R_o \cap R_n) \wedge (r_o \succ r_n)\}|$ item represents the number of resources which are more effective on the new attack surface of s than on the original attack surface. If $\Delta AS > 0$, then the attack surface of s is shifted from R_o to R_n.

However, above definitions and theorems qualitatively describe the attack surface shifting and measurement of shift amount, which is not enough to prove impact of attack surface shifting on security. For this reason, Manadhata also discussed impact of different attack surface shifting methods on the attack surface metrics [12], as shown in Table 2.2.

Defenders can change attack surfaces in the following three ways, but only two of them can shift attack surfaces.

First, by disabling or modifying system features, defenders can shift the attack surface and reduce the attack surface metrics (scenario A). Disabling system features reduces the number of entry points, exit points, channels, and data items, thereby reducing the number of resources on the attack surface. Modifying system features can reduce ratio of damage potential to power consumption of attack surface resources, such as reducing permission of a function or increasing access permission of the function to reduce effect of the resource on the attack surface metric value.

Table 2.2.   Different Assumptions About Attack Surface Shifting

Assumption	Feature	Attack Surface Shifting	Attack Surface Metric Value
A	Disabled	Yes	Decrease
B	Enabled and disabled	Yes	Decrease
C	Enabled and disabled	Yes	Remain unchanged
D	Enabled and disabled	Yes	Increase
E	Enabled	No	Increase

Second, by enabling new features and disabling original features, defenders can shift attack surfaces. Disabling some features means that a resource can be removed from the attack surface, thereby achieving the purpose of attack surface shifting. However, there may be three scenarios for metric values of the attack surface: decrease (scenario B), remain unchanged (scenario C), or increase (scenario D). Enabling a feature will increase the number of resources on the attack surface, thus increasing metric values of the attack surface. Disabling a feature will reduce the number of resources on the attack surface, thus decreasing metric values of the attack surface. Therefore, the overall change in metric values may be negative, zero, or positive. Similarly, defenders can shift attack surfaces by modifying existing features to reduce ratio of damage potential to attack cost of a resource set and increase ratio of another resource set. In short, metric values of the attack surface may decrease, remain unchanged, or increase.

Third, defenders can modify attack surfaces by enabling new features. New features will add resources to the attack surface, improving metric values of the attack surface. However, since the original attack surface still exists and has not been shifted, previously effective attacks will still be valid (scenario E). Defenders can also increase ratio of damage potential to attack cost of the existing resources, so as to increase metric values of the attack surface while keeping the attack surface unchanged. Refer to Table 2.2 for the above three different scenarios.

From the perspective of protection, the order in which defenders choose different scenarios above is A > B > C > D > E. The reason why scenario A precedes over scenario B is that scenario B adds new resources to the attack surface, and new resources will bring new attacks to the system. Although scenario D will increase metric value of the attack surface, it can still be used in moving target defense, especially when increase level of the metric value is low and the amount of attack surface shifting is large.

These conclusions enlighten us that the attack surface shifting brought about by dynamic enablement technology does not always reduce the attack surface metrics and improve system security (assuming that the low metrics of the attack surface do reflect high security of the information system), we also need to enable appropriate features and disable traditional security measures with greater security risks. But as Yih Huang said [36], although the current technology cannot accurately describe capability of the attack surface shifting (moving attack surface), there is no doubt that success of the attack will be more difficult and the loss will be limited.

2.5 Summary

This chapter introduces the basic concept of dynamically enabled defense technology, summarizes classification of relevant technologies for dynamically enabled defense, and then discusses relationship between dynamically enabled defense technology and cyber kill chain, and the relationship between dynamically enabled defense technology and moving attack surface, respectively. These discussions respectively demonstrate the importance and practical effectiveness of dynamically enabled defense technology in defending against cyber attacks from different perspectives.

References

[1] Wengui, Z., Bo, P., and Pan Z. America inside out: Comprehensive national cybersecurity initiative (CNCI). *Computer Security*, 2011, 11: 78–81.
[2] IWG. Federal cybersecurity game-change R&D [EB/OL]. https://www.nitrd.gov/cybersecurity/, 2010.
[3] Al-Shaer, E. Toward network configuration randomization for moving target defense. *Springer New York*, 2011, 153–159.
[4] Evans, D., Nguyen-Tuong, A., and Knight, J. Effectiveness of moving target defenses. *Springer New York*, 2011, 29–48.
[5] Jajodia, S., Ghosh, A. K., Swarup, V., *et al.* Moving target defense: Creating asymmetric uncertainty for cyber threats. *Springer Ebooks*, 2011, (54).
[6] Jajodia, S., Ghosh, A. K., Subrahmanian, V., *et al.* Moving Target Defense? Springer, 2013.
[7] Rahman, M. A., Al-Shaer, E., and Bobba, R. B. Moving target defense for hardening the security of the power system state estimation. *Proceedings of the First ACM Workshop on Moving Target Defense*, 2014.
[8] Okhravi, H., Rabe, M., Mayberr, Y. T., *et al.* Survey of cyber moving target techniques. *DTIC Document*, 2013.

[9] Zaffarano, K., Taylor, J., and Hamilton, S. A quantitative framework for moving target defense effectiveness evaluation. *Proceedings of the Second ACM Workshop on Moving Target Defense*, 2015.

[10] Le Goues, C., Nguyen-Tuong, A., Chen, H., *et al.* Moving target defenses in the helix self-regenerative architecture. Springer New York, 2013, 117–149.

[11] Manadhata, P. K., Kaynar, D. K., and Wing, J. M. A formal model for a system's attack surface. *DTIC Document*, 2007.

[12] Manadhata, P. K. Game theoretic approaches to attack surface shifting. *Advances in Information Security*, 2013, 1–13.

[13] Jain, M., An, B., and Tambe, M. Security games applied to real-world: Research contributions and challenges. *Advances in Information Security*, 2013, 15–39.

[14] Bilar, D., Cybenko, G., and Murphy, J. Adversarial dynamics: The conficker case study. *Springer New York*, 2013, 41–71.

[15] Gonzalez, C. From individual decisions from experience to behavioral game theory: Lessons for cybersecurity. *Advances in Information Security*, 2013, 73–86.

[16] Cybenko, G. and Hughes, J. No free lunch in cyber security. *Proceedings of the First ACM Workshop on Moving Target Defense*, 2014.

[17] Okhravi, H. Getting beyond tit for tat: Better strategies for moving target prototyping and evaluation. *Proceedings of the Second ACM Workshop on Moving Target Defense*, 2015.

[18] Andel, T. R., Whitehurstl, N., and Mcdonald, J. T. Software security and randomization through program partitioning and circuit variation. *Proceedings of the First ACM Workshop on Moving Target Defense*, 2014.

[19] Jafarian, J. H., Al-Shaer, E., and Duan, Q. Openflow random host mutation: Transparent moving target defense using software defined networking. *Proceedings of the First Workshop on Hot Topics in Software Defined Networks*, 2012.

[20] Casola, V., De Benedictis, A., and Albanese, M. A multi-layer moving target defense approach for protecting resource-constrained distributed devices integration of reusable systems. *Springer*, 2014, 299–324.

[21] Arsenault, D., Sood, A., and Huang, Y. Secure, resilient computing clusters: Self-cleansing intrusion tolerance with hardware enforced security (SCIT/HES). *The Second International Conference on Availability, Reliability and Security, IEEE*, 2007.

[22] Shacham, H., Page, M., Pfaff, B., *et al.* On the effectiveness of address-space randomization. *Proceedings of the 11th ACM Conference on Computer and Communications Security[C]*, 2004.

[23] Bhatkar, S., Duvarneyd, C., and Sekar, R. Address obfuscation: An efficient approach to combat a broad range of memory error exploits. *USENIX Security*, 2003.

[24] Li, L., Justj, E., and Sekar, R. Address-space randomization for windows systems. *IEEE Computer Security Applications Conference*, 2006.

[25] Kil, C., Jim, J., Bookholt, C., et al. Address space layout permutation (ASLP): Towards fine-grained randomization of commodity software. *IEEE Computer Security Applications Conference*, 2006.

[26] Whitehouse, O. An analysis of address space layout randomization on windows Vista. *Symantec Advanced Threat Research*, 2007, 1–14.

[27] Durden, T. Bypassing pax ASLR protection. *Phrack Magazine*, 2002, 59(9): 9.

[28] Boyd, S. W., Kc, G. S., Locasto, M. E., et al. On the general applicability of instruction-set randomization. *IEEE Transactions on Dependable and Secure Computing*, 2010, 7(3): 255–270.

[29] Barrantes, E. G., Ackleyd, H., Palmert, S., et al. Randomized instruction set emulation to disrupt binary code injection attacks. *Proceedings of the 10th ACM Conference on Computer and Communications Security*, 2003.

[30] Hu, W., Hiser, J., Williams, D. F., et al. Secure and practical defense against code-injection attacks using software dynamic translation. *Proceedings of the 2nd International Conference on Virtual Execution Environments (VEE)*, 2006.

[31] Jackson, T., Homescu, A., Crane, S., et al. Diversifying the software stack using randomized NOP insertion. *Springer New York*, 2013, 151–173.

[32] Cox, B., Evans, D., Filipi, A., et al. N-variant systems: A secretless framework for security through diversity. *Usenix Security*, 2006.

[33] Kewley, D., Fink, R., Lowry, J., et al. Dynamic approaches to thwart adversary intelligence gathering. *IEEE DARPA Information Survivability Conference & AMP*, 2001.

[34] Moniz, H., Neves, N. F., Correia, M., et al. Randomized intrusion-tolerant asynchronous services. *IEEE Dependable Systems and Networks International Conference*, 2006.

[35] Holland, D. A., Lim, A. T., and Seltzer, M. I. An architecture a day keeps the hacker away. *SIGARCH Computer Architecture News*, 2005, 33(1): 34–41.

[36] Huang, Y., Ghosh A K. Introducing diversity and uncertainty to create moving attack surfaces for web services. *Springer New York*, 2011, 131–151.

[37] Huang, Y., Arsenault, D., and Sood, A. Incorruptible system self-cleansing for intrusion tolerance. *IEEE Performance, Computing and Communications Conference*, 2006.

[38] Cadar, C., Akritidis, P., Costa, M., *et al.* Data randomization. *Microsoft Research*, 2008.

[39] Nguyen-Tuong, A., Evans, D., Knight, J. C., *et al.* Security through redundant data diversity. *IEEE International Conference on Dependable Systems and Networks with FTCS and DCC*, 2008.

[40] Ammann, P. E. and Knight, J. C. Data diversity: An approach to software fault tolerance. *IEEE Transactions on Computers*, 1988, 37(4): 418–425.

[41] Christodorescu, M., Fredrikson, M., Jha, S., *et al.* End-to-end software diversification of internet services. *Springer New York*, 2011, 117–130.

[42] Chen, S., Xu, J., Sezer, E. C., *et al.* Non-control-data attacks are realistic threats. *Usenix Security*, 2005.

Chapter 3

Dynamic Software Defense

3.1 Introduction

In the information security offensive and defensive confrontation, software has always been put in an important position. Malicious software attacks account for an absolute proportion in various types of cyber attacks. Attack methods emerge unceasingly, such as code injection attacks, control injection attacks, malicious tampering, resource consumption, and spoofing attacks, which causes incalculable damage to information systems. At the same time, virus killer, firewall, intrusion detection, patch upgrade, and other protection methods are also developing continuously. However, the existing security protection methods are restricted by the prior knowledge, so they can only respond passively to attacks, and static nature of the system leads to unfavorable situations where the information system is easy to attack and difficult to defend.

As a new security concept, dynamic software defense based on system vulnerabilities from which software attacks are originated, making use of ever-changing, dynamic and random characteristics of software attack technologies, by dynamically changing software attack surfaces to increase difficulty of vulnerability exploits, to change software homogenization phenomenon, in attempt to break current software asymmetry situation of offense and defense, reverse unfavorable situation where cyberspace is easy to attack and difficult to defend, thus ensuring security of information system.

The dynamic software defense technology applies the idea of randomization, based on cryptographic technology, compilation technology, dynamic runtime technology, to implement randomness, diversity, and dynamics process in control structure and code layout of program code, memory layout at execution time, and organizational structure of the execution file. It eliminates software homogenization phenomenon, realizes software polymorphism, reduces or dynamically changes system attack surfaces, increases difficulty of vulnerability exploits by attackers, and effectively resists external code injection attacks, file tampering attacks, data leakage attacks, infection attacks, and other types of attacks against software defects.

Dynamic software defense technology is closely related to software programs. You can bring dynamization technology in development, compilation, linking, deployment, loading, and final running phases of software life cycle. In the development phase, dynamization is mainly applied at the source code level. In 1977, Avizienis and Chen proposed N-version programming to realize multiple versions of the same program, and its initial purpose was to improve fault tolerance of the system [1]. In the compilation and linking phases, dynamization is mainly achieved by modifying the compiler. Compilation is a necessary and fully automated phase in the software life cycle. It is natural to introduce dynamization in a way that is transparent to software developers, modify the compiler, generate any number of program variants by adding, transforming, or removing existing instructions, which have the same running effect on users but different results on code reuse attacks. Dynamization technologies widely used in compilation phase includes randomization of address space layout, etc. In the deployment phase, dynamization is mainly implemented by randomly distributing polymorphism versions of software, randomly deploying multiple versions of the same software program generated during compilation, or implementing dynamization again during patching. This makes the software version obtained by each user different. At present, software polymorphism is the mainstream technology. In the loading phase, software dynamization can be implemented by dynamic loading mechanism of which technologies mainly include address space layout randomization, in-place code randomization, and instruction set randomization technologies at present. Memory address space layout randomization technology randomizes base addresses of process objects (such as stacks, heaps, and program code segments), and dynamically modifies process address space. The basic idea of instruction set randomization is to randomize instructions and hide expected instruction code from attackers. In-place code randomization changes and obfuscates code to prevent damage. In the running phase, software dynamization is mainly implemented by building a binary dynamic execution environment. The most common technology is multi-variant execution technology, which synchronously runs multiple versions of a program and carry out real-time monitoring to prevent the program from being attacked.

In summary, current dynamic software defense technologies mainly include address space layout randomization, instruction set randomization, in-place code randomization, software polymorphism, and multi-variant execution technologies which will be respectively introduced as follows.

3.2 Address Space Layout Randomization

3.2.1 *Overview*

Address Space Layout Randomization (ASLR) was proposed to solve buffer overflow attacks, which is the most successful and widely used software dynamization technology [2,3]. To implement buffer overflow attacks successfully, the attacker must acquire the address space of a process in advance, then through elaborate calculation, use overflow operation to jump execution process of the program to the attack code [4,5]. The basic idea of ASLR is to randomize memory address space distribution of process components and objects, making the process space unpredictable and attackers unable to calculate the exact jump location, thus defending against attacks. Objects that ASLR can randomize include heap address, stack base address, executable file image base address, Process Environment Block (PEB) address, Thread Environment Block (TEB) address, dynamic link library address, and so on.

As an effective method to deal with buffer overflow attacks, ASLR has always been a research hotspot in software protection, and related technologies are constantly developing. The concept of ASLR was first proposed by Forrest [6], and he pointed out that similarity of computer systems posed security risks. Attack methods on one computer can be easily transplanted to other computers, resulting in popularity of attacks and rapid spread of viruses. He first proposed the process address space randomization method to realize diversified computer systems, and gave some address space randomization methods, such as modifying the stack base address, allocating redundant space to local variables, randomizing static variable addresses, etc. Besides, he also designed and implemented a prototype system, in which GCC compiler was modified so that if a local variable required more than 16 bytes of stack space, 8 bytes, 16 bytes, 24 bytes, or 64 bytes were randomly added when allocating space. M. Chew *et al.* randomized the process stack base address by modifying the operating system kernel. The specific implementation method is as follows: When the process is initialized, first put 0–32 KBytes data on top of the process stack, subtract the number of bytes from the stack top pointer, and then start executing the process to realize randomization of the process stack base address. Homebrew implemented ASLR in FreeBSD system [7]. The specific approach is to reduce the stack top pointer by 0–1 MBytes, while filling a random number (0–16 KBytes) of bytes into the stack space of each function, so that the process stack space and the stack space of each function change. This can be done either by modifying GCC during compilation or by modifying the kernel during process loading. Sandeep Bhatkar modified the binary code through LEET tool to achieve ASLR [8]. The distances of Absolute addresses of all units in the process, parameters, and local variables of each function in stacks, and buffer allocated by malloc function in heaps, are randomly increased, and the relative address inside each unit is modified to effectively resist relative address attacks. In 2000, address space layout randomization was the first to be applied in Linux kernel PaX patch [9]. The stack base address, main program base address, and shared library loading address were randomized by patching Linux kernel. The specific implementation method is to randomize 4–27 bits (a total of 24 bits) of the stack base address when the process is loaded, randomize 12–27 bits (a total of 16 bits) of the continuous area base address (including main program image, static data section, and heap), and randomize 12–27 bits of the shared library loading address. ASLR technology in PaX patch, along with the non-executable technology of Linux writable page, together constitutes a complete and practical system protection scheme, which greatly reduces probability of successful attacks and is widely used in Linux system. Since then, ASLR has been used in most major operating systems, including Windows (first for Windows Vista in 2007, then for Windows Server 2008, and Windows 7), Linux, and Mac OS.

ASLR was proposed to solve buffer overflow attacks, and the related technologies were also proposed around how to avoid buffer overflow vulnerabilities. Therefore, to facilitate readers to better understand ASLR technology, the basic principles of buffer overflow attacks are first introduced, and then principles of mainstream ASLR technologies are analyzed, such as stack space layout randomization, heap space layout randomization, dynamic link library distribution randomization, and program image base address randomization.

3.2.2 *Buffer Overflow Attack*

As a mainstream attack method, buffer overflow attacks account for a large proportion in all network attacks and are the most familiar types of attacks for a large number of computer users. This attack method has a long history and can be traced back to Morris worm in 1988 [10]. Morris exploited the buffer overflow vulnerability in the Fingerd software of Unix operating system to write Morris worm, which infected more than 6,000 machines around the world, thus opening "Pandora's box" of buffer overflow attacks. Since then, more and more buffer overflow security vulnerabilities have been discovered and exploited, and many major network attack incidents resulted from buffer overflow attacks, for example, CodeRed worm that broke out on July 19, 2001 [11], Nimda Worm on September 18, 2001, Slapper Worm in 2002, and Sasser Worm in 2004. These viruses, without exception, all exploited buffer overflow vulnerabilities and brought huge damage to information systems, causing incalculable loss [12]. At present, buffer overflow attacks have become one of the biggest threats to cyber security.

Buffer overflow attacks are based on buffer overflow vulnerabilities. The buffer simply refers to a continuous area of the memory in which a program is running. It can be heap section, stack section, or data section where static variables are stored. In brief, buffer overflow means that too much data is written into a buffer beyond the original boundary, and excessively long data overrides data in adjacent areas. Attackers achieve the purpose of executing desired code by precisely structuring data and controlling the amount of data used for buffer overflow. Data sent by attackers contains some special bytecode, known as ShellCode. Once the attack succeeds, these binary instructions will be executed. Since ShellCode will run with the same permissions as attacked process, and most service programs run with superuser permission, it is possible for ShellCode to run with the same permissions, giving attackers full control of the target host. There are roughly three steps of buffer overflow attacks: First, inject attack strings (including ShellCode) into buffer of the vulnerable program; then exploit its vulnerability to rewrite specific data in the memory (such as the return addresses) to redirect the execution process of programs to the pre-embedded ShellCode; finally, attackers run ShellCode to gain control of the compromised host, and then control the compromised host in a particular way.

There are multiple methods for buffer overflow attacks. According to the overflow location, it can be divided into stack overflow, heap overflow, integer variable overflow, and format string overflow, etc. According to source of the attack code, it can be divided into the attacks that need to implant the code and return-into-libc attacks. According to the attack mode, it can be divided into local overflow and remote overflow. Among various types of overflow attacks, heap overflow and stack overflow are the most common ones. The following will respectively introduce stack buffer overflow attacks and heap buffer overflow attacks on Windows to illustrate principles of buffer overflow attacks.

(1) Stack overflow attack

As shown in Figure 3.1, process image in memory can be divided into four areas: code area (.text), data area (.data), heap area, and stack area. The code area stores the binary machine code that is loaded for execution. This area is usually marked as read-only, and any write operation to this area will cause an error. The data area is used to store data such as global variables. The heap area is a memory area for the program to dynamically allocate and reclaim. The stack area is used to dynamically store call relationship between functions, ensuring that the called function can be restored to its parent function to continue running when it is returned.

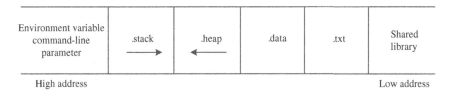

Environment variable command-line parameter	.stack	.heap	.data	.txt	Shared library
	⟶	⟵			

High address   Low address

Figure 3.1.   Memory Structure

```
void function (char *buf_src)
{
    char buf_dest [16];
    strcpy (buf_dest, buf_src);
}
/*main function*/
main()
{
    int i;
    char str [256];
    for (i=0; i<256; i++) str[i]='a';
    function (str);
}
```

Figure 3.2.   Sample Code of Stack Buffer Overflow

Stack buffer overflow attacks usually mean that overflowed buffer is in the stack area. Figure 3.2 shows the sample code of stack overflow. The amount of data that the main function fills into the "function" function buffer exceeds its capacity. If the program does not perform boundary checking, it will lead to a buffer overflow vulnerability.

From the code in Figure 3.2, we can see that size of array str (256 bytes) far exceeds size of destination buffer buf_dest (16 bytes), causing a buffer overflow. In high-level language, the stack is generally used when a function call occurs in the program, it mainly completes the following stack operations: First, the parameters are pressed into the stack, and then the content in the instruction register eip is pressed into the stack as the return address ret. Next, content in the base address register ebp is put in the stack; then current stack pointer esp is copied to ebp as the new base address; finally, the appropriate value is subtracted from esp to leave some space for local variables. Figure 3.3 shows the stack usage before and after the main function calls the "function".

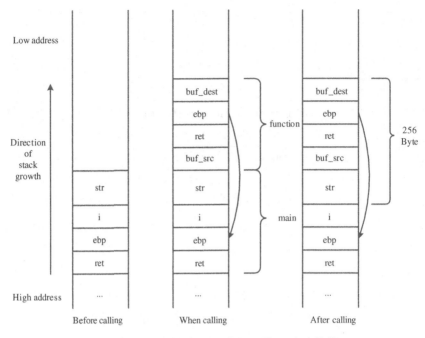

Figure 3.3.   Stack Usage during Function Calls

As Figure 3.3 shows, after "function" function is called, content of str array has overridden content used by the memory space from address buf_dest to buf_dest + 256, including ebp saved when calling "function" function and the return address ret. If the attackers put a piece of ShellCode in the buffer and override the return address of the function to point to the ShellCode (as shown in Figure 3.4), the program will instead execute ShellCode implanted by attackers when the function returns, thus attackers gain the control of the system to achieve malicious attacks.

(2) Heap overflow attack

Heap is a memory area that is dynamically allocated by the application. In the operating system, most of the memory area is allocated dynamically at the kernel level, but the heap segment is allocated by the application and initialized at compile time. The heap segment generally grows upward, that is, if two static variables are declared in a program respectively, address of the first declared variable is smaller than address of the latter declared variable. Heap overflow

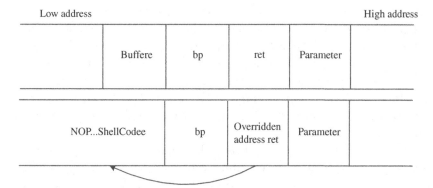

Figure 3.4. Override the Return Address

```
static char buffer (50);
static int (*funcptr)( );
while (*str)
{
    *buffer++=*str;
    *str++;
}
*funcptr ();
```

Figure 3.5. Sample Code of a Heap Overflow Vulnerability

Low address   High address

	Buffer[50]	funcptr	
...			...

Figure 3.6. Storage Location of Variables in the Heap

attacks take advantage of this feature. Figure 3.5 shows sample code of a heap overflow vulnerability.

The code shown in Figure 3.5 corresponds to the storage location of variables in the heap, as shown in Figure 3.6.

Buffer is an array of characters, funcptr is a function pointer, and str is a string that the program gets from the outside. The function pointer is essentially the entry address of a function. Because the program does not perform boundary checking when it copies strings, attackers can override value of funcptr function pointer. When the program executes the funcptr function, it will jump to the overridden address to continue execution. If attackers accurately construct padding data, they can implant ShellCode in the buffer and use its memory address to override funcptr. ShellCode will be executed when funcptr is called.

There are other types of attacks against the heap, such as inclusion of a simple check and recovery system in C language called setjmp/longjmp. Set setjmp (jmp_buf) at check point and use longjmp (jmp_buf, val) to recover the check point. setjmp (jmp_buf) is used to save the current stack frame to jmp_buf. longjmp (jmp_buf, val) will recover the stack frame from jmp_buf. After longjmp is executed, the program continues to execute from the next statement in setjmp () and uses val as return value of setjmp (). jmp_buf is declared as a global variable and is therefore stored in the heap. The register ebx/esi/edi/ebp/esp/eip is stored in jmp_buf. The register eip can be overwritten if jmp_buf is overridden before longjmp is executed. Therefore, after longjmp recovers the saved stack frame, the program can jump to the specified position to execute, and the jump address can be in either the stack or the heap.

Common buffer overflow attacks also include format string overflow attacks, integer variable overflow attacks, etc. Specific technical details of implementation can be referred to the relevant references. As the analysis mentioned above, shows that the implementation method of each buffer overflow attack is different. To achieve effective defense, it is necessary to design corresponding protection technologies. Corresponding to attack technologies, different ASLR technologies are obtained by randomizing stack, heap, string, and other positions that are easily used by buffer overflow. We will introduce ASLR technologies respectively in the following sections.

3.2.3   *Stack Space Layout Randomization*

Stack space layout randomization is the process of randomly changing the size of each function stack frame and variable position in the program. When buffer overflow attacks occur, the same load cannot overflow successfully in all variants, thus limiting universality of

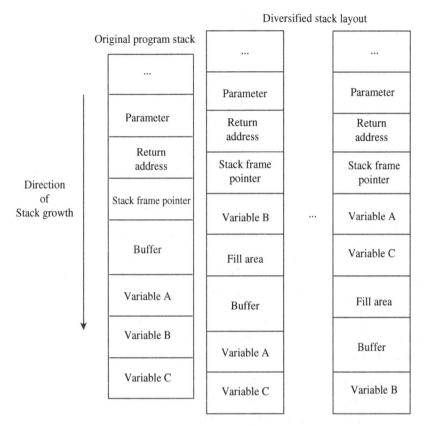

Figure 3.7. Effect of Stack Layout Randomization

attack load. Changing the size of stack frame is achieved by locating the function at compile time and adding a piece of code in the function header that randomly fills the stack frame. Changing the variable position is achieved by randomly adjusting the order of variables in the function during compilation or loading, so that the variable address changes randomly. The effect of stack layout randomization is shown in Figure 3.7.

For Windows operating system, stacks are divided into main stacks and auxiliary stacks when stacks are created. Because stacks are created in different ways, stack randomization can be divided into two categories: main stack space layout randomization and auxiliary stack space layout randomization.

(1) Main stack space layout randomization

The main stack is generated with the creation of main thread. The creation process of main thread is as follows.

(a) Locate the file image.
(b) Convert DOS format name to NT format name.
(c) Call NtOpenFile () to open the file.
(d) Call NtCreateSection () to create the memory area object.
(e) Call NtQuerySection () to get image information.
(f) Call LdrQueryImageFileExecutionOptions () to check whether the debugging is required or not.
(g) Call NtCreateProcessExcellent () to create kernel process.
(h) Call BasePushProcessParameters () to pass parameters for the process.
(i) Call NtCreateThread () to create the first thread of the process.
(j) Call CsrClientCallServer (BasepCreateProcess) to register a new process and thread with the process CSRSS.exe.

NtCreateThread () creates a user-mode thread stack and an initialized thread stack environment when creating the first thread. NtCreateThread () is defined as follows:

> NTSTATUS NtCreateThread(
> OUT PHANDLE ThreadHandle,
> IN ACCESS_MASK DesiredAccess,
> IN POBJECT_AATTRIBUTES ObjectAttributes,
> IN HANDLE ProcessHandle,
> OUT PCLIENT_ID ClientId,
> OUT PCONTEXT ThreadContext,
> OUT PINITIAL_TEB InitialTeb,
> OUT BOOLEAN CreateSuspended)

ProcessHandle is the handle of this process, and ThreadHandle is the handle of main thread. You can call ObReferenceObjectBy-Handle to obtain the thread pointer, which is address of the main stack and starting address of the thread. This address is replaced by a trap function, in which address space layout of the main stack is randomized by hijacking NtAllocateVirtualMemory function to allocate a new randomized stack space and then copying data from original main thread address space to stack space.

NtAllocateVirtualMemory function allocates a new space for the caller. Its allocation rule is to start searching from a fixed high address, find an address space in the current process that satisfies caller's request, and then give the first address of that free space to the caller. Therefore, if search is changed from fixed high address to a random address, then the address space allocated by the function becomes a randomized space.

NtAllocateVirtualMemory function is defined as follows:

NTSTATUS NtAllocateVirtualMemory(
IN HANDLE ProcessHandle,
IN OUT PVOID *BaseAddress,
IN ULONG_PTR ZeroBits,
IN OUT PSIZE_T RegionSize,
IN ULONG AllocationType,
IN ULONG Protect)

Parameter BaseAddress allocates the base address for the stack space, AllocationType allocates the type for the stack space. BaseAddress defaults to 0, which is allocated by the system. The reverse analysis of NtAllocateVirtualMemory function shows that the function always searches down from the address pointed by the fixed pointer MM_HIGHEST_VAD_ADDRESS when it looks for the highest address. This pointer points to value of variable MmHighest-UserAddress exported by ntoskrnl.exe. In NtAllocateVirtualMemory function, a local pointer pointing to the fixed pointer is used for free space search. Therefore, you just need to search for a local pointer pointing to the global pointer in the function space, and then make the local pointer point to another global pointer we defined, which points to a random address. In this way, the result of NtAllocateVirutalMemory function call is a random address space.

The specific method is to hook System Service Descriptor Table (SSDT) to perform function hijacking. Using ntoskrnl.exe (i.e. NtCreateThread and NtAllocateVirtualMemory) to export functions. The location of the local pointer to the MMHighestUserAddress global pointer in the NTalLocateVirtualMemory function is hard-coded by byte search. The process is shown in Figure 3.8.

Boundary of Windows stack is required to be aligned in size of at least 4K, i.e., low 12b bits of the address space are 0; and the

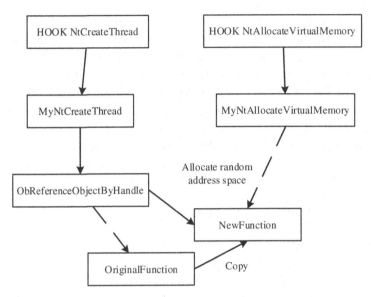

Figure 3.8.　Randomization Process of Main Stack Space Layout

application can only use 2G space (31 bits) for the system space. Thus, randomization granularity of the stack is 19 (31-12) bits.

(2) Auxiliary stack space layout randomization

Multiple threads used by most Windows functions are auxiliary threads, and most of the program functions are completed in auxiliary threads, which run in the auxiliary stack space. The auxiliary thread is created simply by calling CreateThread () function, and calling CreateRemoteThread () within this function to create a specific thread. Therefore, you can randomize the auxiliary stack simply by hijacking CreateRemoteThread () and adopting the method similar to the main stack space layout randomization. CreateRemoteThread () is exported by the dynamic link library Kernel32.dll. Randomization process of auxiliary stack space layout is shown in Figure 3.9.

3.2.4　Heap Space Layout Randomization

Heap is a mechanism that operates on memory and can be used to allocate many relatively small blocks of data. When a process is initialized, the system creates a heap in the process address space. This

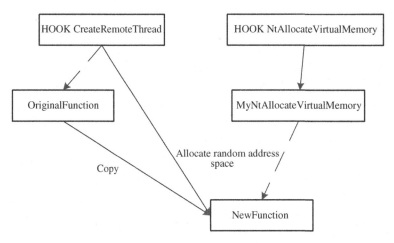

Figure 3.9. Randomization Process of Auxiliary Stack Space Layout

heap is called default heap of the process. Many Windows functions require the process to use the default heap. In addition to default heap of the process, many operations in the process space create some auxiliary heaps. These heaps can be used to protect components, manage the memory more effectively, make local access, and reduce the thread overhead. The heap is in danger of overflow attack during operation, which will pose a security threat to the system. Heap space layout randomization makes it difficult for attackers to predict location of the next allocated memory block by dynamically distributing memory on the heap randomly, thus preventing heap overflow attacks.

The heap is created by calling HeapCreate function exported by kernel32.dll and calling RtlCreateHeap function exported by ntdll within HeapCreate function. The function is defined as follows:

NTSYSAPI HANDLE NTAPIRtCreateHeap(
IN ULONG Flags,
IN PVOID Base,
IN ULONG Resenre,
IN ULONG Commit,
IN ULONG Lock,
IN PVOID RtlHeapPmms)

Base is the starting address of created heap. To implement the heap space layout randomization, similar to the stack space layout

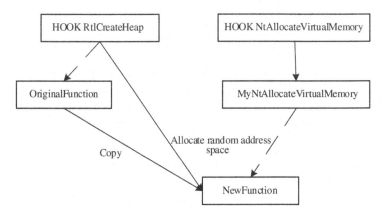

Figure 3.10. Randomization Process of Heap Space Layout

randomization, a trap function is used to replace this address. A new randomized heap space address is allocated by hooking NtAllocat-eVirtualMemory function in the trap function, then data from the original heap address space is copied to the heap space to realize heap address space randomization. The specific process is shown in Figure 3.10.

The boundary of Windows heap is required to be aligned in size of at least 4K, i.e., low 12 bits of the address space are 0; and the application can only use 2G space (31 bits) for the system space. Thus, randomization granularity of the heap space is 19 (31-12) bits.

3.2.5 *Dynamic Link Library Address Space Randomization*

Multiple dynamic link libraries are called when the process is executed. Without randomization, commonly used dynamic link libraries are loaded into the fixed address of memory, which can be easily exploited by attackers. Attackers use illegal destination addresses to replace the fixed addresses to execute ShellCode. The loading address and memory layout of dynamic link library can be changed dynamically by using the randomization technology of dynamic link library address space, thereby preventing buffer overflow attacks effectively.

To understand randomization process of dynamic link library, you need to first know the loading process. Windows system uses

LdrpMapDll function to map the dynamic link library to the user address space, and many other system functions are called within this function. The following is the sequence of calls within this function.

(a) Call LdrpCheckForKnownDll function to check whether the dynamic link library is a KnownDll.

(b) Call LdrpResolveDllName function to get FullPathName and BaseDllName of the dynamic link library.

(c) Call RtlDosPathNameToNtPathName_U function to convert DosPathName to NTStylePathName.

(d) Call LdrpCreateDllSection function to get SectionHandle of the dynamic link library.

(e) Call NtMapViewOfSection function to map the dynamic link library to the process address space.

(f) Call LdrpAllocateDataTableEntry function to assign a data table item of loader.

As you can see, the function that actually maps dynamic link library to process address space is NtMapViewOfSection, and it is defined as follows:

NTSTATUS NtMapViewOfSection(
IN HANDLE SectionHandle,
IN HANDLE ProcessHandle,
IN OUT PVOID *BaseAddress,
IN ULONG_PTR ZeroBits,
IN SIZE_T CommitSize,
IN OUT PLARGE_INTEGER SeetionOffset OPTION AL,
IN OUT PSIZE_T ViewSize,
IN ULONG InheritDisposition,
IN ULONG AllocationType,
IN ULONG Protect)

SectionHandle is the section object handle and BaseAddress is the pointer loading base address. You can call export function (i.e. ObReferenceObjectByHandle) to obtain the object handle (or pointer PSection) of dynamic link library by using this Section-Handle. Then basic information of the dynamic link library can be obtained according to the following data structure defined by Windows. Parameter BaseAddress is a pointer loading base address, and its default value is 0, which means that the system allocates memory space to it according to the Section attribute. If its default value is not 0, the system allocates memory space to it according to the specified address.

In Windows source code, the second domain Segment of Section pointer structure is defined as follows:

```
Typedef Struct_SEGMENT{
PCONTROL_AREA CtrlArea;
PVOID SegmentBaseAddress;
ULONG TotalNumberOfPtes;
ULONG NonExtendedPtes;
ULONG SizeOfSegment;
SIZE_T ImageCommitmen;
ULONG TakePlace2;
PVOID SystemImageBase;
SIZE_T NumberOfCommittedPages;
ULONG TakePlace3;
......
} SEGMET, *PSEGMENT;
```

PVOID BasedAddress is the base address loaded by its dynamic link library by default, and the size of the dynamic link library exists in LARGE_INTEGER SizeOfSection field of SizeOfSection. PCONTROL_AREA CtrlArea structure in SEGMENT contains PFILE_OBJECT FilePointer structure. Pointer of the file object can be obtained through this field, and then path and name of the file can be obtained through FileName.Length field and FileName.Buffer field of file object pointer. Through the above analysis, we can find the base address, size, file path, and name loaded by the dynamic link library by default.

The loading base address of dynamic link library can be modified by hooking NtMapViewOfSection. Since NtMapViewOfSection function is not exported, you can use interrupt service routine of the system to query SSDT (System Service Descriptor Table) to find its address. By hijacking NtMapViewOfSection to modify parameters or return data, we can alter it to data that we need. Randomization process of dynamic link library is shown in Figure 3.11, the doubly linked list mechanism is introduced. Nodes of the linked list store information of each different dynamic link library to ensure that different base address space is allocated for each dynamic link library.

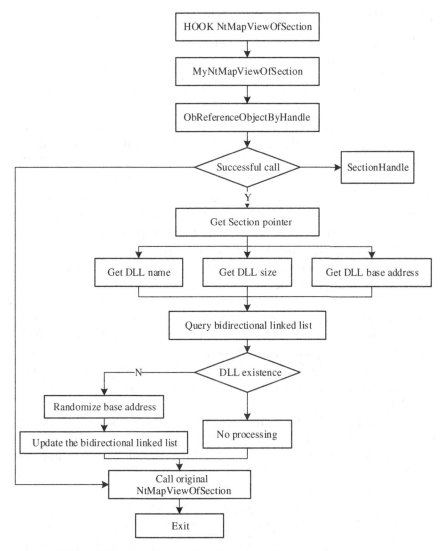

Figure 3.11. Randomization Process of Dynamic Link Library

Boundary of Windows dynamic link library is required to be aligned in size of at least 64K, i.e., low 16 bits of the address space are 0, and the application can only use 2G space (31 bits) for the system space. Thus, randomization granularity of the dynamic link library is 15 (31-16) bits.

3.2.6 *PEB/TEB Address Space Randomization*

PEB is created in kernel mode which contains all the user-mode parameters of the current process that are connected to the system, and can be exploited by heap overflow attacks. Heap overflow attacks can be effectively prevented by randomizing PEB address space.

TEB is created in kernel mode, and this memory block contains system variables stored in user mode. Each thread has its own thread environment block. TEB is exploited by stack overflow attacks. Stack overflow attacks can be effectively prevented by randomizing TEB address space.

PEB/TEB are both created in kernel mode through unexported functions MiCreatePebOrTeb and MmCreatePeb in ntoskrnL.exe. These two functions have different creation procedures for PEB and TEB, but they allocate the starting address space in the same way when creating them. That is, they both search down from the address pointed by the local pointer pointing to the fixed pointer MM_HIGHEST_VAD_ADDRESS, i.e., value of variable MmHighest-UserAddress in ntoskrnl.exe. They find a piece of address space in the current process that is large enough to satisfy the caller's request, and then use the first address of this free space as the starting address of PEB/TEB address space. Figure 3.12 shows the relationship between these two functions and variable MmHighest-UserAddress.

To implement randomization, you only need to search the local pointer pointing to the global pointer in the function space, then have the local pointer point to another global pointer that we

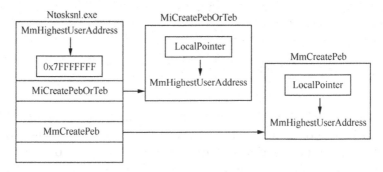

Figure 3.12. MiCreatePebOrTeb/MmCreatePeb and MmHighestUserAddress

defined, which points to a random address. PEB/TEB is allocated to a random free space by calling MiCreatePebOrTeb and MmCreatePebble functions. Since MiCreatePebOrTeb and MmCreatePeb functions are not exported, starting addresses of these two functions can only be searched in hard-coded way in the NtoskrnL.exe space.

3.2.7 *Basic Effectiveness and Existing Deficiencies*

ASLR can be executed in multiple phases, commonly including compile-time randomization and runtime randomization. Compile-time ASLR can generate different versions of the same functional software, which is convenient for software polymorphism. Runtime randomization does not need to modify the program source code. When the program is loaded, it dynamically lays out addresses of the program component and needs to modify operating environment of the operating system.

ASLR greatly increases difficulty of buffer overflow attacks and is a practical and effective defense technology against memory attacks. ASLR is commonly used with data execution protection to provide a better defense effect and has been widely adopted by major control systems.

Although ASLR can effectively improve system capability of defending against buffer overflow attacks, it still has some unavoidable limitations.

(a) Attack non-ASLR-enabled modules. Only after all components are randomized, can defense effect of ASLR be fully exerted. If some code or data has a fixed location in memory, it will be exploited by attackers for overflow attacks. In Windows, Linux, and other operating systems, not all the programs choose to enable ASLR. Attacking modules that are not ASLR-enabled is an important way to bypass ASLR protection.

(b) Guess addresses. Randomization range of ASLR is restricted by factors such as CPU data bus width of the machine, and characteristics of object components. The changing locations of some components are limited, and the randomization range is not large. Attackers can guess jump addresses by brute force cracking to realize buffer overflow attacks.

(c) Override some return addresses. Although the module loading base address changes, low bytes of each module entry point address remain unchanged, and only high bytes change. For example, for the address 0x12345678, the part 5678 is fixed. For example, if there is a buffer overflow, you can use memcpy to override the final two bytes and set it to any value between 0x12340000 and 0x1234FFFF. If you use strcpy to override them, since strcpy will copy ending characters 0x00 at the end, you can override 0x12345678 to 0x12345600, or the value between 0x12340001 and 0x123400FF, so that distance of the overridden address and the base address is fixed, and you can search for available jump instructions near the base address.

(d) Memory information leaks may pose a threat. Memory information leaks allow attackers to snoop into some useful memory layout information or state information of target process, so as to accurately calculate addresses and launch attacks.

3.3　Instruction Set Randomization

3.3.1　*Overview*

According to statistics of the Computer Emergency Response Team (CERT), code injection attacks account for a large proportion of all the cyber attacks and are major threats to information systems. Attackers inject arbitrary code into vulnerable programs through code injection attacks to obtain unauthorized access to the system or extract the sensitive information. The buffer overflow attack mentioned in the previous section is a typical example of code injection attack. Types of vulnerabilities exploited by code injection attacks are diverse, and technologies used are also different. However, there is a prerequisite for implementing attacks: Injected code should be able to run in the environment of the program, that is, the injected code must be compatible with the instruction set of attacked environment. Based on this premise, Instruction Set Randomization (ISR) emerges as inspired by the fact that organisms are protected from environmental threats through genetic variation. Its basic idea is to randomize system instructions so that the code injected by attackers cannot identify the operating environment and generate exceptions.

The idea of ISR was first proposed by Thimbleby in 1991 [13], and has been further developed by different researchers who have developed their own prototype systems. Boyd and Kc *et al.* from Columbia University modified the Bochs emulator [14, 15], constructed the verification system of ISR, and proved feasibility of ISR for Perl, SQL, and other interpreted languages. Barrantes and Ackley *et al.* from the University of New Mexico developed a random instruction set emulator based on an open source binary translation tool – Valgrind [16]. Hu and Hiser *et al.* from the University of Virginia developed a practical ISR prototype system based on Strata virtual machine [17]. Georgios Portokalidis and Keromytis *et al.* from Columbia University realized instruction randomization running environment for x86 software running on Linux based on the binary instrumentation tool PIN [18]. Claire Le Goues and Nguyen-Tuong *et al.* designed and implemented Noncespaces based on ISR technology to prevent XSS attacks by shifting attack surfaces of Web applications [19].

After years of development, ISR technology has made great progress. It is applicable to both compiled language programs and interpreted language source programs. ISR working principles of two types of language programs are introduced as follows.

3.3.2 *Compiled Language ISR*

The premise of successful code injection attacks is that injected code is compatible with the execution environment. ISR focuses on creating an execution environment that is unique to the running processor, so that attackers do not know the language used by the application environment. Therefore, encryption and decryption mechanisms should be introduced to encrypt binary code instructions, generate randomized instruction set, and decode the code when the code is executed to ensure normal operation of the program. ISR system generally consists of two parts: (a) Encrypt the application binary file to generate the randomized instruction set. According to the existing research, it is generally achieved by XOR instructions and specific keys. (b) Build execution environment to decode the randomized instruction code.

Randomized object of ISR technology is a binary executable file. The machine instruction generally consists of opcode and several operands. Randomization of opcode can create new instructions without affecting the processor structure. For example, opcode of software interrupt instruction INT in x86 architecture is 0xCD, and

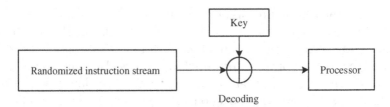

Figure 3.13.   Decoding Process of Randomized Instruction

new instructions can be generated by changing mapping relation-ship between opcode (0xCD) and instruction (INT) without affecting the processor structure. To enhance defense, you can randomize the entire instruction, not just opcode.

The specific execution process is shown in Figure 3.13. Gener-ally, after the instruction is fetched by the system, the randomized instruction is decoded by the key before execution, and then executed by the processor.

Based on the above idea, different researchers use different emu-lators to implement ISR prototype systems, such as SDT-based ISR, Bochs-based ISR, and PIN-based ISR, etc.

(1) SDT-based ISR prototype

Software Dynamic Translation (SDT) is a robust and effective soft-ware dynamic translation system which can provide a virtual exe-cution environment based on a Strata virtual machine. Strata is a software dynamic translation infrastructure [20, 21] that can be redirected, as shown in Figure 3.14. Strata automatically loads the application, checks and transforms application instructions, and then executes them on the main CPU. Transformed application instruc-tions are stored in the Fragment Cache. Strata first captures and saves context of the application (such as program counter, conditional code, and register), and then processes the next instruction. If cur-rent instruction is already in the cache, Strata transfers the control to the cached translation instruction. If the translation instruction is not cached, Strata releases the storage area in the Fragment Cache to store the new translation instruction segment. Strata constantly performs prefetching, decoding, and translation until it encounters the end mark of Fragment.

To implement ISR, SDT extends Strata: (a) Introduce the encryp-tion mechanism before Strata starts executing the application, and

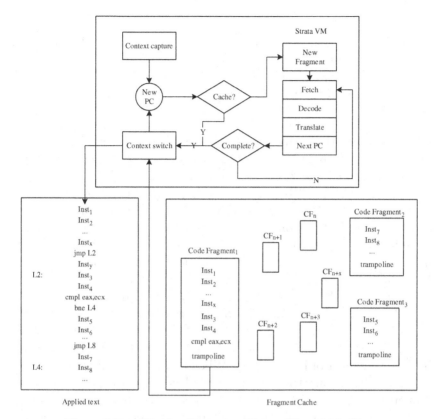

Figure 3.14. Working Diagram of Strata Virtual Machine

use AES to encrypt application content. (b) Abandon Strata's prefetching mechanism, adopt a new prefetching mechanism, and decode and verify instructions before invoking the default target machine prefetching method.

The basic process is as follows.

(a) Initialize system call table.
(b) Encrypt the application.

- Obtain 128-bit encryption key via pseudo-random device/dev/urandom.
- Use mprotect system call to set the text segment as write operation.
- Encrypt the application text with address range table and key.

(c) Fetch the next instruction.

- Fetch 128-bit alignment block and the next 128-bit block pointed by current PC.
- Decrypt two 128-bit blocks.
- Perform decoding and translation phases normally.

(2) Bochs-based ISR prototype

Kc pointed out that implementing ISR in hardware required a slight modification of programmable processors or current processor architectures (such as IA-32) to de-randomize instruction sets before execution, and built an ISR prototype using Bochs emulator. Bochs [22] is an open source emulator based on x86 architecture that interprets each machine instruction. Bochs operates similarly to the real hardware in many ways, for example, it has a CPU that executes a loop in its kernel. Bochs fetches an instruction from its virtual memory by calling FetchDecode() function and decodes it.

Kc chose ELF files as randomized objects, and randomized ELF executable files by modifying objcopy application. Randomization can be implemented either during compilation or during program loading, and then decoded during execution. Key management is an important aspect of ISR security. When a new randomization process starts, it is necessary to know the secret key corresponding to the current instruction executed by the processor. Kc stored the key in an SQlite database, and obtained the key corresponding to the binary file by querying the database through the user space component, and stored it in Process Control Block (PCB) structure of the corresponding process temporarily. When the process is actually executed, the operating system sends the key in PCB to the processor. To this end, the processor needs to provide a special register to store the decoding key, and also needs a special instruction (GAVL) to provide write-only permission for this register in privileged mode. Kc built ISR execution environment by introducing a derandomization unit which is located between fetch instruction and decode instruction. Derandomizing the instructions fetched from the memory, and then send them to CPU for decoding and execution. When using XOR randomization, the process is to simply implement XOR operation between bytes fetched from the memory and keys stored by GAVL.

Kc used Bochs emulator to prove feasibility of hardware-based ISR, and pointed out that the use of hardware emulator would bring

Table 3.1.   Comparison Table of Binary File Execution Time

	FTP	Send Mail	Fibonacci Series
Bochs (s)	39.0	28	93
Direct operation (s)	29.2	1.35	0.322

```
void foo ()  {
    int  a  =  1 ;
    emulate_begin(emurand_args)      ;
    a++ ;
    emulate_and () ;
    printf("a=%d\n",  a)        ;
}
```

Figure 3.15.   EMUrand Emulated Code Segment

considerable performance loss which was usually classified as several orders of magnitude. He compared execution time of binary files for three different applications in Bochs with that in actual system, as shown in Table 3.1. You can see that Bochs environment has a significant impact on efficiency of binary file execution.

(3) EMUrand

Adoption of hardware virtual machine results in unacceptable Bochs-based ISR performance costs. In order to improve efficiency of ISR, Kc *et al.* proposed selective instruction set randomization on the basis of Bochs-based ISR, and built a lightweight emulator EMUrand [15] which was mainly used to improve efficiency of ISR. EMUrand does not randomize all instructions, but first analyzes and locates part of the code that may have a defect, and randomizes only this part of the code.

EMUrand runs in an executable file. It records various states of process instructions, namely general segment, flag, and FPU register, and also marks the randomized code. Figure 3.15 shows that the emulated code segment is enclosed in special tags.

The emulator runs the fetch, decode, execute, and writeback instructions in turn per cycle, and performs randomization before prefetching instructions. Instruction fetch, instruction decoding, execution instruction and rollback instruction are executed in a loop. When the emulator *encounters emulate_begin*, it starts decoding.

Normal operations are not executed until the emulator encounters emulate_end () or detects that the control is returned to the parent function.

(4) PIN-based ISR

Georgios Portokalidis *et al.* designed PIN-based ISR prototype. PIN is a dynamic instruction instrumentation tool launched by Intel Corporation. You can modify the tool to provide an ISR operating environment. The tool provides names of all shared libraries in use and the memory range they occupy in the address space through the callback function by listening to loading operations of all file images, then queries the corresponding one or more keys in the database and saves returned keys and their corresponding memory address range. The data is stored in a structure similar to a hash table. Through this structure, the key can be quickly found through the memory address. Actual derandomization is achieved by creating a callback function. The callback function replaces the default function used by PIN to fetch code from the target process, reads instructions from memory, and uses the memory address to obtain the decoding key.

3.3.3   *Interpreted Language ISR*

With rapid development of Web applications, SQL injection attacks and cross-site scripting attacks greatly increase, bringing new challenges to information system security. ISR is also suitable for SQL, Perl, and other interpreted languages, and has a good protective effect against SQL injection attacks and cross-site scripting attacks.

(1) Perl code randomization

ISR can be implemented on Perl. Randomized objects can be all the key words, operands, function calls in the script. Randomization methods are flexible and diverse, and a relatively simple method to add a random number identification to each element. After adding 9-digit marks (123456789) to all the elements in the code shown in Figure 3.16, you can obtain randomized code, as shown in Figure 3.17. After Perl code is randomized, the malicious code injected by attackers is prevented from execution because it cannot be recognized by the interpreter, effectively preventing Perl injection attacks.

```
foreach $k (sort keys %$tre) {
    $v=$tre->{$k};
    die  " duplicate key $k\n "
        if defined $list{$k};
    push @list, @{$list{$k}} ;
}
```

Figure 3.16.   Original Code

```
foreach123456789 $k (sort123456789  keys %$tre) {
    $v=123456789 $tre->{$k};
    die123456789    " duplicate key $k\n "
        if123456789  defined123456789  $list{$k};
    push123456789 @list, @{$list{$k}} ;
}
```

Figure 3.17.   Changed Code

(2) SQL statement randomization

To understand SQL statement randomization, we should first understand how SQL injection attacks work. The following example introduces SQL injection attack process: consider login page of Common Gateway Interface (CGI) application, enter and submit username and corresponding password, and then execute the following statements.

select*from mysql.user
where username=' ".$uid." 'and
password=password(' ".$pwd. " ');

If the attacker does not input a valid user name, but sets uid variable to "or 1 = 1", it causes CGI script to execute the following query.

selectfrom mysql.user
where username= "or 1 = 1; − −" and
password=password("_any_text_");

The first single quotation mark matches quotation mark after username, and the rest of the attacker's input is treated as an SQL script by the database. In this case, "or 1 = 1" makes the database

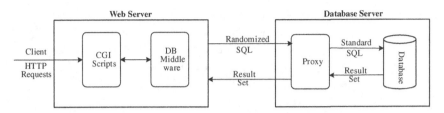

Figure 3.18.   SQL Statement Randomization System Architecture

return all records in the mysql.user table. Because of "or $1 = 1$", the where clause is true.

SQL language randomization adds a random integer to SQL standard operator so that the attacker's input is recognized as an illegal expression, thus preventing attacks.

Figure 3.18 shows SQL randomization system. A proxy is set up between the Web server and the database server, and the proxy decodes received randomized SQL statements and sends them to the database. The proxy is also responsible for hiding database errors that might reveal keys used by the application to attackers. For example, an attacker can perform a simple SQL injection to cause a syntax error and return an error message. This message may reveal some information of the query or table that can be used to infer hidden database properties. By stripping randomization tags in the proxy, you do not have to worry about the database management system inadvertently leaking this content through error messages.

SQL statement randomization tool can read SQL statements, append randomized keys, and rewrite all the keywords. For example, for the following SQL query, the tool picks out keywords from it.

```
select gender, avg (age)
from cs101.students
where dept = %d
group by gender
```

Add a key to each keyword (for example, the key is "123") as follows.

```
select123 gender, avg123 (age)
from123 cs101.students
where123 dept = %d
group123 by123 gender
```

The generated query can be inserted into developer's Web application, then the proxy receives randomized SQL statements, decodes and validates them, and sends them to the database.

(3) Noncespaces

Nguyen-Tuong *et al.* designed Noncespaces mechanism based on the idea of ISR to prevent cross-site scripting attacks. Noncespaces is an end-to-end mechanism that enables server to identify untrusted content, deliver this information accurately to the client, and allow the client to implement security policies on the untrusted content. Noncespaces randomizes (X) HTML tags and attributes to identify and defend against injected malicious network information. Randomization has two functions: First, it can identify untrusted content so that the client can use a policy to limit untrusted content; second, it can prevent untrusted content from destroying the file tree. Because randomized tags are difficult to guess, if an attacker embeds corresponding delimiters in the untrusted content to split contained nodes, it will inevitably cause the syntax analysis error.

Noncespaces aims to allow clients to securely display a variety of files containing trusted and untrusted content at the same time. By implementing a configurable security policy on the browser, Noncespaces eliminates semantic gap between the client and the server and adapts to different security needs. The policy regulates which features of the browser can be used for each type of information, weakening attacker's capability to inject malicious information.

To ensure that the client can determine reliability of all content in the file, the server first divides the content into discrete trust types, and then informs client of content, trust classification, and related policies, as shown in Figure 3.19.

If server's content classification is definite and limited, the server can accurately inform the client of its classification information, and the client can truthfully execute the policy specified by the server, while untrusted content is limited to scope of capabilities that the policy explicitly allows, thus defending against XSS attacks. The server will use the randomization technology to inform the client of trusted content in (X) HTML, and can associate different randomization capabilities with trust types of different content. Names of all elements and attributes in trust types are remapped according to relevant randomization capabilities, so any injection information

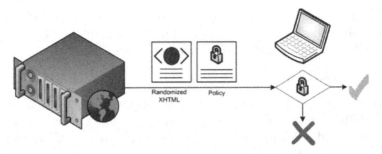

Figure 3.19.   Noncespaces Mechanism

```
1   <!DOCTYPE html PUBLIC "-//W3C//DTD XHTML 1.1//EN"
2         "http://www.w3.org/TR/xhtml11/DTD/xhtml11.dtd">
3   <html xmlns="http://www.w3.org/1999/xhtml"lang="en">
4   <head>        <title>nile.com:++shopping</title>  </head>
5   <body>        <h1  id="title">{item_name}</h1>
6      <p  class='review'>{review.text}
7         --  <a  href='{review.contact}'>{review.author}</a>  </p>
8   </body>
9   </html>
```

Figure 3.20.   Vulnerable Web Page Template

```
1    <!DOCTYPE html PUBLIC "-//W3C//DTD XHTML 1.1//EN"
2          "http://www.w3.org/TR/xhtml11/DTD/xhtml11.dtd">
3    <r60:html  xmlns="http://www.w3.org/1999/xhtml" r60:lang="en"
4          xmlns:r60="http://www.w3.org/1999/xhtml">
5    <r60:head> <r60:title>nile.com:++Shopping</r60:title> </r60:head>
6    <r60:body><r60:h1  r60:id="title"> Useless Do-dad </r60:h1>
7       <r60:p r60:class='review'> </p> <script> attack () </script> <p>
8         -- <r60:a  href=''> </r60:a>  </r60:p>
9    </r60:body>
10   </r60:html>
```

Figure 3.21.   Randomized Vulnerable Web Page Template

cannot correctly name (X) HTML elements and attributes of other trust types.

Figure 3.20 shows a vulnerable Web page template that can be annotated to defend against XSS attacks on this file. For example, using the randomly selected string R60 to represent trusted content and prefix trusted tags and attributes, as shown in Figure 3.21.

```
1    #  Restrict untrusted content to safe subset of XHTML
2    namespace x http://www.w3.org/1999/xhtml
3    #  Declare trust classes
4    trustclass trusted
5    trustclass untrusted
6    order untrusted<trusted
7
8    #Policy for trusted content
9    allow //x:*[ns: trust-class(.,"=trusted")] # all trusted elements
10   allow //@x:*[ns: trust-class(.,"=trusted")] # all trusted attributes
11
12   #  Allow safe untrusted elements
13   allow //x:b | //x:i | //x:u | //x:s | //x:pre | //x:q
14   allow //x:a | //x:img | //x:blockquote
15
16   #  Allow HTTP protocol in the ⟨a href⟩ and ⟨img src⟩ attributes
17   allow //x:a/@href[starts-with(.,"http:")]
18   allow //x:img/@src[starts-with(.,"http:")]
19
20   #  Deny all remaining elements and attributes
21   deny //* | //@*
```

Figure 3.22.   Noncespaces Policy Example for XHTML

Attackers cannot inject malicious content because they do not know the random prefix, and do not interpret it as trusted content. Similarly, attackers cannot embed a closing tag with the prefix in the ending paragraph unit. In XHTML files, attempting to close a closing tag with an unpaired prefix in an open unit will cause XML parsing errors. To prevent attackers from guessing these prefixes, each time a response is rendered, a prefix can be chosen uniformly and randomly, which is Noncespaces technology.

Noncespaces policy specifies capability to invoke the browser in a specified trust type. Figure 3.22 shows an example of a policy for XHTML files. The policy language is designed similar to the firewall configuration language. Comments begin with "#" character and extend to the end of the line. The basic policy consists of a series of allow/deny rules. Each rule makes a policy decision (allow or deny) to a set of file nodes that match XPath expression.

In addition, Noncespaces provides basic XPath capabilities to standardize strings, and also provides additional Boolean functions to compare whether the trust type or attribute value is different from the language default value. The policy example in Figure 3.22 specifies two types of trust object (i.e. the trusted and the trustless). There are no restrictions on tags and attributes that appear in trusted content. Only tags and attributes corresponding to BBCode are allowed in untrusted content: formatting tags, links to other HTTP resources, and images.

When checking whether a file conforms to a policy, the client examines each rule in turn and compares XPath expression with nodes in the file object model of the file. If an allow rule matches a node, the client allows that node and does not consider it when evaluating subsequent rules. If a deny rule matches a node, the client can determine that the file violates the policy and does not render the file.

Anh Nguyen-Tuong *et al.* conducted a function and performance evaluation on Noncespaces to validate its effectiveness on six XSS vulnerability exploitation methods. Experiment results showed that every vulnerability exploitation was successful without Noncespaces enabled, but after Noncespaces was enabled, every vulnerability exploitation was blocked for violation of policy.

Performance evaluation aimed to measure Noncespaces overhead in terms of response latency and server throughput. The test infrastructure consisted of a TikiWiki application for security assessment. VMware virtual machine running security assessment was configured with 512 MB of memory, Fedora Core 3 operating system, Apache 2.0.52 server, and mod PHP5.2.6. The virtual machine ran on a computer which was configured with Intel Pentium IV 3.2 GHz processor, 1 GB of memory, and Ubuntu 7.10 operating system. The client computer was configured with Intel Pentium IV 2 GHz processor, 256 MB of memory, and Ubuntu 8.10 operating system. In each test, an application page was retrieved 1,000 times, and the test was performed for cases with 1, 5, 10, and 15 concurrent requests, respectively. Response latency results showed response time increased by up to 14% after Noncespaces randomization was enabled on the server. The response latency increased by up to 32% over the baseline response time after the policy check proxy server was enabled. The overhead seemed very large on the surface, but the latency increased by no more than 0.6s under interactive use. The test result of Noncespaces' impact on server throughput showed that the throughput decreased by about 10% after the randomization was enabled, and the throughput dropped by 3% when the policy check was enabled. Because the policy check ran on the client, multiple development client requests had little impact on server throughput.

3.3.4 *Basic Effectiveness and Existing Deficiencies*

In theory, ISR can prevent various code injection attacks, making it more difficult to attack protected applications, but it also has its own unavoidable defects.

(a) In order to implement ISR, it is necessary to build a hardware-based or software-based ISR execution environment. The hardware-based environment needs to modify the processor. The software-based environment has a great impact on performance, making ISR impractical.

(b) In general, applications use different libraries, and there are two forms: static and dynamic. But ISR key is associated with the entire process and is difficult to adapt to the dynamic link library, which also limits the application of ISR.

(c) ISR focuses on defending against code injection attacks, especially against remote attacks. If attackers have access to local disks and can acquire binary files and corresponding randomized files, they can easily crack ISR, which limits scope of ISR application.

(d) ISR cannot prevent all code injection attacks, for example, it cannot prevent attacks against functions or pointers. In addition, attackers who can break memory confidentiality can read the key directly from memory, or recover the encrypted code segment and deduce the key by comparing it with the unencrypted code segment in the original executable file.

3.4 In-Place Code Randomization

3.4.1 *Overview*

ASLR and ISR technologies introduced in the previous two sections can prevent injection-type attacks to a large extent. In particular, effective combination of ASLR and Data Execution Protection (DEP) can significantly increase difficulty of injection-type malicious code attacks. However, attack and defense have always been an eternal theme in the field of cyber security. They regard the opposite as target, develop continually in the mutual game. ASLR and DEP technologies blocked a large number of attacks, but facilitated attackers to develop new vulnerability exploiting technology — Return-Oriented Programming (ROP) [23–25]. The technology uses the existing code in the program and assembles it into a continuous code block with Turing-complete compute capabilities, which can bypass double protection of ASLR and DEP and launch attacks on the system. In-place code randomization can effectively defend against ROP attacks by transforming the code.

Based on randomization of binary executable file code segments, in-place code randomization technology uses a set of binary code conversion technologies to disrupt code exploit of ROP attacks, so as to defend against ROP attacks. The following section first introduces the basic principle of ROP attacks, and then focuses on atomic instruction substitution, instruction rearrangement, and other main in-place code randomization technologies.

3.4.2 *How ROP Works*

ROP attacks belong to code reuse attacks, which originate from return-into-libc (RILC) attacks. Currently, there are mainly ROP based on ret instruction and ROP based on JMP instruction.

(1) return-into-libc

Return-into-libc attack is a classic code reuse attack technology [26, 27], which is also the ideological basis of ROP attack. Unlike the traditional overflow attacks, attackers overwrite return addresses of functions as addresses of system library functions and overwrite parameters as parameters of system functions after exploiting buffer overflow vulnerabilities to overflow successfully. This can achieve the purpose of transferring the program control flow and obtaining system control permissions without executing ShellCode in the stack area.

Memory layouts of overflowed functions before and after RILC overflow attack are shown in Figure 3.23. The left side of the figure shows memory layout of overflowed functions before vulnerability overflow, and the right side shows memory layout of overflowed functions after successful vulnerability overflow. System function addresses in the right side of Figure 3.23 are system library function addresses such as system(), exec(), setuid(), and mprotect(). System function parameters are corresponding system function parameters.

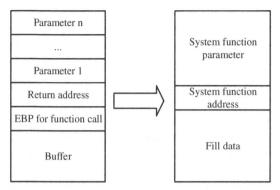

Figure 3.23. Memory Layout Diagram of Functions Before and After RILC Attacks

RILC attacks can exploit key functions of the system to achieve local privilege elevation and change the level of memory protection, etc. In 2011, Minh Tran *et al.* [28] implemented an RILC attack, and proved that the attack method not only met Turing-complete semantic definition, but also work on different operating system versions.

(2) ROP using the ret instruction

Although RILC has been proven to be Turing-complete and has a strong attack capability, it is very difficult to use this method to achieve complex attacks in practice. Based on RILC attacks, ROP attacks utilizing known binary code segments in memory emerge continuously. Unlike RILC calling system library functions directly, ROP attacks using ret instruction select multiple short pieces of binary code (Gadget) terminated by ret instruction in memory and combines them into attack units with special functions in a certain way.

Any strings combination of CISC, a dense instruction set typically represented by x86, might be interpreted as valid instructions. In program code, any instruction ending in 0xC3 can be interpreted as a valid code segment containing ret instruction. As shown in Figure 3.24, if the instruction is interpreted from last two bytes (0x59) of the original address, semantics of the instruction will change into a code segment ending in a ret instruction. This code segment can be called an unintended code segment. In ROP attacks, most Gadgets are composed of such unintended code segments.

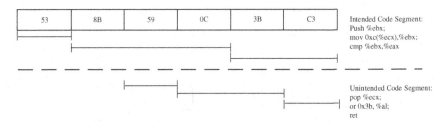

Figure 3.24.   Unintended Code Diagram

ROP attacks using ret instruction direct the program instruction pointer to a piece of ROP attack code which consists of multiple binary code segments (Gadgets) in system memory. After a piece of Gadget code is executed, in order to make the program instruction pointer return and execute the next Gadget, the last instruction in each Gadget must be a ret instruction. When ret instruction is executed, the system pops the word unit at the top of the stack and assigns its value to the instruction pointer, thereby implementing the migration of program execution process between multiple Gadgets.

Ret instructions exist extensively in memory. They are more commonly used in the systems with variable instruction length such as x86 system. A combination of Gadgets ending in ret instruction can implement various in-memory operations in the computer, such as stack operations, conditional jumps, and system calls. Therefore, collection of Gadgets based on ret instruction are Turing-complete for Windows and many other operating system platforms. Figure 3.25 shows ROP attacks which are implemented by exploiting stack buffer overflow vulnerabilities.

The steps for the attacker to launch an ROP attack using ret instruction are as follows.

(a) The attacker inputs well-designed data containing Gadget address into the stack, and uses the data to overwrite the original return address value and adjacent stack space.

(b) The attacker redirects the stack pointer *esp* to Gadget 1 through stack buffer overflow vulnerability.

(c) When the function returns normally, value of eip register is overwritten by Gadget 1 address, and the program executes instruction "xor %cax, %eax; ret" pointed in Gadget 1 address.

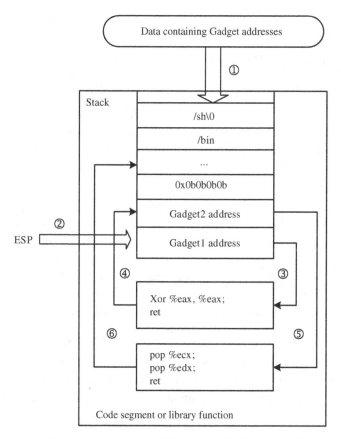

Figure 3.25.   Memory Layout Diagram of ROP Attack Program

(d) After the instruction is executed, it returns to the position in the stack where Gadget 2 address is stored through ret instruction. Value of eip register will be overwritten by Gadget 2 address.

(e) The program executes instructions pointed in Gadget 2 address and then iteratively executes all of the Gadgets specified by the attack.

(f) After executing all of the Gadget code, the attacker has launched an attack successfully.

By analyzing steps of ROP attack using ret instruction, it can be seen that attackers need to control the stack pointer esp and make it point to their malicious data, and then execute ret instructions in all of the Gadgets to ensure continuous execution of all malicious code segments when they launch ROP attacks.

(3) ROP based on JMP instruction

In traditional ROP attacks using ret instruction, Gadget must contain ret instructions. Many detection technologies take advantage of this feature to defend against ROP attacks. To bypass these detection, attackers proposed two technologies which only use indirect jump to realize ROP attacks: POP-JMP [29] and Jump-Oriented Programming (JOP) [30].

(4) POP-JMP

The idea of indirect-jump-based ROP attacks is that there exist instruction sequences in memory that are similar to ret functions, such as "pop x; jmp*x" under x86 platform, where x is any general-purpose register. Gadget that tactfully makes use of these sequences can achieve the same effect as ret attacks. POP-JMP attack process is shown in Figure 3.26.

A ret-like instruction sequence contains two or more instructions. In addition, the number of ret-like instruction sequences in memory is much smaller than the number of ret instructions. If every Gadget is required to end with a ret-like sequence, it is difficult for the collection of Gadgets in memory to be Turing-complete. To do this, you need to find a ret-like instruction sequence as an "instruction trampoline",

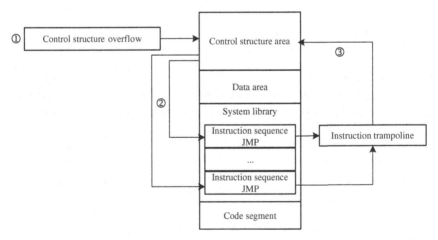

Figure 3.26. Memory Layout Diagram of ROP Attack Using POP-JMP Technology

then select all sequences that jump to the instruction trampoline and end with an indirect jump (such as jmp eax, the instruction trampoline address is stored in eax) instruction as Gadgets. Because there are many indirect jump instructions in memory, a collection of Gadgets composed of these sequences can satisfy Turing-completeness. The typical steps of POP-JMP attack are as follows.

(a) The attacker exploits the memory vulnerability to overflow the control structure area, and directs the program execution process into an instruction sequence (Gadget) of the library function.
(b) The program executes the instruction sequence Gadget, and jumps to the instruction trampoline when encountering an indirect jump instruction.
(c) The instruction trampoline is also stored in the library function. Its address can be stored in a register, and binary sequences that jump to this register in memory constitute the Gadget collection. The instruction trampoline directs the program back to control structure area to realize ret-like operations such as switching the instruction pointer and moving the stack pointer.
(d) The program returns to the second step and continues to execute the next Gadget until all Gadgets have been executed, so the attacker gets the desired result.

(5) JOP

Similar to design concept of POP-JMP, JOP is also a JMP-based ROP attack method. But JOP is implemented by defining Gadget addresses to be executed as per the allocation table and controlling call of each Gadget on the allocation table through the allocator. Comparison between JOP and ROP is shown in Figure 3.27.

JOP attacks differ from ret-based ROP attacks in the following ways.

(a) Gadgets end with different instructions. JOP Gadgets end with JMP, while ROP Gadgets end with ret instruction.
(b) Instruction pointer of the program is switched between Gadgets in different ways. ROP uses ret instruction to switch the instruction pointer through stack operation characteristics, while JOP uses the program to switch the instruction pointer through an allocator.

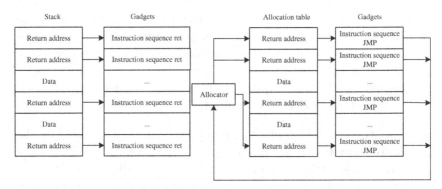

Figure 3.27. Memory Layout Diagram of ROP Attack Using POP-JMP Technology

(c) The attack code is stored in different locations. By making use of stack operation characteristics, ROP attack instructions can only be stored on the stack, while JOP attack instructions can be stored not only on the stack, but also in the other data areas such as the heap.

3.4.3 *Atomic Instruction Substitution*

Execution of a Gadget has a specific sequence set of CPU and memory state corresponding to exploit process. The attacker needs to choose how to link different Gadgets together based on the register, flag, or memory location modified by each Gadget. Subsequent executions of a Gadget depend on results of all previous Gadget executions. ROP code depends on correct executions of all linked Gadgets, so even simple change to Gadget could make ROP attack fail. In-place code randomization is to simply change code and break the Gadget on which ROP depends.

The basic idea of atomic instruction substitution is to implement exact same computation with different instruction combination. In application of code randomization, Gadget instructions are substituted with instructions that are equivalent in function but different in sequence. Although the program produces the same result, it can break Gadget link of ROP. Figure 3.28 (a) shows an example of the atomic instruction substitution technology. The actual code generated by the compiler consists of *mov*, *cmp*, and *lea* instructions, starting at byte B0. However, when you disassemble from the next byte,

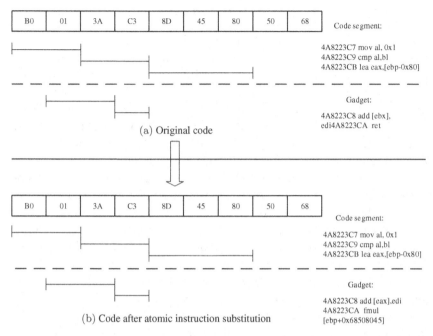

Figure 3.28. Example of Atomic Instruction Substitution

you'll find a very useful Gadget ending with ret. To defend against ROP attacks, you need to substitute a single instruction with the same length and equivalent function for a certain instruction. In addition to the method based on substituting the negative subtraction for addition, there are different forms of instructions with different opcode. For example, add r/m32, r32 stores addition results in register operands or memory operands (r/m32), and add r32, r/m32 stores results in memory (R32). Although two forms of opcode are different, the two instructions are equivalent when both operands are registers. Many arithmetic and logic instructions have this type of double equivalent form. As shown in Figure 3.28 (b), two operands of cmp instruction are both registers, so the instruction can be replaced with the equivalent instruction with different opcode. Although the actual program code has not changed, ret instruction originally contained in cmp instruction has now disappeared, making Gadgets unavailable. In this case, the conversion process eliminates Gadgets entirely, effectively blocking ROP attacks.

3.4.4   *Internal Base Block Reordering*

For a binary file, its internal sequence of instructions is fixed, which is determined by the compiler according to specific input conditions. If different conditions are selected, multiple target files with the same function but different internal instruction sequences can be generated. Therefore, for a binary file, the instruction sequence of its basic block is only one of several reasonable instruction sequences. Based on this discovery, the instruction sequence in the basic block of the binary file can be reordered to disrupt ROP attacks.

Determining ordering relation between instructions is the basis of instruction reordering. The ordering relation must ensure correctness of code, which can be realized with aid of the basic block dependency graph of the program. The basic block dependency graph represents interdependencies between the instructions. The basic block is linear code, and its dependency graph is a directed acyclic graph, in which machine instructions are regarded as vertices, and interdependencies between instructions are regarded as edges. By performing a dependency analysis on the code of the disassembled basic block, dependency graph of each basic block can be obtained. To perform a dependency analysis on the machine code, we first need to carefully handle dependencies between x86 instructions. In addition, we should consider data dependencies between register operands and memory operands, and data dependencies between CPU flags, implicitly used registers, and memory locations.

For each instruction i, we define use[i] and def[i] to represent the registers used or defined by instruction i. In addition to register operands and registers for effective address calculation, instruction i includes all implicitly used registers. For example, use set and def set for pop eax are {esp} and {eax, esp}, respectively, and use set and def set for rep stosb are {ecx, eax, edi} and {ecx, edi}, respectively. We first assume that all the instructions in the base block are interdependent, and then check dependencies between Read After Write (RAW), Write After Read (WAR), and Write After Write (WAW) of each pair of instructions. For example, if any of the following conditions is true, there is a RAW dependency between i_1 and i_2: (a) def $[i_1] \cap$ use$[i_2] \neq \varnothing$. (b) Destination operand of i_1 and source operand of i_2 are both memory locations. (c) i_1 writes at least one flag to be read by i_2.

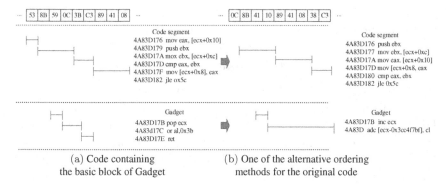

(a) Code containing
the basic block of Gadget

(b) One of the alternative ordering
methods for the original code

Figure 3.29.   Example of Internal Basic Block Reordering

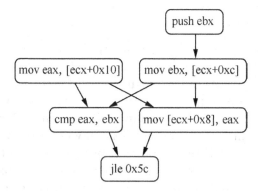

Figure 3.30.   Basic Block Dependency Graph Corresponding to Example of Internal Basic Block Reordering

Figure 3.29 (a) shows the code containing the basic block of Gadget, and Figure 3.30 shows the corresponding Directed Acyclic Graph (DAG) of dependency. Instructions not connected to directed edges are independent instructions, and their relative execution order is not restricted. According to dependency DAG of the basic block, possible ordering of basic block instructions can be determined. Figure 3.29 (b) shows an alternative ordering of the original code. Except for one instruction and one byte value, positions and byte values of all other instructions have changed, eliminating Gadget contained in the original code. Although a new Gadget appears after a few bytes in the code block, attackers cannot rely on this Gadget because alternative ordering will transfer it to another location, and some of Gadget's internal instructions will change constantly.

3.4.5 *Basic Effectiveness and Existing Deficiencies*

In-place code randomization technology can effectively defend against ROP attacks and is an effective supplement to ASLR and DEP protection. However, protection provided by this technology is probabilistic and does not guarantee complete protection against ROP attacks. In addition, this technology also relies on how binary files are disassembled.

3.5 Software Polymorphism

3.5.1 *Overview*

At present, there is a serious asymmetry between cyber attack and defense, mainly due to staticity and unicity of software. Existing software development and deployment are based primarily on cost estimates and ease of use. The source code verified by test is compiled and linked by the same compiler in the same way to generate many software entities of the same version which are sold to different users. Although this benefits software producers, it causes a passive situation where the information system is easy to attack and difficult to defend. This is because attackers only need to concentrate on defect analysis of one software entity, once they find a vulnerability, they can easily apply it to all software of this version, easily launching successful attacks on thousands or even hundreds of millions of computer devices running the same binary code. This asymmetry is reflected in different aspects such as cost of spending and cost of risk. Only one or several attackers analyze a piece of software on several computers, while defenders need to invest a large number of security personnel to guarantee security of tens of thousands of computing devices. Attackers only need to find one vulnerability to launch a large-scale attack, and defenders have to monitor every level of the system carefully. This kind of static production and deployment of software based on cost ignores the importance of security and ultimately leads to greater economic losses.

In order to eliminate huge security risks caused by software staticity, software polymorphism technology emerged [31]. Its basic principle is to use compilers to generate a large number of software entities with the same function and different internal structures for the same source code during the software production process, and distribute software entities to different users. This makes each user use the same software with different internal structures, breaking current serious asymmetry between attack and defense and increasing cost of launching attacks (as shown in Figure 3.31). With development of cloud computing and mobile Internet as well as increasing popularity of the app store model, software polymorphism technology has ushered in an important opportunity for development, and related research has attracted more and more attention.

Compilers are extremely important in software development, and the popular design pattern for compilers today is deterministic: the same source code is always translated into same executable files. In fact, the compiler can do a lot of optimizations during compilation,

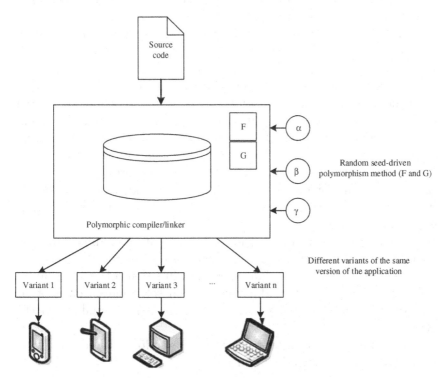

Figure 3.31.   Diagram of Software Polymorphism Technology

adjusting compilation details to user's needs, so the compiler is an ideal place for implementing software polymorphism. According to the input program, the compiler can easily generate a large number of variants with the same external function and different internal structures. These variants are the same in terms of operations specified in the design, but different in the aspects not specified in the design. These variants will behave differently when an attacker attempts to launch an attack without conforming to the specifications. In the process of using the compiler to generate polymorphic software, relevant technologies in ASLR described above as well as variable reordering, function adjustment, and other technologies can be comprehensively used.

3.5.2 *Extensible Compiler for Multi-Phase Instrumentation*

In the process of compilation, various technologies such as randomization and metamorphosis are introduced to obtain polymorphic software. To realize this function, existing compiler needs to be extended, and the extensible compiler for multi-phase instrumentation is one of the main implementation methods.

The extensible compiler for multi-phase instrumentation can realize generic compilation of C/C++/VB/.NET multilingual source code related projects, open its internal access interface for intermediate representations of different levels of abstraction generated during compilation based on the idea of Microsoft open compilation service (Compiler as a Service), and provide instrumentation functions for reading, converting, and modifying corresponding intermediate representations. By supporting the compilation extension module, you can implement the comprehensive application of software anti-attack mechanism on it, including program control flow obfuscation, garbage instruction insertion, generation and scheduling of multi-variant execution functions of complex algorithms, replacement of random instruction set, random encryption and decryption of memory buffer data, memory boundary check, etc.

The compilation process that supports randomization of instructions and data is shown in Figure 3.32.

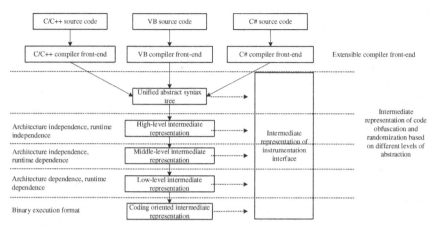

Figure 3.32. Diagram of Compilation Process That Supports Randomization of Instructions and Data

3.5.3 *Program Segmentation and Function Reordering*

Compiler is the basis of software polymorphism. To generate different variants of the same program, compiler is required to combine with various randomization and metamorphosis technologies, such as ISR and ASLR technologies mentioned above, and several common technologies will be described in the following.

The program segmentation and function reordering technology segments the program and reorders functions at compilation time to change the program address space layout. Modern programs are created by putting various modules together, and each module usually corresponds to a separate source file. Each module is divided into different types of sections, such as data section and code section. These modules themselves are usually organized as functions which call each other. Attackers launch some attacks because they know that a global function is stored in a particular location. A simple method of program segmentation and function reordering technology is to randomly change Object File link order during compilation, as shown in Figure 3.33.

Each change of the section order will generate a variant with completely different structure. Randomization intensity is determined by

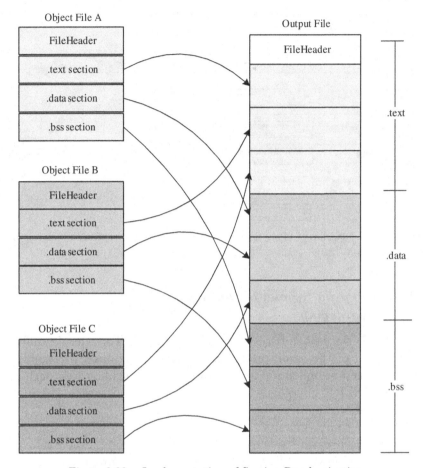

Figure 3.33.   Implementation of Section Randomization

the section granularity, and the smaller granularity, the greater randomization intensity.

3.5.4   *Instruction Filling Randomization*

The generated machine code can be changed by using instruction scheduling, call inlining, code extraction, loop allocation, partial redundancy elimination, and other compiler transformations. To produce randomized output, you can further alter these transformations.

No Operation Sequence (NOP) insertion. Some small code sequences have no real effect at runtime, but they can be used

Figure 3.34. NOP Insertion and Code Sequence Randomization

as filling blocks of code to push forward subsequent instructions by a few bytes. These NOP introduce offsets, increase length of binary file, and can change positions of subsequent code sequences. This change can prevent attacks launched by known bytes at fixed locations. NOP instance code includes movl %eax, %eax, xchgl %esi, %es, leal (%edi), %edi, etc. NOP insertion technology is used to force calibration of the jump target, so that attackers cannot use the existing jump instruction to jump into an appropriate instruction code, but switch to an instruction segment. Figure 3.34 shows an example of NOP insertion and code sequence randomization.

Equivalent instructions. Instruction systems of many architectures provide different instructions. In certain circumstances, these instructions can produce same results and are interchangeable. Substituting these instructions for their equivalent instructions will not cause any performance loss and can significantly change the binary instruction sequence.

For example, the following instructions (and corresponding byte encoding).

movl %edx, %eax	89
xchgl %edx, %eax	92

can be replaced with the following instructions.

leal (%edx), %eax	8D 02
xchgl %eax, %edx	87 D0

After conversion, leal instruction in the code stream is combined with the load address instruction, which becomes a simple register-to-register movement. So-called load address instruction here refers to the use of register addressing to load the address of a memory operand into a register. Other instances use exchange operations or exchangeability of x86 operations in the coding. Although the converted instruction is equivalent to the previous instruction, its binary encoding might be obviously different.

3.5.5 *Register Randomization*

Register randomization means swapping two registers. For example, the stack pointer register esp in Intel x86 architecture can be randomly swapped with another register such as eax. Most attacks rely on the fixed content in registers, and register randomization is proposed for this situation. For example, if an attack puts the system call number in eax and runs the system call, the attack will fail because the system will use the value stored in esp as the system call number. Since there are no registers in hardware architecture that specifically support randomization, registers need to be swapped before instructions that implicitly depend on values in esp or eax are run, such as stack operation instructions or system call instructions. An easier method is to change only the registers used to store variables and temporary variables. Values of these variables will not be used by instructions that require special registers. For example, instruction addl %eax, %ebx can be easily replaced with addl %esi, %ecx.

3.5.6 *Inverse Stack*

Most processor architectures employ an asymmetric design, with stack growth designed as a direction. For example, in Intel x86 instruction set, manual operations of all predefined stacks, such as push and pop, apply only to a downwardly growing stack. By extending stack operation instructions, you can create a variant with a upwardly growing stack [32]. Changing the stack layout makes buffers and variables allocated in the stack completely different. This method can prevent buffer overflow attacks and stack smash attacks that rely on the downwardly growing stack. Figure 3.35 shows a buffer overflow that changes the return value for the downwardly growing stack but does not damage the upwardly growing stack. The overridden area is an unused stack area.

3.5.7 *Basic Effectiveness and Existing Deficiencies*

Software polymorphism creates different variants for the same software, making it difficult for attackers to apply vulnerabilities found

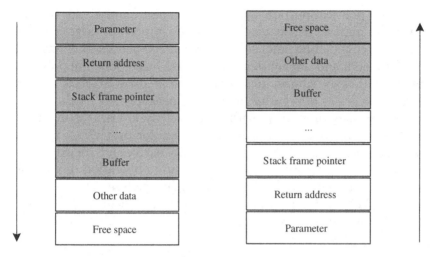

Figure 3.35. Diagram of Inverse Stack against Buffer Overflow

in a piece of software on a large scale. This increases the cost for attackers, reduces possibility of serious worm outbreak, and improves protection capability of the system as a whole.

Software polymorphism technology has the following defects.

(a) It increases the cost for software developers, because they have to generate different versions of software entities for the same source code. At the same time, management and maintenance costs will increase.

(b) Software verification problem. Because each copy of the software is different, it is difficult to apply the existing software verification methods, and users of polymorphic software need other methods to verify binary files.

3.6 Multi-Variant Execution

3.6.1 *Overview*

Software polymorphism technology can increase the cost for attackers and effectively reduce the possibility of large-scale cyber attacks, but it cannot prevent attacks against individual software. With increasing concern about information security by various countries, cyber attacks have long risen from individual behavior to the level of organizations and even nations. To achieve huge economic interests or important political purposes, it is worthwhile to invest a lot of manpower and material resources to attack the important target systems to obtain confidential information or control permissions (such as APT attacks), and impact of attacks is also huge. Software polymorphism technology cannot deal with these kinds of attacks, and we need higher levels of security protection measures.

For information systems with high security levels, it is urgent to use pre-warning and monitoring technology for protection, monitor system state in real time, detect attacks early, and remedy security defects. Multi-variant execution monitors operation of multiple variants of the same program in real time, analyzes and processes abnormal behaviors immediately after detecting them, and can block execution of malicious code before an attack occurs, thus effectively protecting the information system.

3.6.2 *Technology Principle*

Multi-variant execution technology is a technology that can prevent malicious code execution at runtime [33–36]. It runs multiple semantically-equivalent variants simultaneously and compares behaviors of variants at the synchronization point. Under the premise of the same input, once finding an inconsistent behavior, the monitor will start analysis process to determine whether there is an attack behavior.

Jackson *et al.* from the University of California adopted a user-space solution [37, 38] in their architecture. Cox *et al.* designed and implemented N-variant system framework [39] and modified the system kernel to make the monitor run at the core layer. Jackson *et al.* designed and implemented a Multi-Variant Execution Environment (MVEE) by using the multi-variant execution. Multi-variant execution is completed jointly by the compiler and MVEE, as follows: Add pragmas generated by multi-variant execution for program core algorithms or critical control procedures that need critical protection in the source code, so as to generate variants of diversified code at compile time; run multiple variants in the multi-variant execution environment; and synchronize and monitor behaviors of various variants on the system call. If a variant is found to be inconsistent with other variants, it means that the variant has been attacked. At this time, execution of the variant should be suspended, and the result of other variants should be selected as the result of program execution. In MVEE, input from the system is sent to all variants at the same time. This makes it impossible for attackers to send different malicious input to different variants, thus ensuring consistency of variant execution during monitoring.

Multi-variant execution is divided into two parts: variant generation and monitoring execution. Variant generation is based on the compiler implementation. Multi-variant pragmas in the source code are provided by the extensible compiler, like "#DIVERSITY_OPTION=OPTION", where OPTION is a diversified option and can be various technologies mentioned in software polymorphism. The compiler randomizes the corresponding code according to this pragma at compile time, and each compilation can generate multiple (set by the user) variants.

MVEE consists of dynamic operation support environment and multi-variant monitor. Its architecture is shown in Figure 3.36.

Dynamic operation support environment is used to support operation of the variant. It adopts lightweight virtual execution technology to run the program variants in the virtualized operating environment, so that operation of the variant program is independent of the local system and under monitoring of the monitor.

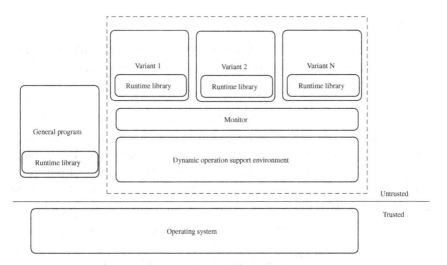

Figure 3.36. Multi-variant Execution Environment Architecture

The multi-variant monitor is used to control execution states of variants while verifying whether they conform to predefined rules. First, MVEE runs multiple variants of the program when the user starts the program, and the monitor does not interrupt the variant execution as long as variants do not access data or resources outside its process space. When a variant requests a system call, the monitor will intercept the request and suspend execution of the variant, then the monitor attempts to synchronize system calls of other variants. All variants need to execute system calls with the same function and equivalent parameters in a short time. When a variant has a different execution result or execution timeout due to an attack, the monitor will take corresponding actions based on the configured policy. By default, it will terminate and restart all variants. It can also eliminate inconsistent variants based on the simple majority rule. Monitoring technology allows multiple program instances of different granularities to run synchronously. The coarse granularity is the system level call, and the fine granularity is the instruction level.

From the perspective of formulation, the monitor determines whether various variants are in a consistent state based on the following rules. If p_1 to p_n are variants of the same program p, they are in a consistent state if and only if the following conditions are true at any system call synchronization point, i.e.,

$$\forall S_i, S_j \in \boldsymbol{S} : s_i = s_j \tag{3.1}$$

$\boldsymbol{S} = \{s_1, s_2, \ldots, s_n\}$ is a series of system functions called at the synchronization point. s_i is a system function called by p_i

$$\forall a_{ij}, a_{ik} \in \boldsymbol{A} : a_{ij} = a_{ik} \tag{3.2}$$

$\boldsymbol{A} = \{a_{11}, a_{12}, \ldots, a_{mn}\}$ is a series of parameters used by the function called at the system synchronization point, a_{ij} is ith parameter of the system function called by p_j, and m is the number of parameters of the system call. If A is null, it means that the system call has no arguments. The parameter equivalence operator is defined as

$$a \equiv b \Leftrightarrow \begin{cases} \text{if type} \neq \text{buffer} : a = b \\ \text{else} : \text{content}(a) = \text{content}(b) \end{cases} \tag{3.3}$$

Type is the type required for parameters of the corresponding system call. Content of the buffer is all the bytes in this series, which are contained in content $(a) := \{a[0] \cdots a[\text{size}(a) - 1]\}$.

For buffers ending with 0, size function returns the first 0 byte encountered in the buffer; for a buffer of an explicitly specified size, size function returns the parameter representing the buffer size in the system call.

$$\forall t_i \in \boldsymbol{T} : t_i - t_s \leq \omega \qquad (3.4)$$

$\boldsymbol{T} = \{t_1, t_2, \ldots, t_n\}$ represents the time when the monitor intercepts system call; t_i is the time when the system call s_i is intercepted by the monitor; t_s is the time when the synchronization point starts and the time when the first system call reaches the synchronization point; ω is maximum hang time for the monitor to wait for a variant. Value of ω is defined in the application policy of the monitor and depends on the application and hardware.

If these conditions are not met, a warning will be triggered, and the monitor will take an appropriate action based on the configurable policy. By default, the monitor will forcibly terminate and restart all variants. But it might also adopt other policies, for example, it only terminates variants that do not meet requirements based on the majority vote.

(1) System call granularity

To synchronize variants, the coarsest granularity solution is to synchronize at the system call level [40]. The reason for selecting this granularity is that in the current operating system environment, it is impossible to break the system without first invoking the system call. Therefore, when various variants do not access the environment outside its process space, variants are allowed to operate independently of each other. When a variant tries to access the environment outside its process space, the monitor will intercept the system call and compare states of variants, as shown in Figure 3.37.

(2) Function call granularity

Function call is a finer granularity level than system call, and the function call synchronization requires detection within variants so that the monitor knows inner status of each variant process. To do this, MVEE needs to contain a dynamic binary tool to detect a variant's access to a new function.

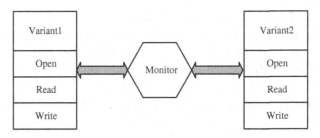

Figure 3.37.   Monitoring Using System Call Granularity

This granularity level enforces restrictions on variant behaviors more strictly, which can effectively prevent attacks. By synchronizing at the function entry, the monitor can detect changes within the program flow before the injected code is executed, and uses this information to establish execution traces. When combined with system call granularity, the execution trace can be combined with the system call trace to show the type of the input that caused change and execution paths of all variants before the change occurs. This method can also be used to detect other kinds of differences, such as mismatches between system calls and function calls.

Synchronization of function call granularity is limited to code optimization type and polymorphism type it can allow. For example, at this granularity, it is not allowed to use function inlining in variants for monitoring unless all variants have the same function inlining relationship. Similarly, when other variants do not have corresponding wrappers, conversions such as insertion of wrapper functions are not allowed.

(3) Instruction level granularity

A more fine-grained method suitable for high-security applications is to monitor at the instruction level, as shown in Figure 3.38.

System call granularity is usually enough to protect a system. At the instruction level granularity, however, programming errors that cause differences in control flow can be detected, and the code injected by an attacker that causes failure can also be detected.

3.6.3   *Basic Effectiveness and Existing Deficiencies*

The multi-variant execution technology is applicable to high security level requirements. By monitoring execution of different variants

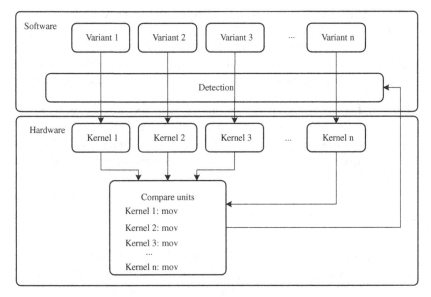

Figure 3.38. Diagram of Instruction-Level Monitoring

of the same program, it is found through comparison that possible attack behaviors can be blocked before attacks take effect to protect the system. But there are some defects in the multi-variant execution technology.

(a) High performance overhead. In multi-variant execution, at least two variants of the same program must be executed synchronously. The monitor must monitor the running result of each variant in real time, which requires higher system performance. In particular, fine-grained monitoring has a greater impact on system performance.

(b) Facing denial of service attacks. When MVEE finds that a variant is exceptional, the system will give an warning, and the monitor will conduct in-depth analysis and processing. If an attacker takes MVEE as the attack target and designs a large number of attack programs, MVEE will repeatedly raise the warnings and analyze the processes, causing more serious performance consumption, and even making the system breakdown.

(c) Low system flexibility. Normal operation of MVEE requires managing each variant independently. For example, in order to patch or upgrade the source code of an application in MVEE, the variant must be rebuilt, especially when this change modifies behavior of the variant that the monitor tries to detect. Existing MVEE does not support dynamic reloading of a variant. When a variant needs to be reloaded, the user must manually restart MVEE.

One of future research directions of this technology is to study more variant diversification methods that can be combined with more system calls or other components of the operating system. In addition, impact of diversification technologies on attacks is also a research focus in the future.

3.7   Summary

Most of the existing attacks are launched against software vulnerabilities, so software security protection is extremely important in information system security. Because software vulnerabilities are inevitable, there is a serious asymmetry between software defense and attack, which is aggravated by software homogenization. The existing mainstream protection technologies still focus on static and passive protection, which makes it difficult to deal with ever-changing attacks, leaving people helpless against unknown attacks. Attack and defense are mutually targeted. Cyber attacks take system vulnerabilities as targets and bypass static and complex protection methods in a flexible and variable way to achieve the purpose of destruction. Inspired by the dynamic nature of attacks, defense can change the original passive response mode, and introduce dynamic mechanisms to present a dynamic, changeable, and random form to attackers. It constantly shifts system attack surface, making attackers unable to re-use vulnerabilities, increasing cost for attackers to find and exploit vulnerabilities, and effectively ensuring system security. Based on this idea, dynamic software defense is proposed to change the traditional fixed thinking mode of security protection and is considered as a game-changing technology.

Dynamic software defense is a comprehensive technology, involving technologies in many fields such as cryptography, compilation, dynamic execution, and disassembly, and is closely related to software life cycle. It can be introduced in multiple phases of software development, compilation, linking, deployment, loading, and

Table 3.2. Comparison of Dynamic Software Defense Technologies

	Specific Technology	Underlying Technology	Effective Phase	Defense Effectiveness
1	Address space layout randomization technology	Compilation technology, dynamic execution technology	Compilation phase, loading phase	Buffer overflow attacks
2	Instruction set randomization technology	Encryption technology, compilation technology, dynamic execution technology	Compilation phase, loading phase	XSS attacks, SQL injection attacks, code injection attacks
3	In-place code randomization technology	Disassembly technology, dynamic execution technology	Loading phase	ROP attacks
4	Software polymorphism technology	Compilation technology	Compilation phase	Suppress attack propagation
5	Multi-variant execution technology	Compilation technology, dynamic execution technology	Operation phase	Attack monitoring and prevention

final operation. This chapter summarizes mainstream technologies of dynamic software defense, and delved into basic information, technical principles, basic effectiveness, and existing deficiencies of each technology. Table 3.2 summarizes and compared main technologies of address space layout randomization, instruction set randomization, in-place code randomization, software polymorphism, and multi-variant execution. These technologies are closely related to each other. For example, the software polymorphism technology will employ many related technologies of address space layout randomization to generate multiple software variants, while the multi-variant execution technology will make use of multiple variant versions generated by the software polymorphism. The existing technologies of dynamic software defense have a good defense effect on specific attacks. How to coordinate and integrate various technologies effectively is a future research area. As cyber attacks and defenses are constantly developing in mutual confrontation, it is necessary to continuously study new dynamic software defense technologies to deal with evolving attacks.

References

[1] Avizienis, A. and Chen, L. On the implementation of n-version programming for software fault tolerance during execution. *Proceedings of the International Computer Software and Applications Conference*, 1977, 149–155.

[2] Shacham, H., Page, M., Pfaff, B. *et al.* On the effectiveness of address space randomization. *ACM Conference on Computer and Communications Security (CCS)*, Washington D. C., 2004, 298–307.

[3] Bhatkar, S., Sekar, R., and Duvamey, D. C. Efficient techniques for comprehensive protection from memory error exploits. *Proceedings of the 14th USENIX Security Symposium, Baltimore, MD*, 2005, 255–270.

[4] Wang, Q. 0-Day Security: Software vulnerability analysis technology (2nd Edition). Beijing: Publishing House of Electronics Industry, 2013.

[5] Marco-Gisbert, H. and Ripoll, I. On the effectiveness of NX, SSP, RenewSSP and ASLR against stack buffer overflows. *Proceedings of the 13th International Symposium on Network Computing and Applications*, 2014.

[6] Forrest, S., Semayaji, A., and Ackley, D. H. Building diverse computer systems. *IEEE Computer Society in 6th Workshop on Hot Topics in Operating Systems*, 1997, 67–72.

[7] Alexander, S. Improving security with homebrew system modifications. *USENIX*, 2004, 29(6): 26–32.

[8] Bhatkar, S., Duvamey, D. C., and Sekar, R. Address obfuscation: An efficient approach to combat a broad range of memory error exploits. *Proceedings of the 12th USENIX Security Symposium*, Washington D. C., 2003.

[9] PaXTeam.PaX. https://pax.grsecurity.net/, 2001.

[10] Eugene, H. S. The Internet worm program: An analysis. *Computer Communication Review*, 1989, 19(1): 17–57.

[11] Zou, C. C., Gong, W., and Towsley, D. Code red worm propagation modeling and analysis. *Proceedings of the 9th ACM Conference on Computer and Communications Security (CCS)*, 2002, 138–147.

[12] He, Z. Research on lightweight buffer overflow protection technology. *University of Electronic Science and Technology of China*, 2008.

[13] Thimbleby, H. Can viruses ever be useful? *Computers and Security*, 1991, 10(2): 111–114.

[14] Kc, G. S., Keromytis, A. D., and Prevelakis, V. Countering code-injection attacks with instruction-set randomization. *ACM Computer & Communications Security Conference*, 2003, 272–280.

[15] Boyd, S. W., Kc, G. S., Locasto, M. E., *et al.* On the general applicability of instruction-set randomization. *IEEE Transactions on Dependable and Secure Computing*, 2010, 7(3): 255–270.

[16] Barrantes, E. G., Ackley, D. H., Forrest, S., *et al.* Randomized instruction set emulation. *ACM Transactions on Information System Security*, 2005, 8: 3–40.

[17] Hu, W., Hiser, J., Williams, D., *et al.* Secure and practical defense against code-injection attacks using software dynamic translation. *Proceedings of the 2nd International Conference on Virtual Execution Environments (VEE)*, 2006, 2–12.

[18] Luk, C. K., Cohn, R., Muth, R., *et al.* Building customized program analysis tools with dynamic instrumentation. *Proceedings of Programming Language Design and Implementation (PLDI)*, 2005: 190–200.

[19] Barrantes, E. G., Ackley, D. H., Forrest, S., *et al.* Randomized instruction set emulation to disrupt binary code injection attacks. *Conference on Computer and Communications Security*, 2003, 281–289.

[20] Scott, K. and Davidson, J. Strata: A software dynamic translation infrastructure. *IEEE Workshop on Binary Translation*, 2001.

[21] Scott, K. and Davison, J. W. Safe virtual execution using software dynamic translation. *Proceedings of the 18th Annual Computer Security Applications Conference (Las Vegas, NV)*, 2002, 209–218.

[22] Bochs emulator web page. http://bochs.sourceforge.net/, 2008.

[23] Davi, L., Sadeghi, A., and Winandy, M. Dynamic integrity measurement and attestation: Towards defense against return-oriented programming attacks. *Proceedings of the 2009 ACM Workshop on Scalable Trusted Computing, Chicago*, 2009, 49–54.

[24] Hiser, J., Nguyen-Tuong, A., Co, M., *et al.* ILR: Where'd my Gadget go. *Proceedings of IEEE Symposium on Security and Privacy, Oakland*, 2012, 571–585.

[25] Checkoway, S., Davi, L., and Dmitrienko, A. Return-oriented programming without returns. *Proceedings of ACM Conference on Computer and Communications Security (CCS)*, 2010, 559–572.

[26] Minh, T., Mark, E., Tyler, B., *et al.* On the expressiveness of return-into-libc attacks *Lecture Notes in Computer Science*, 2011, 6961: 121–141.

[27] Wang, J. Research on ROP attack detection technology based on static features of ShellCode. Nankai University, 2012.

[28] Shacham, H. The geometry of innocent flesh on the bone: Return-into-libc without function calls (on the x86). *Proceedings of ACM Conference on Computer and Communications Security (CCS)*, 2007, 552–561.

[29] Chen, P., Xiao, H., Yin, X. C., *et al.* DROP: Detecting return-oriented programming malicious code. *Lecture Notes in Computer Science*, 2009, 5909, 163–177.

[30] Davi, L., Sadeghi, A. R., and Winandy, M. ROPdefender: A detection tool to defend against return-oriented programming attacks. *Proceedings of the ACM Symposium on Information Computer & Communication Security Cited*, 2011, 22–24.

[31] Frans, M. E. Unibuspluram: Massive-scale software diversity as a defense mechanism. *Proceedings of the 2010 Workshop on New Security Paradigms*, 2010, 7–16.

[32] Salamat, B., Gal, A., and Franz, M. Reverse stack execution in a multi-variant execution environment. *Workshop on Compiler and Architectural Techniques for Application Reliability and Security*, 2008.

[33] Salamat, B., Jackson, T., and Wagner, G. Run-time defense against code injection attacks using replicated execution. *IEEE Transactions on Dependable and Secure Computing*, 2011.

[34] Salamat, B., Gal, A., Jackson, T., *et al.* Multi-variant program execution: Using multi-core systems to defuse buffer-overflow vulnerabilities. *Proceeding Int'l Conference Complex, Intelligent and Software Intensive Systems*, 2008, 843–848.

[35] Salamat, B., Jackson, T., Gal, A., *et al.* Orchestra: Intrusion detection using parallel execution and monitoring of program variants in user-space. *Proc. European Conf. Computer Systems*, 2009, 33–46.

[36] Salamat, B., Wimmer, C., and Franz, M. Synchronous Signal Delivery in a Multi-Variant Intrusion Detection System, 2009.

[37] Jackson, T., Salamat, B., Wagner, G., *et al.* On the effectiveness of multi-variant program execution for vulnerability detection and prevention. *Proceedings of the 6th International Workshop on Security Measurements and Metrics*, 2010, 1–8.

[38] Jackson, T., Wimmer, C., and Franz, M. Multi-variant program execution for vulnerability detection and analysis. *Proceedings of the Sixth Annual Workshop on Cyber Security and Information Intelligence Research*, 2010, 1–4.

[39] Cox, B., Evans, D., Filipi, A., *et al.* N-variant systems: A secret-less framework for security through diversity. *Proceedings of the 15th USENIX Security Symposium*, 2006, 105–120.

[40] Parampalli, C., Sekar, R., and Johnson, R. A practical mimicry attack against powerful system-call monitors. *Proc. ACM Symp. Information, Computer and Comm. Security*, 2008, 156–167.

Chapter 4

Dynamic Network Defense

4.1 Introduction

Dynamic network defense refers to deploying dynamic defense at the network layer, specifically at several network elements, such as network topology, network configuration, network resources, network nodes and network services. Through dynamization, virtualization, and randomization, dynamic network defense breaks staticty, certainty, and similarity of each network element to increase the difficulty of network detection and intranet node penetration so that it could defend malicious attacks on target network by hackers.

At present, methods of cyber attacks are ever-changing, diversified, and endless. High-intensity, complex, and unknown cyber attacks represented by APT are developing rapidly, bringing great hidden danger to cyber security, which imposes great impact and damage and brings incalculable losses. In these cases, attackers usually monitor the target network and collect relevant information to detect weaknesses in the initial phase, and then gradually penetrate into the internal network to obtain internal information as well as control privileges by exploiting vulnerabilities in the layer of network, system and application, which brings great challenges to protect network layer with traditional security protection approaches.

There are several cyber-security software/hardware products deployed in the existing network defense system at the network layer, mainly including firewall, intrusion detection, isolation gateway and traffic detection, aimed to detect attacks and prevent attacks on the

157

target network. These products have improved the security of the network in a way, and they are constantly updated to enhance the ability in defense. However, the network architecture and configuration methods are with an inherent static property so that the defense techniques mentioned above focus on enhancing the ability of confrontation in a static form. On the one hand, attack detection relies on prior knowledge; on the other hand, it is difficult for network defense to prevent data traffic of internal pseudo-legal five-tuple. Most important of all, attackers could continuously analyze the target network and system to accumulate knowledge about them, which even let attackers analyze the potential defects of the intranet architecture or host system to discover vulnerabilities so as to penetrate into the network and breakthrough more intranet nodes to finish the attack mission.

Research shows that the time of early investigation accounts for 95%, and the time of launching an attack only accounts for 5% in the whole process of a cyber attack. Therefore, if we can implement dynamic network defense to interfere in the early detection and reconnaissance by attackers, even provide them with false information, it will be an important and effective way to defend the network. In fact, this idea of interference and dynamic change has a long history in the network confrontation. Attackers first introduced such dynamic change techniques in cyber attacks, for example, rebound port Trojan, IP proxy springboard, protocol conversion attack, hopping encryption attack, and time slot hopping are all typical network-layer dynamic attack techniques.

(1) Rebound port Trojan

The port of the rebound port Trojan is random. Resulting from the firewall usually pays less attention to detect and analyze the internal Web data traffic connected to the outside, the infected host actively connects the network to the hacker host, and the relevant traffic is disguised as Web data traffic, rather than the hacker host actively set up a network connection like a traditional Trojan. Obviously, the rebound port Trojan with random port works well in penetrating firewall.

(2) IP proxy springboard

IP proxy springboard is a quite effective hiding attack technique. Hackers forward attack traffic through a series of proxy hosts which have an independent IP address, and each forwarding is hidden by processing, making it difficult for victims to trace real attackers. From the view of proxy host topology, hopping IP proxy can be divided into two basic types – breadth hopping proxy technique and depth hopping proxy technique. In the former case, attackers use different proxy servers for traffic forwarding at different times or hopping time slots, while the latter uses proxy servers to launch cyber attacks on victims through multiple cascades.

(3) Protocol conversion attack

Protocol conversion attack is a hidden means of a cyber attack. Attackers usually use some features of TCP/IP protocol to implement protocol conversion of attack traffic, such as exceptional traffic handling mechanism. After a router receives a TCP data packet from an unknown address, it will return an ICMP data packet at the network layer to the source address of the data packet, informing it that the destination network is unreachable. Attackers can use this feature to launch cyber attacks on their victims.

(4) Dynamic encryption attack method

Dynamic encryption attack method is a dynamic encryption process performed by attackers to prevent network managers from deciphering control instructions on the network "zombie computer", which can effectively avoid victims' monitoring and tracking. This hopping encryption method generally includes two ways, encryption seed hopping and encryption algorithm hopping. Since the principle of this hopping attack is simple, it will not be more discussed here.

(5) Hybrid hopping attack

Hybrid hopping based on multiple hopping forms refers to a comprehensive attack method that uses the above-mentioned various dynamic methods. For example, a hybrid jump attack technique that integrates ports, addresses, protocols, and encryption methods, and uses Snake proxy springboards. It converts UDP data packets used for attacks to TCP data packets, thus successfully breaking through the blockade on UDP ports. It supports up to 255 intermediate proxy springboards, and data transmission and instruction delivery are carried out by means of hopping encryption among proxies at each level.

These techniques essentially implement dynamic changes to communication ports, IP addresses, and other identifications at the network layer, so that attackers could hide attack behaviors in the process of attack, and also achieve a better attack effect through this dynamic way. This provides a good enlightenment for implementing dynamic defense at the network layer.

(1) The goal of dynamic network defense

The overall goal of dynamic network defense is to block the first step of the entire attack chain, that is, to cut off network reconnaissance and target node access. From the perspective of attack effect, dynamic network defense helps to increase difficulty for attackers to detect the target network, confuse attackers, and prevent them from trying to connect to the target system and obtain its properties (version, vulnerability, configuration, etc.), and increase difficulty for attackers to collect information on the target machine, thus blocking or misleading subsequent attacks.

(2) The technical system of dynamic network defense

Dynamization, virtualization, and randomization techniques could be coupled with various network elements respectively such as link communication, network architecture, key equipment, and network service, to break the staticity, certainty, and similarity of each network element. It makes the entire network's topology structure, interconnection protocol, communication content and communication mode be changeable at the interconnection level.

To be specific, implementing dynamization at the network link communication level mainly includes the dynamization of physical communication signals and the dynamization of communication protocol. These techniques have been widely applied in anti-jamming wireless communication by changing the parameter setting of a communication system in a rapid and active way. For example, pseudo-random hopping of communication frequency makes attackers difficult to monitor and barrage jamming. What' more, hopping time, hopping space, hopping power, hopping code, hopping procedures, and hopping structure can be combined into several complex anti-jamming techniques to enhance the anti-jamming capability in wireless communication. In fact, this is a typical defense approach by dynamic and changeable communication signals. Since this approach involves the communication fields and relevant techniques are mature, it will not be more discussed in the book.

Dynamization of network architecture mainly refers to virtualization, randomization, and dynamization of network core resources such as network topology, network nodes, and network configuration. These techniques include the random hopping technique for links and network addresses, node random access technique, dynamic encryption/decryption technique based on channels, network configuration dynamization management technique, etc. They are the core and focus of dynamic network defense.

Dynamization of critical network equipment represented by core router and switch mainly includes two aspects: On the one hand, the dynamic protection of software and hardware can be realized through relevant dynamic techniques at the software and hardware level, to defend against attacks on the hardware system or operating system level of the equipment itself. For this part of the content, please refer to relevant content of runtime platform and dynamic software defense chapters in this book. On the other hand, according to their specific network communication functions and network services, dynamization technique can be used to achieve dynamic exchange of information, dynamic routing selection to resist attacks on internal networks or protect network data flow.

Dynamization of network services and applications mainly includes virtualization, randomization, and dynamization of specific network services, which makes network service fingerprint present dynamic and virtual change to the outside, In addition, this level can also rely on overlay networks and management configuration systems such as trusted network and flow redirection network to build an application-level network with specific security requirements.

The entire techical system of the dynamic network defense mentioned above is shown in Figure 4.1, which includes four levels of physics, link, switching and routing, applications and services from bottom to top. Among them, the physical layer mainly completes dynamic change of physical signals and communication protocol; the link layer mainly completes management of link state and resources, and can change link communication protocol and link communication address in a dynamic and random way. the switching and routing layer mainly completes dynamic access and generation of nodes, dynamic virtual generation of networks, dynamic communication and routing of nodes, etc.; the application and service layer mainly completes service fingerprint randomization, dynamic virtualization of

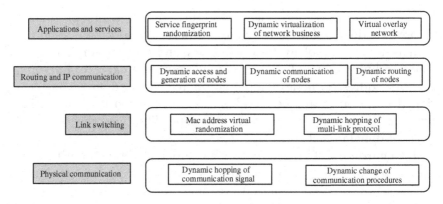

Figure 4.1.   Diagram of Dynamic Network Defense Technical System

network business, overlay network virtualization, etc. It should be noted that no matter what kind of network dynamization technology, or at which level, it should be discussed in terms of who to change, what to change, how to change, and relevant effectiveness. This not only affects security effectiveness of defense technique itself, also affects service performance of the original system.

This essence will focus on dynamization methods and techniques for network architectures, protocols, and services. Nature propety, objective, and effect of dynamic network defense, as well as various dynamization methods, technologies, and their effects will be further discussed.

4.2 Dynamic Network Address Translation Technology

4.2.1 *Overview*

Dynamic Network Address Translation (DyNAT) is a typical dynamic change method of network node identification, from which it is easy to think of the mature Network Address Translation (NAT) technique, first proposed in 1984. NAT belongs to the Wide Area Network (WAN) access technique which is used in network technology to solve the problem of insufficient Internet IP addresses in internal networks. NAT is a typical dynamic network address translation technology which can translate private (reserved) addresses of internal network into legitimate Internet IP addresses. At present, NAT technique is implemented at the network and link layers of practical routers and switches.

From the perspective of internal cyber security, NAT technology can not only solve the problem of insufficient internal network IP addresses and translate them into legitimate external network addresses, it also hides real addresses in the internal network from the external network, providing a certain degree of security. However, relevant research have shown that there are many ways to bypass NAT and enter the internal network only by using NAT translation at the exit point, such as using Trojan technology to regard a host in the internal network as a springboard, or using source routing protocols to attack, etc. Therefore, NAT itself plays a very limited role in ensuring security of the internal network. In practice, NAT needs to be integrated with other security products such as firewalls.

Based on traditional NAT technique, Dorene Kewley *et al.* at Sandia National Laboratories under the U.S. Department of Energy further expanded the scope and mechanism of the network node identification changes and proposed DyNAT [1,2], which can be used to prevent information collection on internal networks and nodes by attackers. The core idea of this technique is to constantly change the terminal node identification by changing the fixed address of the terminal node and providing the corresponding mechanism and method. The technology implements encryption and other scrambling processing for information related to the host ID in the header of the network data packet (not including payload part of the data packet), introduces a dynamic updating mechanism based on time or network properties (such as the number of sent data packets) to the key, and starts translation before the data packets access the network, and restores changes before data packets access the host. This method of periodically changing communication protocol fields can be used to prevent attackers from attacking personal terminal hosts, destroy the effect of man-in-the-middle sniffing, prevent attackers from scanning the internal network, and block information collection on terminal nodes by attackers, because only legitimate users know the right way to change the mapping of protocol-related fields.

4.2.2 Technical Principle of DyNAT

Before introducing the technical principle of DyNAT, we will first define what is internal cyber security defense. Internal cyber security defense usually refers to approaches of protecting the internal network to prevent it from being invaded. Current cyber security defense techniques mainly adopt strong boundary defense, that is, firewall, security proxy, application-level gateway, etc. are used in the inner and outer network boundary areas, even the intrusion detection system is used to reduce the capability of external attackers to access the local network. However, once attackers are able to access the local network, traditional internal defense plays a very limited role in preventing internal network penetration and network resource abuse.

As a technique to protect the internal network and defend against external attackers, the core idea of DyNAT is to constantly change protocol-related fields of terminal node identification by changing the fixed address of the terminal node.

In practical application, it is necessary to determine the applicable mechanism and method category of DyNAT according to application scenarios and specific defense objectives of the target network. Sandia National Laboratories built a DyNAT discriminant tree and summarized dynamic changes, dynamic change mechanisms, related deployment and application execution mechanisms of DyNAT technology, as shown in Figure 4.2.

1. Change of DyNAT

DyNAT is essentially a protocol obfuscation technique. The main object of change is some field information related to the host ID in the network data packet header and method of change is to randomize encryption/decryption. Due to the actual meaning of the communication five-tuple in the IP network, depending on the position of change, this randomization makes it difficult for attackers to determine current network operations, two sides of communication, services used, locations of important systems and other information in the network.

According to TCP/IP protocol hierarchy, from bottom to top, the variable protocol field implements scrambling on the source/destination address of Media Access Control (MAC) at the link layer, IP source/destination address at the network layer, IP Type of Service (TOS) field, Transmission Control Protocol

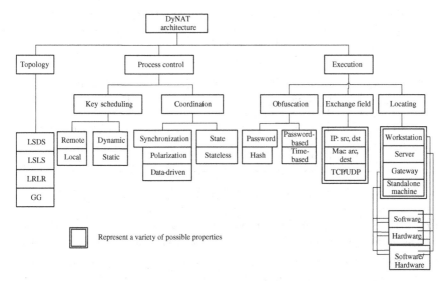

Figure 4.2. DyNAT Architecture Diagram

(TCP) source/destination port at the transport layer, TCP sequence number, TCP window size and User Datagram Protocol (UDP) source/destination port, etc. This scrambling process can scramble the whole area or a part of these fields. For example, MAC source/destination address and IP source/destination address can be randomized only for host bits.

Dorene Kewley *et al.* proposed that this scrambling randomization process can use a high-strength encryption scheme to dynamically change the key based on time or certain network properties (such as the number of sent data packets). The key used for scrambling can be statically generated on each host. It can have both static and dynamic characteristics, and it can be completely dynamically generated. DyNAT variable protocol fields are shown in Table 4.1.

2. Change mechanism of DyNAT

Kewley *et al.* proposed three trigger mechanisms for randomization change: time synchronization mechanism, time voting, or polling mechanism, and data packet or data frame mechanism.

(1) Time synchronization mechanism

The time synchronization mechanism uses a clock to determine when to change DyNAT encryption. The time is determined by the change

Dynamically Enabled Cyber Defense

Table 4.1.   DyNAT Variable Protocol Field List

Layer	Variable Item Name	Position 1	Position 2
Layer 2	MAC address	Source	Destination
Layer 3	IP address	Source	Destination
	IP service type	Source	Destination
Layer 4	TCP port number	Source	Destination
	TCP sequence number	Source	Destination
	TCP window size	Source	Destination
	UDP port	Source	Destination

rate of the DyNAT code. Time synchronization is critical for all participating nodes since time will become a part of dynamically encoded key as index information. The key can be a time-based exponentially increasing output. It consists of two or more parts, for example, each participating node contributes a part of the static "secret" of the generated key, and time or exponentially increasing time output makes the additional part. There can also be more inputs, including the overall key structure, but the dynamic part is always based on a common clock change.

(2) Time voting or polling mechanism

The time control method also relies on the clock to determine when to change DyNAT encoding mechanism. It needs to be implemented in a non-distributed manner and requires a controller node to coordinate changes of DyNAT encoded values. The main difference from the distributed time sequence method based on time synchronization is that, although the node controller referenced by the time element provides consultation time for the change rate of DyNAT code, time does not play a role in distributed key generation. That is, the key itself is not relevant to time, and time is only used to control the negotiation process and protocol for code obfuscation time.

(3) Data packet or data frame mechanism

The method based on packet or data frame negotiation must include a predetermined scheme which does not rely on any time or time-based coordination mechanism. The change rate depends on data packets or frames. With this method, each time a DyNAT change is started, a session is initiated to record the number of packets or frames. Data packets or frames also provide a way to adjust

Table 4.2.   Objects Protected by DyNAT

Network Structure Type	Level
LAN segment based on switch	Access
LAN segment based on contention	Access
LAN to LAN connection	Distributed
Gateway to gateway connection (network separated by Internet or remote connection)	Distributed
LAN segment and gateway connection	Distributed

indexes. Indexes can be used as variables to help build change keys for data packets or frames. The change rate is optional, but participating nodes must be coordinated.

3. Protected areas and deployment locations

Network structure types of areas and objects which the technique can be used to protect include five categories: (a) Local Area Network (LAN) segment based on the switch; (b) LAN segment based on contention; (c) LAN to LAN connection (local router connection); (d) gateway to gateway connection (network separated by the Internet or remote connection); (e) LAN segment and gateway connection. See Table 4.2 for details.

DyNAT can provide a variety of different actual deployment schemes for different protected objects, which depends on the level of protection required. It can be deployed in hosts, workstations, servers, routers, gateways, etc. There are three types of deployment: software, hardware, and a combination of software/hardware.

For example, in deployments where LAN clients connect to servers locally or remotely via routers, DyNAT software/hardware deployment locations are as shown in Figures 4.3 and 4.4.

4.2.3   *Working Example of DyNAT*

Taking the remote communication between clients and servers as an example, we will introduce the working process of DyNAT, as shown in Figure 4.5. DyNAT dynamically transforms host identity information in the TCP/IP data packet header before the data packet enters the public part of the network.

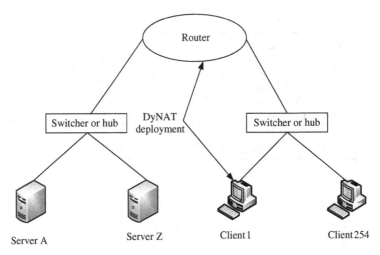

Figure 4.3.   DyNAT Deployment Where Local Servers Directly Connect to LAN Clients

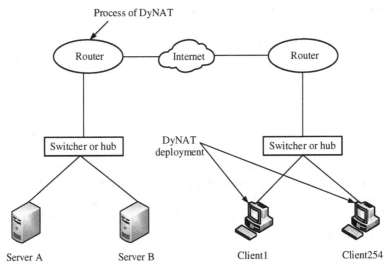

Figure 4.4.   DyNAT Deployment Where Remote Servers Connect to LAN Clients

Before the client's source address information is routed to the receiving server, it is translated in its data packet header. Translation algorithm relies on pre-established key parameters based on the time change. The receiver translates the header domain back at DyNAT

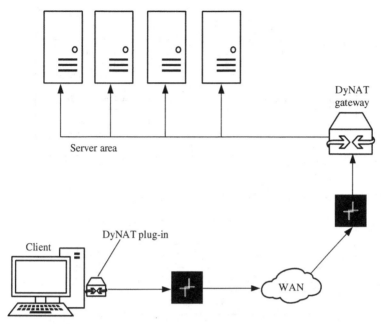

Figure 4.5. DyNAT Working Process When a Client Remotely Connects to Servers

gateway to obtain the real host identity information. Data packet containing the original identity information is sent to the server area for normal processing.

The host identity information can be anything in the header that can uniquely describe network connection between two hosts. In the experiment, identity information included the host address and TCP/UDP port number in the server IP address. In layers 2 and 3 of the network, we can hide real information about servers and their services. This concealment helps defend against most network-layer traffic analysis tools. Figure 4.6 shows an example of TCP header parameter translation.

As you can see from Figure 4.6, only the host address part of the destination address has been translated. In this way, data packets can still be routed normally. The number of bits of the translated address depends on the type of IP address. In the experiment, class B and class C addresses are used. DyNAT needs to translate 16-bit address for class B addresses and the last 8 bytes for

	Version	Header length	Type of service	Total length		
IP	Reassembly flag			Flag	Fragment offset	
	Time to live		Protocol code	Header checksum		
	Source network address			Source host address		
	Destination network address			Destination host address		
	Optional option					

	Source port		Destination port	
TCP	Sequence number			
	Acknowledgement number			
	Offset	Reserved	Flag	Window field
	Package checksum			Urgent pointer
	Optional option			

Figure 4.6.   TCP/IP Header Field Translation

class C addresses. The Destination port for UDP data packets is processed in the same way as that for TCP data packets.

The translation method here is performed by using an encryption algorithm. The source side and destination side of DyNAT will calculate an initial secret value. In this experiment, a time-based mechanism is used to periodically change this secret item, so that change the result of translation calculation, which makes it difficult for attackers to construct and maintain the network topology. In this experiment, these translations are implemented in the form of software in the source host and DyNAT gateway at the destination to protect specific server information. The secret translation mechanism between clients and servers can be synchronized through the clock. To correct potential synchronization problems, DyNAT software will retranslate data packets which have been translated using the previous time slot key.

In the experiment, Windows NT client runs a traffic generator to simulate the actual data flow generated through NT TCP/IP protocol stack. The data packets created by the network protocol stack are translated into the destination address information and destination port information by DyNAT source software, data packet checksum is recalculated, and modified data packets are forwarded to the network and routed to the server. After the server gateway receives data packets from the public network interface, it retranslates the target host identity information, recalculates the checksum, and forwards data packets to the internal private server network. The server responds to the client by processing accordingly.

The experimental results show that DyNAT reduces attacker's capability to identify the server and services provided on the server by translating destination addresses of client and server data packets.

4.2.4 *IPv6 Address Translation Technology*

Dunlop *et al.* also proposed Moving Target IPv6 Defense (MT6D) technology [3–5] for IPv6 address privacy protection [3–5]. The technology protects host and network privacy by constantly changing the IP addresses of the sender and receiver, which provides a powerful moving target defense solution for the platform and application layer.

(1) Problem with stateless address autoconfiguration function

MT6D is designed to address the privacy leak problem when people use IPv6 Stateless Address Autoconfiguration (SLAAC) function. SLAAC is a way for hosts using IPv6 protocol to configure their own network addresses without centralized management, which is different from the DHCP dynamic host configuration method used in the IPv4 network environment. IPv6 allows hosts to configure their own IP addresses, which can reduce the administration burden on network administrators.

The problem with using SLAAC is that the host address or Interface Identifier (IID) remains the same whether or not the host is connected to a subnet. This default address system, the 64-bit Extended Unique Identifier (EUI64), takes MAC address as IID. As a result, once the attacker finds out the subnet list and the host's MAC address, that host might be tracked and is more likely to become the attack target for hackers from anywhere in the world.

Huge IPv6 address group can frequently change client IP addresses, which facilitates implementation of the privacy extension function. It can protect clients from cyber attacks, which is very important for clients. Privacy extension is of not much help for server security because IP addresses of servers are relatively static and fixed to ensure reliable server connections. Privacy extension lacks effectiveness on server security and cannot prevent all the cyber attacks. For example, Web servers or corporate VPN servers, cannot frequently change addresses. In addition, privacy extension is mainly used for Web communication and other applications (such as VoIP and VPN), and it has little effect on their security. Moreover, systems with privacy extensions are more likely to be targets for attackers. Privacy extension technique of the Windows operating system also relies on another IPv6 address for neighbor discovery, local DNS, and other functions. The address must be static and accessible to other hosts. If hackers intercept the address, the target host may be attacked.

(2) Technical principle of MT6D tunnel

MT6D improves privacy security by dynamically changing IP addresses of the sender and receiver, enabling two sides of the communication to realize anonymous and secure communication, which is similar to frequency hopping technique. When two hosts, in reality, communicate in an IPv6 network, attackers intercept multiple pairings of independent host addresses. Attackers cannot know which address pairing is the real two sides of communication, nor can they simply attack an address. A key function of MT6D is that address changes can be made in the middle of a thread when two hosts are communicating, without causing a reset or crash of communication.

MT6D establishes a channel and encapsulates all data flows into it, as shown in Figure 4.7, without modifying TCP three-way handshake rule. The tunnel limits TCP thread overhead by balancing all four layers of protocols. Changing the address in the middle of a thread will not interrupt the existing thread, nor will it result in additional three-way handshake communication.

(3) Deployment

The Deployment of MT6D is shown in Figure 4.8. It can be embedded in the terminal host as software, or deployed in the front end of the protected entity as an independent security gateway.

Virginia Tech has a few network environments in the United States that fully support IPv6 protocol. In fact, it is the largest IPv6 campus network in the United States, containing about 30,000

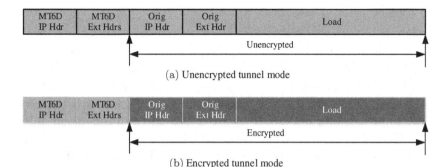

(a) Unencrypted tunnel mode

(b) Encrypted tunnel mode

Figure 4.7.   MT6D Establishes a Tunnel to Encapsulate IPv6 Data Packets

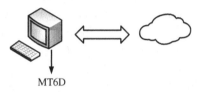

(a) MT6D is embedded in the terminal device as software

(b) MT6D is implemented as an independent gateway

Figure 4.8.   MT6D Deployment

network nodes. This scale allows us to carry out MT6D real-world environment test.

(4) Difference between MT6D and IPSec

MT6D also encrypts information flow. It can be considered as an enhanced IPSec. IPSec can encrypt network data flow, but it requires fixed IP addresses. If a host or gateway is equipped with IPSec, attackers can attack the host or gateway by launching denial-of-service attacks.

MT6D provides network-layer encryption and dynamic addresses. Attackers can neither listen to data packets encapsulated through MT6D, nor lock the host address to launch denial-of-service attacks, which is the same with IPsec.

(5) Effects

MT6D can prevent a variety of cyber attacks against a certain address, such as denial-of-service attacks, and can also defend against attacks in application layer, which is implemented by making host IP addresses fuzzy dynamically on both sides of the communication. Because of the huge number of IPv6 network addresses, it is theoretically impossible for hackers to locate a host through range scanning. Even if hackers get the IP address of the target host, the attack time is limited to the time before the host address is retranslated.

Meanwhile, although the technical concept of MT6D is also applicable to IPv4 networks, there still exist two problems. First, the IPv4 subnet is so small that attackers can scan IP addresses of the entire subnet within a few minutes, which is easy for attackers to lock the target host. Second, IPv4 does not have enough addresses available for address translation, and direct use of MT6D can cause address conflicts.

The IPv6 subnet is 64-bit, which means that the entire IPv4 address space can be placed in an IPv6 subnet, taking up less than one-four billionth of the total space. At present, it is impossible to implement a detailed scan of such a large subnet efficiently.

Also, IPv6 has a large enough address space, and it is rare that address conflict occurs during address transformation. Therefore, it's better to use MT6D in an IPv6 network.

In an IPv6 environment, although every computer accesses the Internet directly, MT6D can help protect privacy and eliminate potential risks.

4.2.5 *Basic Effectiveness and Existing Deficiencies*

From the phases of attack killing chain, dynamic network address translation technique increases difficulty for attackers to detect the network and access key nodes. The main effectiveness includes the following aspects: (a) This technique can be used to defend against resource attacks such as denial-of-service attacks depending on the location of the changed protocol fields. (b) It increases the difficulty for attackers to execute spoofing attacks. (c) It uses dynamic address change based on a key mechanism. Change of encryption key and uncertainty of network address mapping increase difficulty for attackers to capture and replay the network traffic. Although this technique increases the workload of attackers, it cannot prevent attackers from collecting required information. Attackers can still analyze the type of network flow through traffic analysis, and can also collect relevant network information by analyzing data load of data packets.

At the same time, this technique also brings some additional overhead and costs, mainly reflected in the following aspects: (a) increase the network overhead. Depending on different deployment and scrambled fields, the network overhead may be very huge. For example, when MAC address is scrambled on the switching network, this may cause the switch memory to be over-occupied, which makes it easier to determine Address Resolution Protocol (ARP) network flow of the switch port to route data packets. (b) increase the cost of deployment and implementation. The actual deployment requires changes to the operating system, hardware, and infrastructure, which is not transparent to users.

In addition, DyNAT technique also has some limitations, mainly including: (a) If other subprotocols such as VLAN or MPLS are used in the intranet, it may reduce the effectiveness of this technique. If the data packet header does not scramble this extra information, the information about the internal network will be leaked. (b) DyNAT technique does not change the size and time sequence of data packets, and does not use pseudo data packets, so it cannot prevent traffic analysis. (c) DyNAT technique only limits the accessibility of nodes and does not provide any protection for externally accessible services. (d) Because it is opaque to the host, plug-ins are required to be installed on the client side and the server side accordingly, which is not easy to deploy and apply.

Dynamic network address translation technique typically embodies the idea of dynamically changing terminal identification information. In actual engineering use, this technique can be further extended to enhance its capability to resist traffic analysis and adopt more scrambling methods, including changing the time sequence of data packets sent by the system, changing the size of data packets by inserting padding data, sending parameters such as pseudo data packets. This technique can also be combined with IPSec to encrypt valid data payload, which would make it impossible for attackers to analyze the content of data packets, thereby increasing effectiveness of this technology.

It is worth mentioning that methods and ideas of improving cyber security through these kinds of early dynamic network address translation technologies (such as NAT and DyNAT) had a long history before the SDN concept emerged in recent years. However, limited to implementation and performance issues of controllable measures for network infrastructure, practicability and availability of such early technologies were limited. With the gradual support of related equipment providers for OpenFlow related protocols in recent years [21], it is possible for these dynamization technologies to be used for engineering applications in the actual network. It also provides the possibility of unified scheduling and automatic control of different types of network equipment in a wider range of applications and makes the development and application process more convenient.

4.3   Randomized Allocation of Network Address Space Technology Based on DHCP

4.3.1   *Overview*

Network Address Space Randomization (NASR) refers to that the host is able to get network addresses randomly. Dynamic Host Configure Protocol (DHCP) is a typical randomized allocation of network address technique and is an application layer protocol in TCP/IP protocol cluster. It is mainly used to assign dynamic IP addresses to LAN client computers and assigned IP addresses belong to the address set consisting of multiple addresses, which are usually consecutive, reserved by the DHCP server.

When we use DHCP services, a DHCP server must be configured on the network, and other machines act as DHCP clients. When DHCP client program makes an information request for using a dynamic IP address, DHCP server will provide an available IP address and subnet mask to the client based on currently configured addresses.

DHCP-based NASR technique [6] was originally proposed as a method to prevent worm propagation and attacks based on IP address lists. Like other methods of preventing worm attacks, NASR is only a partial solution for preventing worm attacks. This method requires modifying the implementation of the DHCP server so that it can change the host IP address frequently enough. This technique is essentially an IP address hopping technology. With this hopping, blacklist of IP address list attacked by worms becomes invalid before the virus spreads and launches, thus slowing down propagation of worm viruses. In fact, this technique cannot prevent any specific attack, but it helps reduce effectiveness of scanning attacks. Meanwhile, this technique has no effect on other types of worm attacks based on DNS blacklists, and cannot be used to completely defend against worm attacks.

4.3.2 *Principle of Network Worm Propagation*

Before introducing the principle of randomized selection of network address space, we first analyze how worm viruses propagate and spread.

Network worm is a kind of program code that could be executed automatically without the intervention of a computer user, which is combined with hacker technique and computer virus technique. It uses node hosts with vulnerabilities to spread from one node to another in the network system. The operation mechanism of network worms can be divided into three phases: discovering susceptible targets, infecting susceptible targets, and executing attack code. Among them, discovery of susceptible targets depends on the selected propagation method, and a good propagation method can enable network worms to find susceptible hosts on the Internet with the least resources and expand propagation in a short time.

According to the way network worms discover susceptible hosts, propagation methods can be divided into the following three categories: random scanning, sequential scanning, and selective scanning. Selective scanning is the main development direction of network worms, which can be subdivided into selective random scanning, target list-based scanning, routing-based scanning, DNS-based scanning, and divide-and-conquer scanning. DHCP-based NASR discussed in this chapter is to prevent worm viruses that use a target list-based scanning method.

The propagation method of target list-based scanning is that network worms pre-generate a list of targets that may be susceptible (that is, there are some defects or vulnerabilities) before searching for susceptible targets, and then attempt to attack and spread the list. When we use target list scanning, network worms usually distribute the initial worm infection source in different address spaces to improve propagation speed. Nicholas C Weaver from University of California, Berkeley, has studied and implemented an experimental Warhol worm based on well-constructed target list scanning, and theoretically inferred that the worm could infect the entire Internet within 30 minutes. More recent researches have shown that worms can infect 1 million hosts in less than 2 seconds.

Current researches on worm prevention are mainly focused on scanning and detection mechanisms, hoping to block connection of worms to realize prevention. However, if the worm virus does not present its known characteristics, it is impossible to effectively resist worm attacks by relying solely on detection technique. At the same time, after the discovery of the worm, the response mechanism may not respond to a very fast target list attack worm in a timely manner. Therefore, some other special defense measures should be considered to prevent worm attacks.

The analysis shows that when susceptible hosts in the target list addresses are not connected or the program is exceptionally aborted, the propagation speed of the attack list will be naturally delayed, which slows down propagation of the virus. Such a result will also add a large number of new scanning connections to infection source hosts, thus exposing traces of worm attacks. Therefore, the randomized selection mechanism of network address space intends to increase the delay of the attack list purposefully. It is an IP address hopping mechanism.

4.3.3 Abstract Model of Network Address Space Randomization

The purpose of randomized selection of network address space is to make the host change IP address frequently enough so that the information collected on the attack list is out of date, which prevents worms from spreading effectively. Its abstract system model is as follows.

Make address space $R = [1, 2, \ldots, n]$, host set $H = [h_2, \ldots, h_m]$, where $m < n$, and function A maps all hosts h_k to address $A(h_k) = r$, $r \in R$.

Suppose that at time t_a, the attacker can generate an attack list $X \subset R$ immediately, which contains the addresses of vulnerable hosts that were opened at that moment. If the attack begins at time t_x, all the hosts $\boldsymbol{X}$ are still open and vulnerable, and have the same address as the time t_a, then worms can infect hosts $\boldsymbol{X}$ very quickly. Suppose that at time $t_b(t_a < t_b < t_x)$, the host is allocated a new address from the address space R, then at the attack time t_x, probability that the address x_k in the attack list still matches open hosts is $p = m/n$, and then the number of hosts that the attacker can successfully infect is $(m/n)|\boldsymbol{X}|$.

It can be seen from this model that density m/n of address space is a crucial factor for detection efficiency of randomized selection mechanism of network address space. Supposing that for a collection of similar nodes that have the same vulnerabilities and infection probability, if only a subset of one host group is susceptible to some type of attack, randomized selection mechanism of network address space will have a better effect on reducing the number of locally infected blacklist nodes and the number of failed attempts.

4.3.4 *System Principle and Deployment Implementation*

A basic implementation of NASR is to configure a DHCP server to limit its address lease to an appropriate time interval and then it could be randomized. DHCP server allows a client to make a request to re-enable a lease before the last lease expires. In this way, even if the client makes a request to re-enable a lease before it expires, the Mandatory address change still requires some small changes on the DHCP server. Fortunately, no changes to the protocol or the client are required. Researchers have implemented an improved version of DHCP server which can implement NASR, called Wuke-DHCP, an ISC-based open source DHCP implementation (https://www.isc.org/download/#DHCP). In order to minimize the impact of address changes, the prototype system introduces two modules – the active monitoring module and the service fingerprint module. The prototype system is shown in Figure 4.9.

The active monitoring module detects the open connection of each host to avoid interruption of host service due to address interruption. Only long TCP connections, such as FTP download, are considered in this prototype. Use a traffic monitor to examine network traffic of all the hosts in the subnet and respond to a large number of active

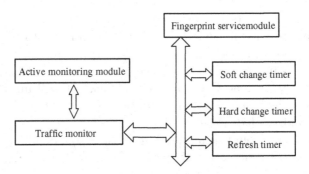

Figure 4.9.   Prototype Diagram of DHCP Server Composition

connections that are sensitive to address changes. The fingerprint service module verifies network traffic and identifies the services running on each host.

The fingerprint service module has two tasks: First, by providing a connection error, observe whether the terminal system can tolerate it, and provide some contextual information for the active monitoring module to make address change decisions. Second, avoid assigning an address to a host that has an obvious overlap in services and potential vulnerabilities with hosts that have recently used the address. To do this, we can choose hosts running different operating systems, such as Windows or Linux platforms. Implementation of fingerprint detection is preliminary, and only uses the port number information obtained from passive monitoring to determine the operating system and application characteristics. For example, TCP connection at port 80 indicates that the host is running a Web service, and port 445 indicates that the host may be a Windows platform. At the same time, more technical support is needed in operation settings, such as the passive detection technique and the active detection technique.

In the implementation of the DHCP server, three timers are used to control host address change.

(a) Refresh timer. It is used to determine the delivery of lease communication with the client. When the timer expires, the client is forced to issue a query to the server, which decides whether to refresh with the same address.

(b) Soft change timer. It is used by the server at intervals to specify the time interval for address changes when the traffic monitor cannot report the survival state of the host.

(c) Hard change timer. It is used to explicitly specify the maximum time a host can hold the address. If the timer expires, the host is forced to change the address regardless of whether connection is broken or not.

To use this method of address change based on DHCP, we should also take full account of the limitations of address change and tolerance of the host.

Addresses of some nodes cannot be changed, while addresses of some other nodes are not allowed to change too frequently. It is necessary to consider whether the host has active connections to be aborted, and whether the application can recover from the short-term connection problem caused by the address change. For example, the address of the DNS server is usually hardwired in the system configuration. Even for the host DHCP configuration, changing the address of the DNS server will need synchronization of the continuous lease, so that all hosts can refresh their DHCP leases while DNS server precisely changes its address.

Both E-mail and Web servers use domain name resolution. When implementing a randomized selection mechanism of network address space, the domain name must be accurately mapped to the correct host IP address. Therefore, DNS real-time clock needs to be set long enough, so that client and DNS server does not need to cache historical data when an address changes. Randomized selection mechanism of network address space also needs to interact with the DNS server to update address records in time and ask whether it is reasonable to increase the burden of DNS.

Based on the above idea, researchers simulated worm outbreak by experiments with different parameters and measured the worm propagation time. The results are shown in Figure 4.10. It can be seen that randomized selection of network address space achieves the purpose of slowing down the worm outbreak. From the 500th second when the randomized selection mechanism of network address space was used until the 1000th second when the host frequently changed its address, the number of hosts infected with worms changed very quickly and reached the peak in the number of infectable hosts quickly when no measures were taken. However, under randomized address selection mechanism, because hosts corresponding to addresses in the attack list frequently changed their addresses, worms

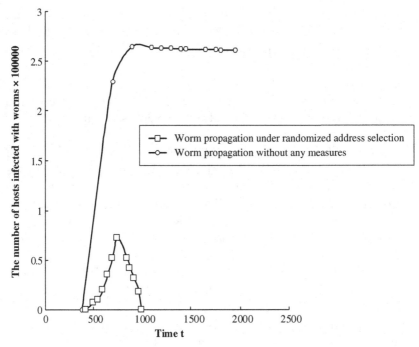

Figure 4.10. Diagram of Changes in the Number of Hosts Infected With Worms Without Any Measures and After Implementation of Randomized Address Selection Mechanism

failed to infect addresses in the attack list and the number of infected hosts decreased rapidly. Randomized selection mechanism of network address space caused many failed infection attempts and invalid re-scanning after failure, because the host's changed address and its previous address were not used, and different hosts running the same service might not use these addresses. Therefore, hosts would no longer be vulnerable to be infected with worms.

4.3.5 *Basic Effectiveness and Existing Deficiencies*

Preventing worm attacks against IP address list based on changing DHCP is a typical application of network address space randomized allocation technology, and its implementation principle and deployment method are relatively simple. This technique can force hosts to change their network addresses frequently, and has significant defensive effects under certain conditions. On the one hand, this technique can force the worm attack based on IP address list infection to further expose its hosts' scanning behavior. On the other hand, the technique is highly implementable and does not require any terminal changes. It is transparent to the host and easy to deploy. Although it only limits worm infection on IP attack list in terms of security effectiveness, this is an effective attempt at dynamic network defense technology.

However, this technique has obvious limitations: Firstly, it can only slow down certain types of attacks and just randomly select IP layer addresses. Secondly, it needs to rely on other active defenses, or cooperate with distributed detection mechanisms and other means to complete the overall function. In other words, the performance of this technique itself needs to be improved. Thirdly, it is only deployed locally in the subnet, without considering effectiveness under wide deployment. Fourthly, this method cannot prevent attackers from reaching hosts using other types of protocols, nor can it prevent attacks against clients (such as browsing malicious websites). Finally, it is worth mentioning that density of address space (the number of addresses to be allocated/the total number of allocable address spaces) is a crucial factor to invalidate the IP address list after randomized selection of network address space is used. Therefore, the address space to be randomly allocated should be increased as much as possible. However, in practical use, allocable address space is usually not large enough for ease of management. If DHCP configuration is adopted to enhance security effectiveness, compromise of address range should be considered.

DHCP itself is designed to facilitate network users to configure IP addresses and network parameters, so the protocol has some defects in its own security. Furthermore, the most significant feature of DHCP is that the client and server are coupled loosely, and it does not need to make changes to the client. Although this method is easy to deploy, it requires additional consideration of interference with the application.

Similarly, like other dynamic network address translation technologies (such as NAT, DyNAT), the method that relies solely on DHCP itself to improve cyber security has limited practical effects. It should be combined with other relevant security techniques, relying on SDN technology and OpenFlow related standards, to make these dynamization technologies available for engineering applications in practical networks.

4.4   Synchronization-Based End Information Hopping Protection Technology

4.4.1   *Overview*

In end information hopping technique for end-to-end data transmission, both sides or one side of communication changes end information such as ports, addresses, time slots, encryption algorithms, and even protocols pseudorandomly according to the protocol, so as to destroy enemy attacks and interference, and realize active network protection. End information hopping technique belongs to the node information hopping technique at the network layer.

From the perspective of categories of hopping participants, the end information hopping can be one-side hopping of the server or two-side hopping of peer hosts. Due to the complexity of implementation of two-side hopping systems, current researches and prototype system implementation mainly focus on one-side information hopping of server.

In recent years, the defense technology based on end information hopping has attracted extensive attention from researchers and has been applied in network defense to some extent. In APOD [7, 8] project in 2003, the U.S. military proposed a hybrid hopping defense policy for port and address hopping, and developed a network protection method of anti-port scanning and anti-DoS (Denial of Service) attacks based on false port address hopping. In this method, the real address and port of the server do not hop, and only the fake address and port are used for address port replacement in data transmission communication to confuse external attackers. In China, Lin and Jia *et al.* [9–11] from Nankai University proposed an active network protection system model based on end information hopping, which destroys attacker interference and achieves network protection by changing end information such as communication ports, addresses, time slots, and even protocols in end-to-end data transmission pseudorandomly. The system adopts an encryption algorithm for hopping and synchronization, and a prototype system has been developed by Java mobile agent technique, which proves that the end information hopping technique has stronger capability to resist DoS attacks.

In addition, Lee *et al.* [12] studied anti-DOS attacks based on port hopping. The research team divided network communication time into discrete time slots with equal intervals, and the network service port was determined by time slot, key, and generation function. Trusted users obtained the key through legal authorization, while attackers could not obtain the key to lock the target port of the attack. Badishiy *et al.* [13] also used port hopping for network communication, and resisted DoS attacks and interception attacks through randomly changed communication ports. In order to realize port synchronization between server and client, they used an ACK message that has been successfully confirmed in the communication process as a factor of the port generation function, and combined it with the shared key to generate the port used for communication. Mills *et al.* [14] used port hopping to realize covert communication, and discussed the port synchronization, key management, time slot selection, and other issues to be solved during the implementation of port hopping.

From the perspective of end information elements of dynamic hopping, the end information hopping is a comprehensive and effective defense means. At present, the relevant technique and theoretical research are still at the stage of continuous improvement and experimental verification, and most theoretical research results are limited to the prototype system, which is still far from being applied to the real network service. In terms of network protection methods, if they can be used together, especially the complex and changeable hybrid hopping technique, it will help improve the effectiveness of existing networks defense against DoS attacks.

4.4.2   *Principle of DoS Attacks*

The ultimate goal of end information hopping is to prevent DoS attacks. DoS attack is one of the most influential and most harmful attacks in current cyber attacks, and it is a typical destructive attack. Let's first introduce principles and defense difficulties of such attacks.

The National Institute of Standards and Technology (NIST) specifically defined the DoS attack as behavior that prevents or weakens authorized operations on network, system, application, etc., by exhausting system resources such as CPU, memory, bandwidth, disk space, etc.

DoS attacks usually do not modify data information in the target system, but adopt relatively easy attack methods. Principle of DoS attacks generally include the following three categories.

(a) Generate a large amount of burst data traffic, resulting in the reduction of network performance of the target system and its capability to communicate with the outside world. For example, UDP Flooding attacks forge UDP communication with Chargen service of host A, and the reply address points to another host B that enabled Echo service, so that network bandwidth between host A and host B would be exhausted. Smurf attacks point to the reply address of ICMP request packet to the broadcast address of the target network, and all hosts respond to the ICMP packet, thus flooding the attacked target network.

(b) Use characteristics of network service or protocol to send requests beyond its processing capabilities, which make the server unable to provide network services to legitimate users in a short time. For example, SYN Flooding attacks take advantage of vulnerabilities of TCP's three-way handshake protocol to send request traffic that exceeds the server's receiving capability in a short time, which make legitimate clients unable to connect to the server.

(c) Exploit vulnerabilities in the operating system or application to send specially constructed data packets that cause the system or software to crash. For example, Ping of Death attacks use ICMP fragment packets to cause a buffer overflow during reassembly of data packets. Teardrop attack is also a fragment packet-based attack mode, and some operating systems will crash when they are subjected to pseudo fragments that contain overlapping offsets.

4.4.3   *Technical Principle of End Information Hopping*

Theoretically, hopping content in the end information hopping protection technique can include all kinds of identification elements related to the end information, such as time slot, port, address, encryption algorithm, and even protocol. At present, relevant research results and application fields mainly include the following aspects.

(1) Port hopping

Port hopping is one of the most typical applications of hopping ideas in network defense in recent years. Its main principle is that the server's service port number changes randomly in the process of information transmission. Both sides of the communication transmit information under a certain synchronization policy. Legal clients can follow the hopping of the server port number to maintain synchronization and complete communication, while illegal clients or attackers cannot predict the port number used by the server at a particular moment, and thus cannot obtain all the communication content or perform effective attacks.

(2) Address hopping

With further research and application of the port hopping technique, researchers consider whether resources involved in hopping can be further expanded, so that network addresses can also be dynamized like ports, which brings more confusion to attackers. Current research results (such as APOD) focus on dynamically changing some TCP service elements (such as IP and port) during communication, and address hopping is usually combined with port hopping to resist TCP flooding attacks.

(3) Protocol hopping

Protocol hopping technique means that a large number of available protocols are stored in the protocol library in advance, including both network communication protocol and data encryption protocol. During communication, it can hop between different protocols and dynamically select the next protocol. This hopping can be implemented during network communication between two nodes, or during data transmission between different parts of the equipment. At present, research results of implementing communication protocol hopping has not been reported, but related studies have proposed a communication mechanism based on encryption protocol hopping, that is, the encryption protocol used in data transmission is dynamically transformed, such as from AES, Twofish to Triple DES. The real-time and dynamic segmented encryption protocol is more secure than a single fixed encryption protocol during communication.

(4) Hybrid hopping

Hybrid hopping is a hopping technique that integrates the above-mentioned hopping methods. Hybrid hopping with higher security protection capabilities can reduce network threats from attackers. Among them, the Snake proxy hopping technique uses hybrid hopping, including address hopping and protocol hopping, when using the proxy.

Among the above hopping methods, the implementation of port hopping is relatively simple without considering the influence of the complex network environment. It is also relatively easy to detect exceptional traffic, and only needs to detect traffic of the current port. However, if the port hopping policy is designed improperly, it is vulnerable to interception attacks. Resulting from attackers intercepting all data packets issued by the host and then conducting traffic analysis. The implementation of address hopping is relatively complex, which requires consistency of data communication among multiple hosts (or multiple IP addresses of one host), but it is less likely to be attacked by opponents than port hopping. However, compared with the numerous available ports (the maximum number of available IPv4 ports is 65,535), the number of available IP addresses is relatively fewer and the cost is higher. This hopping method works better if the application environment is limited to LAN. The implementation of network protocol hopping is the most complex, and network compatibility is relatively low, but its security is higher. So far, research achievements of network protection technique based on communication network protocol hopping are reported rarely.

The following takes the one-side end information hopping system of server as an example [9–11] to briefly introduce working mode of the defense system based on end information hopping. Its logical diagram is shown in Figure 4.11. The system should include four modules: service module, control module, synchronization module, and client module. The service module is implemented in a server cluster, that is, multiple servers with the same hardware performance and software system are connected to work together. The control module can use an ordinary server, whose main task is to coordinate operations among various modules and strictly control the operation policy of the hopping system. The synchronization module mainly provides synchronization services to clients so that remote

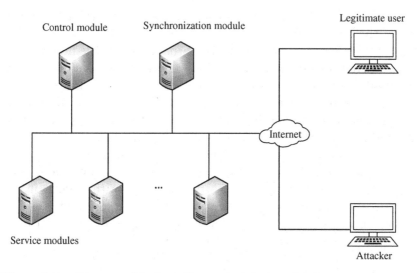

Figure 4.11. Diagram of Defense System Based on End Information Hopping

clients can synchronize with the service module seamlessly. The main task of the client module is to communicate and cooperate with the synchronization module to achieve synchronization.

(a) The service module is the core of the entire hopping system, which is responsible for providing network services to remote legal users, such as Web services, FTP services, and so on. Each server in the service module cluster has its own independent IP address and can change the network service port based on commands from the control module. In general, the network service requests sent by legal users have time continuity. Therefore, in order to meet the service requirement, the server needs a certain amount of time. This conflicts with the idea of hopping. For example, a legal user requests to Web server A for downloading a big file. When the file is in the middle of downloading, server A needs to hop to server B, then server A needs to migrate this file download service to server B seamlessly through service migration technique.

(b) The control module is the headquarter of the entire hopping system. It is responsible for calculating the network information (IP, port, protocol, etc.) of the next hopping server terminal and notifying the corresponding server and synchronization module.

The control module involves stability and anti-attack capability of the entire system.

(c) The synchronization module is a broadcaster of the hopping system. It provides synchronization services to legal users, so that legal users can accurately locate the server network information which is providing network services. The synchronization module is a difficult point in implementing the entire hopping system, and involves the security of the hopping system. If attackers can get network information of the service module from the synchronization module, the entire hopping system will become useless.

(d) There exists the same synchronization algorithm both in the client module and synchronization module. According to the consistent synchronization policy provided by the synchronization module, such as calculation algorithm based on timestamp factor, it can calculate network information of the service module, and then request normal network services.

4.4.4 *Core Technology of End Information Hopping*

To complete the hopping process of the above-mentioned end information hopping system, the system should focus on solving such problems as hopping coordination mode, hopping item selection, synchronization policy, service switching, attack model, and adaptive policy. Among them, hopping item selection, synchronization policy, network service hard switching technology, and adaptive policy are core techniques of end information hopping.

(1) Hopping item selection

Selection of end information is very important, which determines service performance and security performance of the hopping system directly. In the Internet environment, a variable range of end information includes port, address, protocol, and other basic network protocol stack information. With the increase and combination of available end information types, range of changes that can be provided to the server also increases. It is more difficult for attackers to accurately locate the server, but it also increases the operational complexity of the whole system.

(2) Hopping synchronization method

Hopping synchronization involves service performance and security performance of the hopping service. The server and the client use the unified synchronization policy of both sides to achieve synchronized hopping communication, which is the major difference between this technique and DyNAT and DHCP. DyNAT and DHCP rely on the network layer's own protocol to automatically allocate and randomize the address, port, and other information without considering synchronization. This technique can defend against traditional cyber attacks because attackers cannot get hopping rules of end information. At present, several common synchronization policies mainly include the following.

(3) Strict time synchronization based on time slice

Strict time synchronization is the simplest and easiest way to achieve synchronization, which does not require complicated calculation methods or too much system customization. It only requires a hopping diagram to correspond the time with the end information used in communication. The server opens the network service according to the end information corresponding to the current time, and the client sends the network request traffic according to the end information corresponding to the current time. As long as the hopping diagram is not cracked by attackers, synchronization security of end information hopping can be guaranteed. In general, strict time synchronization will slice time into equal length slices, and each time slice corresponds to unique end information.

(4) ACK acknowledgement synchronization based on data packets

Due to congestion and transmission delay in the computer network, strict time synchronization will cause serious synchronization failure. The client sends data traffic to the end information opened by the server, but it takes a certain amount of time for network transmission. When the data traffic arrives at the server, if the end information has already hopped, it means that synchronization fails. Therefore, we can consider ACK acknowledgement synchronization based on TCP.

ACK acknowledgement synchronization mechanism maintains an ACK message counter on client and server. The counter can record the number of ACK messages that have been sent successfully, and then take the number of ACK messages as a generation factor to generate the end information used in communication. Because no strict time correspondence is required, network delay and congestion will not cause synchronization failure. However, ACK acknowledgement synchronization is vulnerable to interception attacks. If attackers eavesdrop on the server network from the beginning of communication, they can accurately know the number of ACK messages that have been successfully sent.

(5) Timestamp-based synchronization

In order to overcome the synchronization failure problem in strict time synchronization and leakage problem of the number of ACK messages in ACK response synchronization, researchers proposed the timestamp synchronization technique. The client first sends a timestamp request to the server every time before sending data packets. The server generates an instant timestamp immediately, and uses the private end information generation algorithm combined with the instant timestamp to calculate the exact end information, then returns the instant timestamp to the client. After the client receives the timestamp, it also uses the same generation algorithm to calculate the same end information to achieve synchronization.

Timestamp synchronization requires the client to request a timestamp from the server every time before sending data packets. Data packets from the client can only be received by the server if they reach the service within a valid time of the timestamp. This synchronization technique can not only avoid time delay and network congestion of the computer network, but also resist interception attacks from network attackers.

Synchronization is an important part of end information hopping technique. No matter what kind of synchronization method is used, it requires coordination of changes on both sides of the communication. It is necessary to fully consider the network delay and service delay issues, which are also current research hotspots of the end information hopping technique.

(6) Network service hard switching technique

Service switching focuses on how to ensure continuity of network services when they hop from one end information service to another. Service switching is an important core technique in the end information hopping, and it is also a current research hotspot of this technique. Its performance determines the service performance of the hopping service. At present, there are conversion technologies which have been applied maturely, including Socket migration, hopping agent, and other techniques. Among them, Hopping Agent (HA) technique is a more effective service switching implementation scheme. By deploying multiple hopping agents between client and server, it realizes the hopping process and hopping policy on HA, hiding the real server behind HA. Each HA has an independent external IP address and can receive and send data packets. The IP address of the server is interal so that it cannot directly access the external network. After the client gets the server information through the synchronization module, it communicates with the corresponding HA. HA is responsible for forwarding data packets between client and server, and it can switch between the active state and the inactive state. Only the active HA can forward data packets. It seems like the client is communicating with a server whose IP address and port are constantly changing, but the real IP address and port of the server are actually unchanged.

(7) Adaptive hopping policy

The end information hopping technique copes with cyber attacks by means of dynamic change and alternation between truth and falsehood. Its ultimate goal is to make attackers lose their attack targets. Therefore, as an important part of the end information hopping, change rules (i.e. hopping policies) of the end information should be able to change dynamically to cope with the intricate network environment and evolving cyber attacks.

It is difficult for simple hopping with a fixed policy to cope with the threat of follow-up attacks. Attackers can grasp hopping rules of end information to a certain extent through some network technical means such as monitoring and interception, thereby effectively decreasing their attack range (range of end information hopping), and concentrating the original sparse and scattered attack traffic to a smaller range to improve the attack effect. Therefore, an adaptive hopping policy that can adapt to the complex network attack environment is extremely necessary, because the server needs to choose the optimal hopping policy according to real-time network conditions, so that the hopping technique can adapt to changes in the network environment and improve defense effect automatically. Adaptive hopping needs to comprehensively consider the time adaptive policy, space adaptive policy, and time-space hybrid adaptive policy, so that the policy can not only defend against threat of cyber attacks, but also ensure high efficiency of service performance.

The above four core techniques are also the key points and difficulties to be considered for each dynamization technique of dynamic network defense.

At present, most of the research on this technique focuses on research and development of the prototype system as well as verification of emulation experiment results, especially verifying availability, feasibility, and anti-attacking capability of this technique in the real network applications and in resisting cyber attacks. Lin Kai, Shi Leyi *et al.* carried out an SYN flood attack experiment in the above-mentioned prototype system environment under a specific experimental configuration. The experiment tested changes of the average service response time of the end information hopping prototype system under different rates of SYN flood attack to reflect the performance of service availability. The response rate of the service reflects the capability to resist DoS attacks, they obtained several meaningful experimental results and conclusions.

(a) Anti-DoS performance of end information hopping is much better than non-hopping services and simple port hopping services, and is approximately proportional to the number of available hopping addresses. The more the available hopping addresses, the better the performance. Slow hopping of end information can cause opponents to make directed attacks, thus causing the performance to deteriorate. However, due to network congestion and delay, too rapid hopping will lead to frequent switching of services and reduce service performance. This shows that a good end information hopping policy can greatly improve the performance of the system to resist DoS attacks, but the hopping rate should be optimized according to the network scale, degree of congestion, and other conditions.

(b) It is difficult to disperse the network traffic without a hopping policy, which undermines the anti-interception performance of the network. The end information hopping technique can effectively scatter the network traffic. In addition, using the pseudo-random hopping encryption algorithm significantly increases complexity for interceptors to parse out data messages completely, which is very beneficial for interfering with interception attacks by opponents.

4.4.5 *Basic Effectiveness and Existing Deficiencies*

Synchronization-based end information hopping is a dynamic network defense technique that implements end information hopping of one or two sides through a unified synchronization policy agreed upon by both sides. Compared with the traditional network protection techniques, it has the following advantages.

(1) Strong anti-attacking capability

The traditional network protection techniques only resist attacks in the implementation phase or post-processing phase, while the end information hopping makes the attacker lose his attack target and cannot lock the server in the preparation phase of the attack. Based on the idea of dynamic change of end information, combined with temptation and concealment methods, cyber attacks can be difficult to achieve.

(2) Anti-interception capability

In the process of data communication, dynamic change of end information makes it difficult for attackers to intercept data packets effectively. As the target of the network, interception is often an IP address or a LAN, it is generally difficult to achieve network interception for multiple data communications that do not belong to the same LAN.

By increasing or decreasing the size of the end information state space gradually, the end information hopping technique can improve or reduce service performance and anti-attacking performance of the end information hopping on the basis of the original performance of the hopping technique.

However, synchronization and global coordination of this technique are very complex. Both sides of communication are required to cooperate in the process of the end information change, which is not transparent to users, and is difficult for actual deployment. At present, research results of network protection technique based on end information hopping is still at the stage of theoretical research and prototype system verification. Especially for the complex and changeable hybrid hopping technique, its theoretical research is limited to the prototype system, and there is still a certain gap from the network service and application deployment applied in practice. However, the theoretical research and experimental results show that this technique has a good active protection performance when defending against strong DoS and interception attacks, which is of great significance for active network defense. Moreover, this technique is highly scalable, and effective theoretical and practical researches can be carried out in terms of synchronization policy, hopping policy, hybrid hopping, peer hopping, etc., which has positive effects on DoS and DDoS protection.

4.5 Overlay Network Protection Technology Against DDoS Attacks

4.5.1 *Overview*

The Overlay network is a method to construct a network, which has nothing to do with specific technologies levels. It is built on top of one or more existing networks. By adding additional, indirect and virtual layers, it can improve some properties in some domains of the underlying real network to increase the network performance. The essence of the overlay network is to adjust the structure and distribution of network resource utilization. Current research on overlay networks is mostly limited to support for specific applications, and different applications need to establish different overlay networks [15].

Generally, overlay network nodes have the function of routing function, data storage function, and data processing. Virtual links between overlay nodes usually correspond to one or more underlying physical links. Even if a certain network is exceptional, the application system can query alternative paths according to the overlay network, so as to improve the reliability of network transmission. In addition, the application system can choose the optimal path according to different service quality requirements on the overlay network. From the perspective of application-level networks, overlay networks can shield dynamic changes of internal physical networks and heterogeneity of physical resources. At the logical network level, it can dynamically change, reconfigure, and manage paths according to application requirements, and respond to dynamically changing links or nodes in a timely manner.

Characteristics of the overlay network include hiding dynamic changes of underlying physical networks and meeting specific requirements of high-level applications such as task scheduling, security, and management [20] by providing a virtual logical network. Therefore, according to characteristics of specific application requirements, we can construct a specific overlay network structure, establish a virtual network based on node interaction, realize isolation of the runtime environment and physical resources, shield heterogeneity of physical networks, and enhance the adaptability of the application system to distribution, autonomy, dynamics, and evolution characteristics of physical networks. It can be used as an effective security application mode. Multi-layer overlay network protection technology based on Dynamic Backbone (DynaBone) [16] also builds a multi-layer overlay network to dynamically reroute network flows in real time, so as to protect the virtual overlay network and defend against denial-of-service attacks.

4.5.2 *Overlay Network Architecture*

The Overlay network is a virtual network that overlays an existing network. Overlay network nodes and connections between them are logical. Overlay network nodes can be routers, servers, or even network terminals. Virtual links between them correspond to one or more physical links. The overlay network actually uses software engineering to implement a new network application mode at the application layer on the basis that the underlying network provides basic connections. Figure 4.12 shows the diagram of the overlay network.

Overlay network nodes generally have the function of routing function, data storage function, and data processing, while virtual links between overlay nodes correspond to one or more underlying physical links. Even if a certain network is exceptional, the application system can query alternative paths according to the overlay network, so as to improve the reliability of network transmission. In addition, the application system can choose the optimal path according to different service quality requirements on the overlay network.

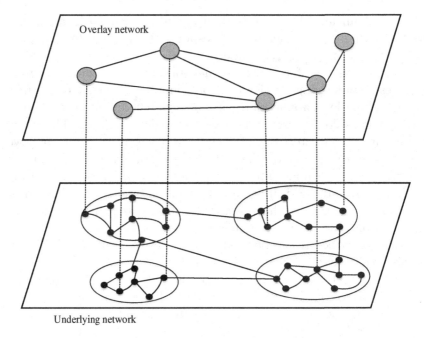

Figure 4.12.   Diagram of Overlay Network

Resilience Overlay Network (RON) is a distributed overlay network Architecture. It uses RON nodes distributed on the Internet to detect a link failure and periodic performance deterioration in just a few seconds and recover it quickly, while it takes a few minutes for the current Internet Border Gateway Protocol (BGP) to do that.

RON nodes automatically detect the quality of underlying Internet links that connect to them, use collected information, and compare which path factor the application is more sensitive to (such as time delay, packet loss rate, link throughput, etc.) to determine if packets of an application are forwarded directly by the Internet link or via another RON node, so that routing selection of the application can be more optimized.

4.5.3 *Principle of DDoS Attacks*

Single node-based DoS has relatively a little attack traffic. It cannot cause serious consequences, and is easily tracked and exposed. Distributed Denial-of-Service (DDoS) attacks use zombie computer technique such as botnets to implement distributed denial of service, which can not only generate a huge amount of attack traffic through traffic aggregation, but also hide behind botnets to avoid being tracked.

Due to its high attack intensity and high concealment, DDoS attacks have become the preferred method of attackers. Arbor Networks' global infrastructure security report pointed out that scale and scope of DDoS attacks was increasing year by year, traffic bandwidth of cyber attacks was also significantly increasing and average traffic bandwidth of a single DDoS attack was as high as 10 Gbit/s or above.

At present, it is extremely difficult to defend against DDoS attacks, and in other words, there is no effective way to defend. Because DDoS attacks can not only easily generate attack traffic far beyond the server's network bandwidth, but can also choose a variety of attack methods, different attack methods are used for different network services. To defend against DDoS attacks, the main challenges are as follows.

(1) Distributed attack sources

Due to the existence of botnets, DDoS attacks can use several hosts scattered on the Internet to generate the aggregated traffic composed of a lot of small traffic. This amounts to an all-out attack on the server from all sides, similar to "wolfpack tactic" against aircraft carriers in naval warfare. Its horror is self-evident.

(2) Spoofed IP source addresses

IP spoofing is a common camouflage tactic used by attackers. When sending attack traffic, the attacker uses a fake or random IP address as the source address to hide the true source of the traffic. This makes it difficult to track back and find out the real culprits behind cyber attacks.

(3) Dynamic attack rate

A DDoS attack does not expect the server to detect its attack behavior immediately, but hopes to be discovered after the attack has caused a certain attack effect or never be discovered. So, some low-speed denial-of-service attacks have appeared, such as pulsing denial-of-service attacks. Pulsing denial-of-service attacks use the protocol defects of the TCP congestion control mechanism to cause instantaneous network congestion, so that the sliding window of TCP is reduced rapidly. Slow denial-of-service attacks are more covert and more difficult to detect.

(4) Diversified attack methods

There are thousands of vulnerabilities in computer networks. In a DDoS attack, the attacker may use a mixture of different attack methods to attack the server at the same time, which makes a single, static protection technology unable to cope with it.

Therefore, a single, static technology (such as detection and analysis) has a very limited defense effect on DDoS. The end information hopping technique in the complex hopping mode is a dynamic protection method proposed to deal with defects of the existing static protection.

4.5.4 *Technical Principle of DynaBone*

The multi-overlay dynamic network protection technique based on DynaBone relies on the construction of multi-layer overlay networks and its dynamic configuration as well as management system. Its main idea is to protect virtual overlay networks through dynamic rerouting of network data flow, so as to prevent DDoS [17, 18].

The core idea of DynaBone is to build a larger external virtual overlay network which internally relies on multiple internal virtual overlay networks. It can provide security objectives such as encryption, dynamic routing, and configuration diversity through multi-layer overlay networks. DynaBone provides a way to choose a path. It deploys multiple different network defense methods and means in different internal overlay layers, and distributes the external data traffic to different levels according to different states and throughputs of their respective internal networks, finally forming a dynamic backbone network which can not only improve network performance and prevent DDoS, but also route network traffic automatically.

(1) Structure of DynaBone multi-overlay network

DynaBone's parallel internal overlay, known as the internal layer, provides a single, consistent network service to the outside, which can be regarded as an external overlay network. At the entrance of DynaBone, a Preset Multiplexer Module (PRM) is provided, which determines the distribution of data packets in the internal levels

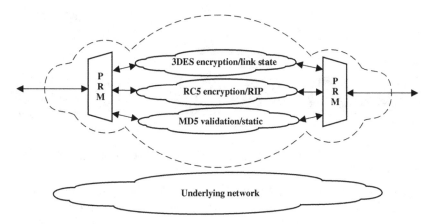

Figure 4.13.   Diagram of Dynabone Dynamic Concurrent Overlay Network

through the attack data and performance monitoring data. If an internal overlay network is attacked and the link fails, other overlay layers can be used to balance the network traffic. Its logical diagram is shown in Figure 4.13.

(2) Composition of DynaBone

DynaBone has two components: overlay layers and feedback-based PRM.

(3) Overlay layers

Based on the unique capability of X-Bone system, overlay layers provide a cyclic overlay structure. Each overlay network is a separate virtual network deployed over a real network. It includes hosts, routers, and channels. Channels are paths on underlying networks, that is, links on overlay networks.

Hosts are data packet sources, and routers are used for data packet forwarding, just like the traditional networks. Individual components (such as routers or hosts) can participate in more than one overlay network or participate in the overlay network with multiple different roles (routers or hosts) at a time. Figure 4.14 (a) shows an IP network. Over this network, a ring network (as shown in Figure 4.14 (b)) and a star network (as shown in Figure 4.14 (c)) are configured using different subnets made up of nodes in the underlying network. These networks are connected by a set of channels. These channels

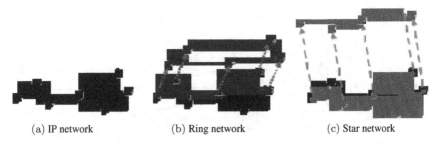

(a) IP network   (b) Ring network   (c) Star network

Figure 4.14.   Diagram of Overlay Network Channels

determine the topology of overlay networks. They can traverse multiple links of the underlying network, or traverse multiple times on a single connection.

Internal overlay networks have the following characteristics.

(a) Each internal network can use different network protocols and routing protocols or host different services to increase their diversity.

(b) Each host in external overlay networks is unaware of these internal networks and behaves as if there was only one network. At the entrance to the internal overlay network there are several sensors to monitor performance and possible attack flows.

(c) Determine which internal network to use depending on different network conditions.

(d) If it is detected that an internal overlay network is under attack or is meeting performance problems, it can be routed through a different overlay (DynaBone's dynamic network).

This technique is built on X-Bone, a dynamic network overlay technique [19], which allows multiple synchronous virtual overlays to coexist and allows the network topology to be dynamically created and used by applications. Hosts and network equipment can participate in multiple overlays. It can also be set to make each physical path in the network unique to different overlays.

X-Bone is a dynamic configuration and management system for overlay networks on the Internet. Overlay networks are used to configure the infrastructure at the top of the existing network, to isolate experiments on new protocols and separation capabilities, or to provide a simplified topology network environment. Current overlay network systems include commercial VPN, IP tunnel network

(M-Bone), and emerging research systems providing quality assurance services.

X-Bone system provides high-level interfaces that users and applications can configure on demand, such as creating an overlay network of six routers in a ring, each containing two hosts. X-bone automatically identifies available components and configurations, and monitors them.

DynaBone extends the X-Bone architecture by configuring a PRM converter for feedback and traffic distribution on a series of hierarchical internal overlay networks. PRM converter is located in the external overlay network.

(4) PRM

PRM is used to dynamically redirect the network traffic from external overlays to internal overlay layers that can provide network services. PRM includes multiplexers, multi-output converters, monitors, and preset control components, as shown in Figure 4.15. Among them, multiplexers are used to distribute the traffic from external networks to internal overlay networks. According to the multiplexing algorithm, each data packet, each session, each connection, or data packets containing a specific format is copied to multiple internal overlay networks. Tag information can also be added if needed, for example, to facilitate the receiver to reconstruct the sequence or to extract the data in a specific format. Multi-output converters are used to collect internal data packets. They may also need to reorder data packets, strip off duplicate content, and extract data from a specific format encoding. The multiplexing algorithm needs to be comprehensively determined based on built-in or user-defined policies, channel management, and interface of the existing bandwidth reservation and allocation mechanism. Policies and channel management are used to determine which channel to use. The monitor is used to coordinate and analyze states of internal overlay network layers. It may send heartbeat packets by itself, or trigger an external mechanism to comprehensively analyze network state, for example, to regulate mechanism for cyclically tracking performance of internal overlay network layers.

Three components coordinate with each other through preset control components. The controller determines how to configure the

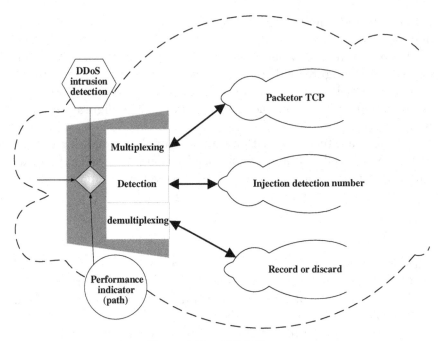

Figure 4.15.　PRM Diagram

multiplexers and distribute the traffic based on the attack situation detected by external sensors.

4.5.5　*Security Policy of DynaBone*

DynaBone is constructed to defend against DDoS attacks because any single layer of the network being attacked can be disconnected without affecting the connectivity of the entire overlay group. When internal overlay layers of DynaBone are attacked, PRM will convert the traffic to non-attacked overlay layers, as shown in Figure 4.16. All of these processes are transparent to users and applications at the top level.

DynaBone allows the internal network to be unavailable due to attacks. It can use the remaining multiple internal overlays concurrently to effectively block DDoS attacks, and it also allows the performance of all services to be degraded slowly. Defects of an individual protocol or an attack at a fixed address can only break one layer of overlay network at a time. Only if all overlay

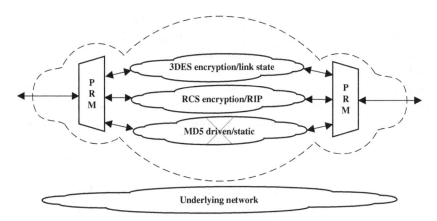

Figure 4.16. Diagram of PRM Converting Traffic under DDoS Attack

networks are successfully attacked at the same time will the service become unavailable at all. Moreover, the service will be automatically restored, and can redistribute the traffic to the other overlay layers.

DynaBone structure also provides some other functional configurations. The use of different overlays and inconsistent traffic distribution will allow attackers to obtain some information that enables them to interrupt services of overlay layers with heavy loads. Although this will not completely destroy the entire architecture, it may cause a slow recovery of the original service, because the whole overlay layer configures some traffic confidentiality techniques in a coordinated manner, such as hiding real data packets in randomized data flows. Other techniques, such as honeypots, dynamically adding new overlay layers, and relocating dangerous services, can also be configured in this architecture.

The Diversity of DynaBone technique is that it can use a variety of existing network protocols and security algorithms in different internal overlay layers, thereby deploying optional, concurrent, and parallel internal overlay networks. At present, DynaBone software has been used in 50 concurrent internal networks. Researchers got effective results under certain test conditions.

4.5.6 Basic Effectiveness and Existing Deficiencies

The Application of security protection technique based on overlay networks is an application-level dynamic network application mode and an important idea of dynamic network defense. Dynamic path change, reconfiguration, and security management are completed at the application level to shield differences in physical networks and difficulties of dynamic routing. But this technique relies on the robustness and stability of the underlying network, and all its operations in the application layer network may increase the overhead of the underlying network. At the same time, control messages passed between nodes will bring more network traffic, and reconfiguration and routing may bring uncertain network overhead. Therefore, further experimental verification and application are needed.

The multi-overlay dynamic network protection technique based on DynaBone aims to protect the availability of services on networks and ensure that traffic is rerouted dynamically or routed simultaneously through multiple paths. Depending on network protocols and routing protocols deployed at different internal virtual network layers, it may increase the latency and reduce the bandwidth. Moreover, there is a lack of effective experiment and emulation verification regarding the impact of more routing paths and heavier load on the network infrastructure. In addition, this technique has some limitations: (a) It relies on the perfect detection mechanism to detect when the overlay network is attacked. (b) Internal overlay layers may not be adequately isolated from each other, and the loss of certain hosts/network equipment/routes may seriously affect the entire network. (c) This technique is a relatively ideal prototype system model, which is still far from the actual use. (d) The protection capability of this technique is limited. It cannot provide any protection after an attacker gets access to a certain host.

4.6 Summary

From the perspective of the whole attack chain, the goal of dynamic network defense is to implement defense in the initial phase of the attack, especially in the phases of reconnaissance and target node access. It helps to increase the difficulty for attackers to detect the target network in the reconnaissance phase. It is used to confuse attackers and prevent them from trying to connect to the target system and obtain its properties (version, vulnerability, configuration, etc.) in the target access phase, which increase difficulty for attackers to collect information on the target machine.

This chapter analyzed dynamic network address translation based on DyNAT, network address randomization based on DHCP, end information hopping based on synchronization, security update distribution based on overlay networks, multi-overlay networks based on dynamic paths, and other network dynamization techniques and methods. For each technique, what information should be dynamized, how to implement and synchronize dynamic changes, policies of dynamic changes and their defense effectiveness were discussed, respectively. Comparative analysis of these dynamization techniques is shown in Table 4.3.

The common point of these dynamization techniques is to leave network structures, network communication, and network services to present multi-dimensional changes like temporal and spatial dimensions, which make it impossible for attackers to effectively implement attacks with conventional attack methods. At the same time, each technique has its own characteristics and application scope depending on its own unique change objects and change policies. These techniques are not mutually exclusive with traditional network-level security protection measures and products and are complementary to them. The traditional defense can play a role in authorization attack protection, confidential authentication, and application data security protection, while dynamic defense makes it more difficult for attackers to carry out attacks through dynamic changes of network architecture and communication content, thus multiplying security effectiveness.

Dynamically-enabled network defense is a network protection technique that can actively improve its own defense capability. In future studies, on the one hand, we should enhance the effectiveness verification and performance evaluation of dynamic hybrid change technology to achieve a trade-off between security and performance. On the premise of ensuring normal services, loss of certain service performance is in exchange for the improvement of security performance. On the other hand, we should actively research and develop diversification technologies with high practicality, which should be combined with current SDN and OpenFlow-related engineering standards, making it possible for these dynamization techniques to be applied to engineering applications in large-scale networks. They can implement unified scheduling and automatic control of different types of network equipment within a larger network, make the development

Table 4.3.   Comparative Analysis of Network Dynamization Technologies

Serial Number	Technical Name	Dynamization Objects	Dynamization Policies	Defense Effectiveness	Deployment
1	Dynamic network address translation based on DyNAT	MAC addresses, network addresses, ports, IP sequence numbers, etc.	End information scrambling based on encryption	Scanning, detection	Both sides of communication
2	Network address randomization based on DHCP	Network addresses	Frequently randomize allocation of network host addresses	Worm attacks based on IP address lists	Server side
3	End information hopping based on synchronization	End information such as ports, addresses, time slots, encryption algorithms and even protocols	Unified synchronization policies negotiated by two sides	DoS attacks	Server side or both sides
4	Multi-overlay dynamic network defense based on dynamic backbone	Paths of network data flow	Multi-layer overlay networks	Prevent DDoS attacks, attacks that manipulate network content and other resources attacks	Overlay networks and configuration management system
5	MT6D	IPv6 addresses	Randomize address allocation for both sides of virtual communication	Hide actual addresses to prevent scanning and detection	Both sides of communication

and application process more convenient, and facilitate upgrading and reconstruction of the existing network protection equipment. Therefore, dynamic defense techniques are not only suitable to current network facilities, but also applicable to future network systems and applications.

References

[1] Kewley, D., Fink, R., Lowry, J., *et al.* Dynamic approaches to thwart adversary intelligence gathering. *Proceedings of DARPA Information Survivability Conference & Exposition II*, 2001, 176–185.

[2] Price, C. M., Stanton, E., Lee, E. J., *et al.* Network security mechanisms utilizing dynamic network address translation LDRD project. *Sandia National Labs*, 2002.

[3] Dunlop, M., Groat, S., Urbanski, W., *et al.* Mt6d: A moving target IPv6 defense. *IEEE Military Communications Conference*, 2011, 1321–1326.

[4] Dunlop, M., Groat, S., Marchany, R., *et al.* IPv6: Now you see me, now you don't. *Tenth International Conference on Networks (ICN 2011)*, 2011.

[5] Groat, S., Dunlop, M., Marchany, R., *et al.* Using dynamic addressing for a moving target defense. *6th International Conference on Information Warfare and Security*, 2011.

[6] Antonatos, S., Akritidis, P., Markatos, E. P., *et al.* Defending against hit list worms using network address space randomization. *Computer Networks*, 2007, 51(12): 3471–3490.

[7] Atighetchi, M., Pal, P., Webber, F., *et al.* Adaptive use of network-centric mechanisms in cyber-defense. *Proc. 6th IEEE Int'l Syrup. Object-Oriented Real-Time Distributed Computing*, 2003, 183–192.

[8] Webber, F., Pal, P., Atighetchi, M., *et al.* Apod final report. Technical Report Technical Memorandum, BBN Technologies LLC, 2002.

[9] Shi, L. and Jia, C. Research on end hopping for active network confrontation. *Journal on Communications*, 2008, 29(2): 106–110.

[10] Jia, C., Lin, K., and Lu, K. Plug-in policy for DoS attack defense mechanism based on end hopping. *Journal on Communications*, 2009, 30(10): 114–118.

[11] Lin, K. and Jia, C. End hopping based on message Tampering. *Journal on Communications*, 2013, 34(12): 142–148.

[12] Lee, H. C. J. and Thing, V. L. L. Port hopping for resilient networks. *Proceedings of 60th IEEE Vehicular Technology*, 2004, 3291–3295.

[13] Badishiy, G., Herzberg, A., Keidar, I., *et al.* Keeping denial-of-service attackers in the dark. *Springer Berlin Heidelberg*, 2005, 4(3): 191–204.

[14] Mills, D. L. Internet time synchronization: The network time protocol. *IEEE Transactions on Communications*, 1991, 39(10): 1482–1493.

[15] Andersen, D., Balakrishnan, H., Kaashoek, F., *et al.* Resilient overlay networks. *Proceedings of ACM Symposium on Operating System Principles (SOSP)*, 2001.

[16] Touch, J. D., Finn, G. G., Wang, Y. S., *et al.* DynaBone: Dynamic defense using multi-layer Internet overlays. *Proceedings of DARPA Information Survivability Conference and Exposition*, 2003, 2: 271–276.

[17] Wang, H., Jia, Q., Fleck, D., *et al.* A moving target DDoS defense mechanism. *Computer Communications*, 2014, 46(6): 10–21.

[18] Jia, Q., Sun, K., and Stavrou, A. Motag: Moving target defense against Internet denial of service attacks. *IEEE International Conference on Computer Communications and Networks*, 2013, 1–9.

[19] Touch, J. Dynamic Internet overlay deployment and management using the x-bone. *Computer Networks*, 2000, 36(2): 59–68.

[20] Li, J., Reiher, P. L., and Popek, G. J. Resilient self-organizing overlay networks for security update delivery. *IEEE Journal on Selected Areas in Communications*, 2004, 22(1): 189–202.

[21] Jafarian, J. H., Al-Shaer, E., and Duan, Q. OpenFlow random host mutation: Transparent moving target defense using software defined networking. *Proceedings of the 1st Workshop on Hot Topics in Software Defined Networking*, 2012, 127–132.

Chapter 5

Dynamic Platform Defense

5.1 Introduction

Platforms mainly refer to software/hardware environments supporting application execution, which includes processors, operating systems, virtualization platforms, specific application development environments, etc. Among them, hardware mainly includes processor architectures, such as x86, Sparc, ARM, MIPS, and Alpha. There are several processor models for each architecture, and each model is different in terms of CPU frequency, instruction set, number of processed bits, register, supported interface, etc. Operating systems usually have different types and versions, and there are mainly two types – Windows and Linux. Windows includes Windows 95, Windows 98, Windows XP, Windows Vista, Windows 7, Windows 8, and other versions. There is little difference between these versions. There are many customized versions based on Linux kernel, such as RedHat, Ubuntu, Fedora, CentOS, and Debian. Virtualization platforms mainly include hardware-level virtualization and operating system-level virtualization. Hardware-level virtualization products include VMware, Xen, KVM, etc., while operating system-level virtualization products include Jail, Virtual Zoo, Open VZ, etc. For Web application development, Web servers include Apache, Tomcat, IIS, etc., and Web applications are developed in forms of CGI, ASP, PHP, J2EE, .NET, etc.

At present, the design of application systems often adopts a single design architecture which remains unchanged for a long time after delivery. This gives malicious attackers enough time to detect and learn the architecture and vulnerabilities of the system. Despite great efforts of security managers, each system that seems secure enough has some vulnerabilities. So with continuous development of attack technologies, it is impossible to completely eradicate new security vulnerabilities. Once system vulnerabilities are discovered and successfully exploited by malicious attackers, the system will face serious threats such as service exception, information theft, and identity theft.

According to dynamic enablement, if a dynamically changing system operating platform can be built, making the observation of system operating environment uncertain for internal and external attackers. It is impossible or difficult to build an attack chain based on vulnerabilities or backdoors, thereby improving capability of the system to defend against attacks. Platform dynamization is an effective way to solve inherent defects of traditional system design with a single architecture. By building a diversified operating platform and dynamically changing the application operating environment, it makes the system present randomization, uncertainty, and dynamics. This can shorten the time during which applications are exposed on a platform and create reconnaissance fog, which makes it difficult for attackers to find out the specific structure of the system and launch attacks effectively.

Platform dynamization technology overturns the traditional protection measures that use firewall, intrusion detection, anti-virus, and other technologies. It does not rely on static sealing, blocking, checking, and killing methods, but on constructing a diversified operating platform and randomly changing the application operating environment to increase difficulty for attackers to attack the system. On the one hand, platform dynamization technology allows the use of "virus-containing" software/hardware components, and its protection effectiveness is achieved by enhancing random changes of the platform, rather than eliminating vulnerabilities. On the other hand, although platform dynamization technology is a brand-new system security protection method, it does not exclude traditional protection methods. The use of platform dynamization technology on the basis of traditional protection methods can help obtain additional protection effects.

At present, there are mainly four dynamic platform defense technologies: platform dynamization based on reconfigurable computing, application live migration based on heterogeneous platforms, diversification of Web services, and platform dynamization based on intrusion tolerance. The four platform dynamization technologies are representative and effective methods at present. Each of these technologies will be discussed in detail in terms of technical background, principle, effectiveness, and deficiencies as follows.

5.2 Platform Dynamization Based on Reconfigurable Computing

Reconfigurable Computing (RC) is proposed to solve high-performance and high-efficiency computing problems. By utilizing flexibility of programmable logic devices, the devices can realize different functions according to different computing tasks at runtime. Expanding the equivalent scale of hardware by reusing programmable logic devices can save hardware resources and input/output pins, and reduce power consumption of the system.

A reconfigurable system is usually a heterogeneous computing environment, including general-purpose processors and programmable logic devices that execute different software/hardware tasks respectively. Programmable logic devices can load different configuration data under the control of processors to perform reconfiguration at runtime, and can realize unintermittent processing tasks in the reconfiguration process to ensure continuity of task execution.

Using the characteristic that a reconfigurable system supports reconfiguration at runtime, a diversified operating platform can be built to solve the security problems of the system. Therefore, the purpose of platform dynamization technology based on reconfigurable computing is different from that of reconfigurable computing. Its purpose is not to realize high-efficiency computing, but refer to reconfigurable system to improve system security and explore diversified platform construction methods based on dynamic enablement.

Specifically, platform dynamization technology based on reconfigurable computing uses diversified software/hardware task partitioning and differentiated logic circuit design to design multiple executable files and configuration data that satisfy the application tasks and run on general-purpose processors and programmable logic devices, and randomly change the loaded executable files and corresponding configuration data files during the system running. Since the change of programmable logic devices' configuration data will change its circuit logic structure, the application operating platform can be dynamized by randomly changing configuration data files of the system.

5.2.1 *Overview*

Reconfigurable computing is a new computing mode that has emerged in recent years. It makes use of hardware programmability of reconfigurable logic devices to reconfigure logic devices for specific applications and change their functions to meet the changing application requirements [1]. In particular, dynamic reconfiguration allows the reconfiguration of logic devices during application execution without interruption.

A reconfigurable system itself has the capability to prevent malicious attackers from scouting and snooping the system to a certain extent, because the system needs to load different configuration data for different computing tasks, which can present certain platform dynamics. However, dynamics is associated with corresponding computing tasks and lacks randomness. After a period of reconnaissance, attackers can master the corresponding relationship between computing tasks and platform states, and then launch attacks. Meanwhile, for the same computing task, configuration data loaded by the system is the same, which is not dynamic. Therefore, the uncertainty and randomness of platform change cannot be realized simply using the reconfigurable system without improvement and change.

With the help of reconfiguration technology, especially the dynamic reconfiguration technology, we can build random, diverse, and dynamically changing operating platforms for different tasks or the same task, and perform dynamic changes in time and space dimensions in a way that defenders can control. Dynamic changes in time dimension mean that the logic function of a reconfigurable system can be changed dynamically as needed, and data processing of the entire system is completed by using different software/hardware configuration data at different times. Dynamic changes in space dimension mean that the programmable logic resource invoked by each kind of configuration data are different, which is embodied in different organizational structures of logic circuits. Dynamic changes in both time and space dimensions make it difficult for attackers to carry out effective reconnaissance and detection on the system, thereby eliminating attack behaviors in the initial phase of the attack chain.

5.2.2 Technical Principles

This section will first prove theoretically that system reconfiguration can improve the defense capability of the system, then introduce the concept of reconfigurable computing. Based on the theoretical proofs, it will summarize the current commonly used reconfigurable system architecture and its design process, and discuss the design method of platform dynamization for a typical heterogeneous system composed of traditional general-purpose processors and programmable logic devices in detail.

1. Theoretical analysis of system reconfiguration in improving security Intuitively, system reconfiguration can enhance the uncertainty and increase attack difficulty of attackers. The theoretical proof will be given in the following.

Based on the verification method [2] of Valentina Casola *et al.*, supposing that an attacker's reconnaissance time on the system is $[0, T]$, and the number of system reconfiguration is n (n is an integer not less than 2) in time period $[0, T]$, the security improvement achieved by system reconfiguration can be expressed as

$$Pr(success([0, T], n)) \leqslant Pr(success([0, T], 0)) \qquad (5.1)$$

where $Pr(success(I, n))$ represents the probability that the attacker can successfully attack under the condition that the number of system reconfiguration is n in time period I.

To prove equation (5.1), we convert the left-hand side of this equation to

$$Pr(success([0, T], n)) = 1 - Pr(\neg success([0, T], n)) \qquad (5.2)$$

where $Pr(\neg success([0, T], n))$ represents the probability that the attacker fails to attack in time period $[0, T]$. We divide $[0, T]$ into

n smaller time periods, and suppose that the system in each small time period uses different reconfiguration methods. The probability of the attacker's failure can be expressed as

$$Pr(\neg success([0,T],n)) = Pr(\neg success\left(\left[0, \frac{1}{n} \cdot T\right]\right)$$

$$\cap \neg success\left(\left[\frac{1}{n} \cdot T, \frac{2}{n} \cdot T\right]\right)$$

$$\cap \cdots \cap \neg success\left(\left[\frac{n-1}{n} \cdot T, T\right]\right) \quad (5.3)$$

Since attack events in each small time period are mutually independent, $Pr(\neg success([0,T],n))$ can be expressed as

$$Pr(\neg success([0,T],n))$$

$$= \prod_{i=0}^{n-1}\left(1 - Pr\left(success\left(\left[\frac{i}{n} \cdot T \cdot \frac{i+1}{n} \cdot T\right]\right)\right)\right) \quad (5.4)$$

Supposing that for each reconfiguration method of the system, the attacker takes the same length of time to attack successfully, the probability of the attacker's successful attack in a given time is proportional to the length of time. For $i \in [0, n-1]$, there is

$$Pr\left(\neg success\left(\left[\frac{i}{n} \cdot T, \frac{i+1}{n} \cdot T\right]\right)\right) = \frac{Pr(success([0,T]))}{n} \quad (5.5)$$

By substituting equation (5.5) into equation (5.4), we can get

$$Pr(\neg success([0,T],n)) = \prod_{i=0}^{n-1}\left(1 - \frac{Pr(success[0,T])}{n}\right)$$

$$= \left(1 - \frac{Pr(success([0,T]))}{n}\right)^n \quad (5.6)$$

For the real number $x \in [0, 1]$ and positive integer n, there is

$$\left(1 - \frac{x}{n}\right)^n \geqslant 1 - x \quad (5.7)$$

The following proves that Eq. (5.7) is true. Based on the binomial principle, $\left(1 - \frac{x}{n}\right)^n$ can be expressed as

$$\left(1 - \frac{x}{n}\right)^n = \sum_{k=0}^{n} \binom{n}{k} \left(-\frac{x}{n}\right)^n = 1 - x + \sum_{k=2}^{n} \binom{n}{k} \left(-\frac{x}{n}\right)^k \quad (5.8)$$

To prove the above equation, we only need to prove that $\sum_{k=2}^{n} \binom{n}{k} \left(-\frac{x}{n}\right)^k$ is not less than 0. Because when $k = 2$, the value of $\sum_{k=2}^{n} \binom{n}{k} \left(-\frac{x}{n}\right)^k$ is greater than 0, we only need to prove that the absolute values of all items are gradually decreasing. Now let's see if the ratio of the two consecutive items is greater than 1.

$$\left| \frac{\binom{n}{k} \left(-\frac{x}{n}\right)^k}{\binom{n}{k+1} \left(-\frac{x}{n}\right)^{k+1}} \right| = \frac{\frac{n!}{k! \cdot (n-k)!}}{\frac{n!}{(k+1)! \cdot (n-k-1)!}} = \frac{n \cdot (k+1)}{(n-k) \cdot x} \quad (5.9)$$

Because $n \cdot (k+1) \geqslant n$, and $(n-k) \cdot x \leqslant n$, Eq. (5.9) is not less than 1.

By combining Eqs. (5.6) and (5.7), we can get

$$\left(1 - \frac{Pr\left(success\left([0, T]\right)\right)}{n}\right)^n \geqslant 1 - Pr\left(success\left([0, T]\right)\right) \quad (5.10)$$

By combining equations (5.2), (5.6), and (5.10), we can get

$$1 - Pr(success([0, T], n)) \geqslant 1 - Pr(success([0, T])) \quad (5.11)$$

that is

$$Pr\left(success\left([0, T]\,, n\right)\right) \leqslant Pr\left(success\left([0, T]\right)\right) \quad (5.12)$$

Therefore, equation (5.1) can be proved. The above process theoretically proves that the system reconfiguration can improve the difficulty for attackers to attack.

2. Concept of reconfigurable computing

Reconfigurable computing was first proposed by Gerald Estri *et al.* from University of California, USA, in 1960s [3]. Before the advent of reconfigurable computing, a program was implemented in two main ways. One is to use a general-purpose processor, in which computing tasks are accomplished by software programming. When the task changes, we only need to rewrite software to implement the new task. Advantages of this method are high flexibility, strong versatility, good portability, and short development cycle. However, the processor executes software instructions one by one in a serial way. The efficiency of instruction execution is not high and the computing speed is slow, so it is difficult to realize high-performance parallel processing. The other method is to use Application-Specific Integrated Circuit (ASIC). ASIC is designed for a specific task. It uses hardware resources in the device to perform computing tasks in parallel, and has the advantages of fast processing speed, high computing efficiency, and low power consumption. However, as ASIC adopts a custom circuit, it can only be used to complete fixed tasks after it is designed. When the task changes, the original ASIC cannot be used, and a hardware circuit needs to be redesigned. Therefore, the method lacks flexibility.

With the development of programmable device technology, especially the appearance of Field Programmable Gate Arrays (FPGA), reconfigurable computing has gradually become a new research hotspot in the field of computing. Reconfigurable computing can realize different computing tasks through flexible configuration of programmable devices, which has the flexibility of general-purpose processors and the efficiency of ASIC.

Figure 5.1 shows architectures of the processing systems constructed with the general-purpose processor, ASIC, and programmable device [4]. The general-purpose processor architecture converts an application into a series of instructions through a compilation process. These instructions use computing units of the general-purpose processor to process data in sequence. ASIC maps specific functions to specific circuits, and adopts acceleration mechanisms such as pipeline and parallel processing to process input data sequentially. The reconfigurable processing architecture implements

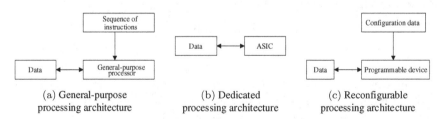

(a) General-purpose processing architecture

(b) Dedicated processing architecture

(c) Reconfigurable processing architecture

Figure 5.1.   Three Computing System Architectures

different processing tasks by loading different configuration data. It combines the advantages of the above two methods — flexibility of a general-purpose processor and efficiency of ASIC.

Reconfigurable systems can be divided into statically reconfigurable systems and dynamically reconfigurable systems [5, 6]. When using static reconfiguration, the entire circuit system generates a configuration file and downloads it to the reconfigurable device before the system executes tasks. While the system is running, configuration of the reconfigurable device remains unchanged. This reconfiguration method is the simplest way to configure the control circuit, but it is not suitable for applications with high real-time requirements. Dynamic reconfiguration means that during the entire operation, the system can reconfigure the reconfigurable device in real time as needed to achieve new logic functions without interfering with the correct operation of the system. With this configuration method, multiple configuration files supporting different functions can be generated in advance, and the corresponding configuration files are selected to be loaded according to task requirements during the system operation.

Dynamic reconfiguration is divided into dynamic global reconfiguration and dynamic partial reconfiguration. Dynamic global reconfiguration means that the entire reconfigurable device needs to be reconfigured when a system function changes. Before reconfiguration, the result and state of the previous operation are extracted and saved in the external storage. After new configuration is completed, data in the storage is called to make the system continue to work. System functions are suspended during reconfiguration, and the execution of application is not continuous. In addition, during reconfiguration of the device, all resources need to be reconfigured, the configuration data is large and the configuration time is long. Dynamic partial reconfiguration means that during the system operation, only some resources of the reconfigurable device are reconfigured, while the other resources run correctly and are not affected by reconfiguration. Compared with global reconfiguration, dynamic partial reconfiguration only configures very little data, so reducing the configuration time accordingly. The dynamically and partially reconfigurable system can change system functions by dynamically modifying the configurations of partial resources. In this process, the system maintains right running, so the operation of the entire system has time continuity. The partially and dynamically reconfigurable system can not only realize time division multiplexing of logical resources, improving resource utilization, but also performs computing and configuration operations simultaneously, effectively improving execution performance of the system. At present, it is mainly FPGA that have the partial and dynamic reconfiguration function.

It can be seen from the concept of reconfigurable computing that if a reconfigurable system is used, by pre-generating multiple configuration files (also called configuration variants) that support applications, and randomly changing configuration variants loaded in the system during system operation, the platform can present a randomly changing logical architecture, thereby making it difficult for attackers to detect and attack the system. Partially and dynamically reconfigurable systems can be used for applications that require both real-time performance and uninterrupted service in the process of reconfiguration.

3. Reconfigurable system structure

Generally, the fixed computing component of a reconfigurable system is CPU, and the variable component is FPGA. According to the coupling relationship between CPU and FPGA, reconfigurable systems can be divided into the following three categories [7].

(1) FPGA acts as an independent peripheral

As shown in Figure 5.2, FPGA communicates with CPU through I/O bus, which is the loosest coupling mode. FPGA is a completely independent device, and its work can be completely free from the interference of the host. The host may only control the configuration of FPGA. Due to the limited communication rate, it is usually applicable to the case where there is less communication between CPU and FPGA. The advantage of this structure is that it is simple to implement, CPU is separated from FPGA, and both can be designed separately. The disadvantage is that the I/O interface tends to be a bottleneck that limits the system performance.

(2) FPGA acts as a coprocessor

As shown in Figure 5.3, the speed of communication between CPU and FPGA is much faster in this coupling mode. CPU can configure FPGA as a coprocessor with corresponding functions, and provide the data to FPGA for processing. FPGA completes computing tasks

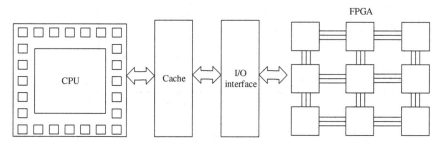

Figure 5.2.   Structure of FPGA as Independent Peripheral

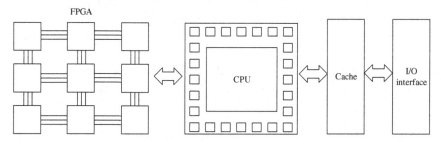

Figure 5.3.   Structure of FPGA as Coprocessor

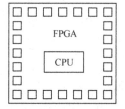

Figure 5.4.   Structure of FPGA Embedded with CPU

independently and returns the results to CPU. In this mode, FPGA can also work independently and complete the relatively complex computing tasks. While FPGA is working, CPU can also perform other tasks in parallel.

(3) FPGA is embedded with CPU

As shown in Figure 5.4, FPGA is internally embedded with a hardcore or softcore CPU to form a System on Programmable

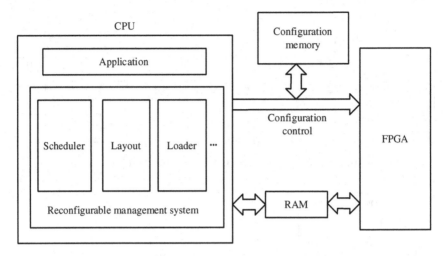

Figure 5.5.   Abstract Model of Reconfigurable System

Chip (SoPC). At present, this structure has been greatly used. For example, Xilinx Virtex-IIPro and Virtex-4 series FPGAs are embedded with hardcore Power PC, Virtex and Spartan series chips can be embedded with softcore MicroBlaze, and the latest Virtex-7 series is embedded with ARM. This coupling mode reduces the communication delay and data access overhead, and also reduces design complexity of the reconfigurable system.

From the structures of the above three types of reconfigurable systems, no matter which architecture is adopted, the abstract model of the reconfigurable system can be simplified into a heterogeneous system consisting of a general-purpose CPU and FPGA, as shown in Figure 5.5. The reconfigurable management system runs on CPU and is mainly used for system resource management and task scheduling. The management system includes a scheduler, a layout, a loader, etc. The scheduler is responsible for assigning computing resources to tasks and determining when to load and execute them, the layout is responsible for management and maintenance of programmable resources, and the loader is responsible for loading the corresponding configuration data to FPGA.

As Figure 5.5 shows, dynamization of reconfigurable system can be implemented by the reconfigurable management system running on CPU. For specific processing tasks, reconfigurable management

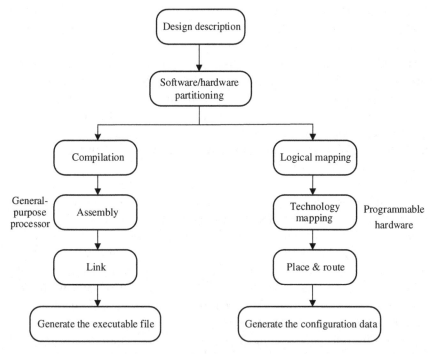

Figure 5.6.   Development Process Diagram of a Reconfigurable System

system randomly selects pre-generated software executable files and hardware configuration data (also called software variants and configuration variants), and loads them to CPU and FPGA, respectively, to run. During operation, software variants and configuration variants with the same function can be randomly switched for different tasks or the same task, thus increasing dynamics and uncertainty of the system.

(4) Development process and dynamization implementation methods of a reconfigurable system

Figure 5.6 shows the development process diagram of a reconfigurable system [8, 9]. The specific steps may be slightly different for different systems. First, it requires to describe the design. This process is to describe the application system functions to be implemented. Second, software/hardware partitioning of application tasks is performed to divide application tasks into two parts: Some tasks that are executed sequentially or belong to the control flow are mapped to the general-purpose processor for implementation, and the other tasks that can be executed in parallel or implemented at high speed are mapped to the reconfigurable hardware for implementation. After software/hardware partitioning is completed, the whole development process is divided into two processes: One is the traditional, general-purpose processor-oriented development process, which compiles the design description and links it as an executable file composed of instructions and data to be executed by the processor; the other uses the traditional hardware logic design process to convert function description into a circuit structure.

In the process of developing programmable hardware, logic mapping is first performed to map the operations of application tasks to the logical unit. For FPGA, logical mapping is to map each operation to a logical gate circuit. Technology mapping is performed after logic mapping. For FPGA, the logic gate circuit generated by logic mapping needs to be converted into a look-up table. Place & route is to solve the problem of circuit module construction and wiring on programmable hardware after technology mapping. Signal transmission delay can be effectively reduced by putting adjacent modules together to reduce the length of connection. Finally, the mapped circuit will be converted into configuration information for programmable hardware. In application, configuration information can be downloaded to the programmable hardware through the system interface to complete configuration of programmable hardware.

As the process shown in Figure 5.6, there are two ways to implement dynamization of the system platform. The first way is to design software/hardware partitioning. For the same task or different tasks, a variety of software/hardware partitioning methods are adopted on the emphasis of diversity rather than the best performance. For each of the software/hardware partitioning methods, the executable files running on the general-purpose processor and the configuration data running on the programmable hardware are generated, respectively. During the system operation, the corresponding executable files and configuration data are randomly selected to be loaded. The second way is to design the implementation process of programmable hardware. For certain functional requirements, a variety of logical design, technology mapping, place & route methods are adopted to generate multiple configuration data files which are randomly selected to be loaded into the programmable hardware during system operation. Although the two platform dynamization implementation methods have a certain impact on system performance, both of them can make the reconfigurable system have the characteristic of changing logical resource structure, and make it difficult for malicious attackers to carry out effective reconnaissance on the system architecture, improving the system's capability to defend against attacks.

(5) Changing space analysis of platform dynamization

For the convenience of analysis, the executable files and corresponding configuration data for implementing an application task are regarded as a configuration variant of the platform dynamization change space. The more the number of configuration variants, the wider the optional scope of platform change, and the greater the difficulty for attackers to detect. For reconfigurable systems, the diversity of platforms is equivalent to the diversity of configuration variants.

The original purpose of reconfigurable computing is to achieve high-performance computing tasks through the use of programmable logic devices. During the system operation, the configuration data of programmable logic devices are changed dynamically to handle different computing tasks. For different computing tasks, the reconfigurable system requires corresponding configuration data to be generated. From this point of view, reconfigurable computing itself also includes a certain dynamization process. Although different computing tasks have different configuration data, which have a certain diversity, the configuration data is bundled to computing tasks, which does not have randomness. To maximize diversity of the system, the number of configuration variants need to be increased greatly. From the perspective of platform dynamization, for different computing tasks, it is necessary to generate multiple configuration variants corresponding to each task, and randomly change loaded variants during the system operation.

According to Figure 5.6, the design of configuration variants mainly involves two phases: partitioning of software/hardware tasks and implementation of software/hardware tasks.

The purpose of software/hardware task partitioning in reconfigurable computing is to obtain an implementation that meets the requirements of time, cost, and power consumption from system design space, which essentially maximizes the computing efficiency.

Generally, software/hardware partitioning is a Non-deterministic Polynomial (NP) complete problem. Therefore, the objective of researchers is to quickly find the approximate optimal solution with heuristic algorithms, such as mountain climbing, genetic algorithm, simulated annealing, and tabu search algorithm [10]. Platform dynamization technology makes use of software/hardware task partitioning method of reconfigurable computing, however its main purpose is not to obtain the best partitioning method, but to obtain diversity of the partitioning method, in some cases at the expense of performance. Different methods of software/hardware partitioning lead to different software functions implemented in the general-purpose processor. Because the implementation method of each software is different, and the address space adopted is also different, the random changes of software variants loaded in the general-purpose processor can effectively defend against certain software vulnerability attacks and buffer overflow attacks.

At the implementation stage of software/hardware tasks, the flexible use of different logical design, technology mapping, place & route methods can generate different configuration data files for certain functional requirements, implementing multiple configuration variants loaded in programmable hardware.

Figure 5.7 shows Verilog code of the two-input adder. The logic circuit synthesized by Xilinx Synthesis Tool (XST) is shown in Figure 5.8. To generate configuration variants with the same function, we delay the output result of the adder by one clock cycle. The corresponding Verilog code is shown in Figure 5.9, and the synthesized circuit is shown in Figure 5.10. By comparing Figure 5.8 and Figure 5.10, it can be seen that a different logic circuit diagram is obtained after the output is delayed by one clock. Delay increase is only a simple way to change the logic circuit. For more complex functional requirements, different functional unit partitioning and different functional module combination can be used to achieve different logical circuit structures. In general, hardware engineers with different design habits implement different logic circuits for the same functional requirement. This example shows that there are many design methods to implement different configuration data in the logical design process.

During the technology mapping and place & route process, a dedicated layout constraint tool such as Xilinx's PlanAhead can be used

```
module        MyAdder (
input                   clock,
input                   para1,
input                   para2,
output reg   [1:0]    sum);
alawys  @(posedge clock)
      begin
            sum <= para1+para2;
      end
end module
```

Figure 5.7.   Verilog Code of Two-Input Adder

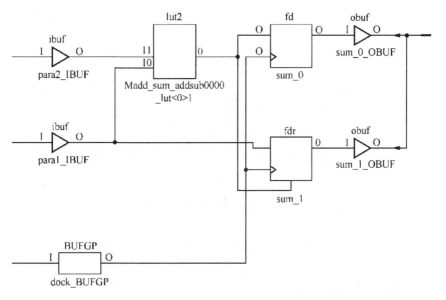

Figure 5.8.   Logic Circuit Diagram of Synthesized Adder

to limit the logical circuit generated by logical mapping to a certain area of FPGA. The more the FPGA resources, the simpler the logic circuit, and the more the areas available.

In summary, with help of the development tools provided by programmable hardware manufacturers, a variety of configuration data files can be easily and conveniently implemented by using programmable hardware. Random change of the configuration data loaded in programmable hardware can dynamically change the execution time, power consumption, electromagnetic radiation, and other characteristics of programmable hardware, making it difficult for

```
module        MyAdder (
input                    clock,
input                    para1,
input                    para2,
output reg   [1:0]    sum);
reg              [1:0]    sum_buf;
alawys   @(posedge clock)
    begin
          sum_buf <= para1+para2;
          sum <= sum_buf;
    end
end module
```

Figure 5.9.   Verilog Code with Increased Output Delay

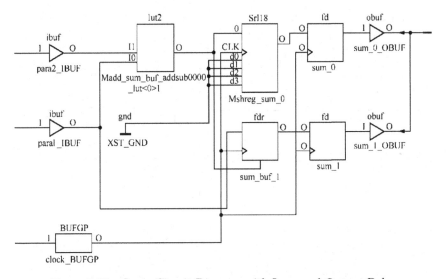

Figure 5.10.   Logic Circuit Diagram with Increased Output Delay

attackers to establish a connection between leaked physical signals and processed data, and thus effectively defending against bypass attacks.

5.2.3   *Basic Effectiveness and Existing Deficiencies*

Employing the reconfiguration characteristics of programmable logic devices, the platform dynamization method based on reconfigurable computing randomly changes the executable files running in the general-purpose processor and the configuration data files running in programmable logic devices during system runtime. This method shorten the exposure time window of the system, thereby breaking the attack chain in reconnaissance phase. At the same time, dynamic changes of the executable files can effectively prevent attacks against a certain software vulnerability and buffer overflow attacks. Dynamic changes of the configuration data files can effectively prevent the bypass attacks against programmable hardware.

If there are not enough variants of executable files and configuration data files in the platform, or the changing speed speed is not fast enough, attackers may find a way to attack the system platform. If the storage configuration data files do not adopt the security protection measures that prohibit unauthorized access, attackers may tamper with the configuration data and further attack the platform. Moreover attackers may obtain the stored configuration data and make a reverse analysis on system functions. In addition, due to the need to generate multiple configuration variants, complexity of system management and task scheduling is increased.

5.3 Application Live Migration Based on Heterogeneous Platforms

Application live migration based on heterogeneous platforms constructs multiple heterogeneous system platforms, including heterogeneous hardware and operating systems, and enables the applications running on these platforms to randomly migrate across different platforms in a controlled manner, thus reducing the exposure time of a single platform to make it difficult for malicious attackers to detect system effectively, and ultimately achieving the goal of improving system defense capability.

5.3.1 *Overview*

Reconnaissance on the platform where the application is running is the first step attackers must perform before launching attacks. Through reconnaissance, attackers know the specific environment where the application runs, and find out vulnerabilities of the environment, so as to prepare for launching attacks. If the application is always running on a single platform, attackers will have enough time to implement continuous reconnaissance and attempt attacks on the platform. Once the intrusion succeeds, it will cause great damage. From the perspective of defenders, if the operating platform of the application can be dynamically changed and the application can be randomly migrated across heterogeneous platforms, it will be difficult for attackers to figure out the specific running environment of the application. This can improve the system security defense capability.

Application live migration based on heterogeneous platforms is a technology that dynamically changes the application operating platform. It achieves diversity and randomness of the operating platform by randomly and dynamically changing the application operating environment, including hardware platforms and operating systems, so as to enhance capability of the system to defend against attacks. This technology uses operating system-level virtualization and checkpointing compilation technologies to create a virtual execution environment, and migrate applications across different platforms while saving application operating states (including the execution state, file state, network connection, etc.). By randomly and dynamically changing the platform, the platform information collected by attackers in reconnaissance phase becomes invalid during attack, which increases difficulty for attackers to attack the system to some extent.

5.3.2 *Technical Principles*

Implementation of application live migration across heterogeneous platforms involves two key technologies [11]: operating system-level virtualization and checkpointing compilation. The principles of these two technologies are described respectively, and based on these, the implementation methods of operating state migration and application operating environment migration are discussed in the following.

(1) Implementation method of application live migration across heterogeneous platforms

Implementation of application live migration across heterogeneous platforms means that the application can achieve the following objectives.

(a) Support heterogeneity at the instruction set architecture level, that is, applications can run on processors with different instruction sets.

(b) Support heterogeneity of operating systems, that is, applications can run on different operating systems.

(c) Be able to save application states, including execution state, operating state, network state, and so on. When you migrate an application across heterogeneous platforms, you should not only restart the application on the target platform, but also ensure the consistency of application operating states on the source and target platforms.

(d) Support cross-platform programming languages such as C language, which can run on different platforms. Although Java virtual machine provides a sandbox environment for applications to operate, making Java language a platform-independent language, a lot of software is developed based on C language. If the technology is subject to Java language, its application range will be limited.

Application live migration technology based on heterogeneous platforms needs to implement migration across different hardware and operating systems under the premise of saving application operating environment and state. Operating system-level virtualization and checkpointing compilation technologies can achieve the objective of application live migration across heterogeneous platforms. Operating system-level virtualization helps build a sandbox environment for applications to operate, and implement the migration of their operating environments (such as file systems, open files, and network connection, etc.). Checkpointing compilation is a process of compiling an application to adapt to platforms with different architectures and migrate the running state of the application across platforms.

Figure 5.11 shows the complete process of application migration across heterogeneous platforms. First, operating system-level virtualization is used to implement migration of the application operating environment. Then, checkpointing technology is used to save the execution state of the application and restore it on the target platform. In Figure 5.11, applications on different platforms are binary code generated by compilation corresponding to the platforms.

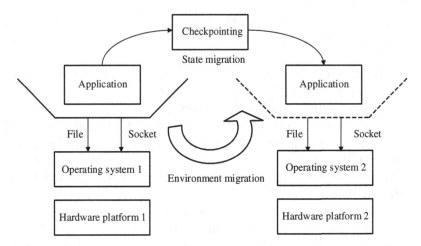

Figure 5.11. Application Migration Process across Heterogeneous Platforms

(2) Operating system-level virtualization and operating environment migration

The operating environment which saves applications is the prerequisite for implementing application migration across heterogeneous platforms. The application operating environment includes file systems, configuration files, open files, network connection, etc. Although many environment parameters can be saved through virtual machine migration, virtual machine migration is only applicable to homogeneous operating systems and hardware. Application live migration is implemented across heterogeneous operating systems and hardware, and virtual machine migration cannot meet this requirement.

Application live migration technology based on heterogeneous platforms implements the migration of the application operating environment through operating system-level virtualization technology. The concept of operating system-level virtualization and the method of operating environment migration will be described in the following respectively.

1. Concept of operating system-level virtualization

Operating system-level virtualization technology usually uses partitioning method to provide multiple independent application operating environments on the basis of the existing operating system (host),

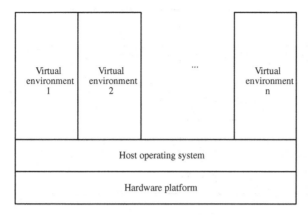

Figure 5.12. Principle of Operating System-Level Virtualization Technology

and each partition has complete critical system resources, including independent root file systems, system libraries, system software and application software, users and user groups, process trees, network configurations (such as IP addresses, routing rules, and firewall rules), etc. [12] Applications in different partitions are mutually independent, as if they were actually running on multiple separate computers. All partitions are based on the host system and use the same kernel as the host system, making full use of the host system's hardware drivers and other resources. The principle of operating system-level virtualization technology is shown in Figure 5.12.

Operating system-level virtualization is not to create multiple virtual machine environments in a physical system, but to have one operating system create multiple application environments that are independent of each other. In order to distinguish the isolated process (process group) from the virtual machine – a virtualization solution for a complete operating system – these processes are often called containers rather than virtual machines [13]. With only one layer of operating system kernel, containers are lighter than virtual machines, start up faster, have less memory and scheduling overhead, and more importantly, access to I/O devices such as disks does not need to go through the virtualization layer, which does not bring performance loss. Currently, the main operating system-level virtualization products include Jail running on FreeBSD system, Virtual Zoo, and its open source version OpenVZ developed by SWSoft and running on Windows/Linux platform, etc.

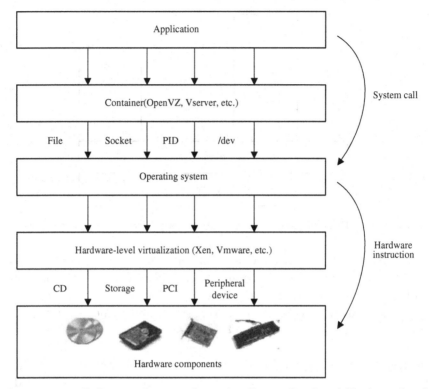

Figure 5.13. Differences between Operating System-Level and Hardware-Level Virtualization

The differences between operating system-level and hardware-level virtualization are shown in Figure 5.13. Hardware-level virtualization uses the virtual machine monitor to generate many virtual machine instances that can run independent operating systems on the hardware platform. It virtualizes hard disk partitions, storage sectors, hardware components, CPU, etc. In essence, it is the actual logical abstraction of hardware and configures resources from the perspective of hardware. Currently, the commonly used products supporting hardware-level virtualization include VMware Workstation, Xen, KVM, etc. Operating system-level virtualization mainly acts on file systems, storage areas, sockets, and kernel objects, and runs applications in multiple independent execution containers.

Generally, the main differences between operating system level and hardware-level virtualization contains following four aspects.

(a) Operating system-level virtualization takes the original system as a sample, and virtualizes a nearly identical system; hardware-level virtualization virtualizes the hardware environment, and then actually installs the system. (b) Operating system-level virtualization can only virtualize the same system, while hardware-level virtualization can virtualize different systems, such as Linux, MAC, and Windows family. (c) Multiple systems virtualized by operating system-level virtualization have strong correlations, reflected in the following aspects: First, multiple virtual systems can be configured simultaneously, changing the original system is equivalent to changing all systems. Second, if the original system is damaged, all virtual systems will be affected. The multiple systems virtualized by hardware-level virtualization are mutually independent, and have no connection with the original system. Damage of the original system will not affect virtual systems. (d) Operating system-level virtualization has a low performance loss because they are virtual systems rather than actual entities installed by hardware-level virtualization. Hardware-level virtualization requires high performance for computers. Both creation and management of virtual machines suffer low efficiency, and computer system resources are severely depleted during runtime.

2. Operating environment migration method

Application operating environments include file systems, configuration files, network connection, etc. Although many operating environment parameters adopt hardware-level virtualization technology and can be saved to the target platform through virtual machine migration, at present, virtual machine migration only supports homogeneous hardware platforms and operating systems, and cannot support application migration in heterogeneous environments. This technology uses operating system-level virtualization to build the runtime sandbox environment for applications and implement migration of the operating environment.

When a malicious attack is detected or the migration of an application is performed in period, the application container can be migrated from the source platform to the target platform by synchronizing file systems of the source container and the target container. During synchronization, state of the same file is synchronized to the target platform because the operating system keeps track of the application actions on the files in real time.

According to OpenVZ documentation, a network connection can typically be virtualized in three ways [14]: layer 2 virtualization, layer 3 virtualization, and socket virtualization. Only with layer 2 virtualization does each container have its own IP address and routing table information. Therefore, in order to migrate the container's IP address, layer 2 virtualization is required. To ensure network connectivity during migration, the virtual network IP address of the source container is first migrated to the new container. The state of each TCP socket is then transmitted. During migration, network migration is seamless for applications. Applications can send and receive data packets continuously.

3. Checkpointing compilation and operating state migration

When an application is migrated across heterogeneous platforms, the application operating state should also be migrated in addition to the application operating environment. Migration of application operating state can be achieved by using the checkpointing method. Specifically, perform checkpointing on the running application first, save state of the application to the checkpointing file, then migrate operating state of the application to the target platform by mirror file.

(1) Checkpointing requirements and implementation methods

Checkpointing technology is an effective fault-tolerant method and is often used to restore the application operating state. This technology saves state of the running process in a process image. When the process fails, the system can resume execution from the checkpoint according to the saved process image file. Similarly, checkpointing technology can also migrate the process operating state.

In order to achieve migration of application operating state, checkpointing must meet the following three requirements.

(a) Flexibility: The checkpointing program should be able to support different hardware architectures and operating systems in a heterogeneous environment.

(b) Transparency: When performing checkpointing, you should avoid making a lot of code changes to the existing program.

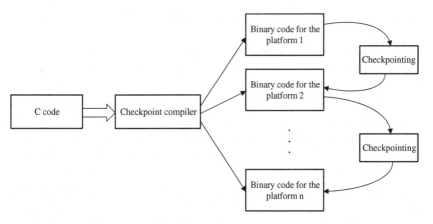

Figure 5.14.   Diagram of Checkpointing Compilation Method

(c) Scalability: Checkpointing should be able to handle complex programs and large amounts of data without impacting system performance.

The checkpointing compilation process shown in Figure 5.14 can meet the flexibility requirement. This compilation method can support any combination of various operating systems and hardware structures. The executable program generated by compilation contains the inserted checkpointing code and can run on the target platform.

Transparency can be achieved with automatic code analysis and checkpointing code insertion. With this approach, users do not need to change code to indicate where to perform checkpointing and what data needs to be checkpointed.

Using compressed checkpointing file format is an effective way to implement scalability. With this approach, the checkpointing file can still be as small as possible even when the amount of processed data increases.

(2) Checkpointing methods for the process

There are two possible checkpointing methods for the executing process [15]: Data Segment Level Checkpointing (DSLC) and Variable Level Checkpointing (VLC). Please note that these are two different types of checkpointing methods.

Data segment level checkpointing saves the overall state of the application (including heap and stack) in a checkpointing file. Although data segment level checkpointing saves the overall state of the process, because the checkpointing file contains large amounts of data on the platform, such as heap and stack, this approach has higher data storage overhead and lower checkpointing performance.

Variable level checkpointing only saves the variables related to restart operation in the checkpointing file. Variable level checkpointing is more suitable for migration across heterogeneous platforms because the checkpointing file contains less data and reduces the storage and recovery overhead of checkpointing. To reconfigure the overall state of the process, variable level checkpointing must re-execute some of the platform-dependent values in the code, which are stored in the heap and stack.

Using the variable level checkpointing method, code needs to be recompiled to find the variables related to the application restart operation [16], and then save these variables and their storage locations to the checkpointing file. During checkpointing execution, the process needs to be suspended, and then the storage location is saved in the file. To ensure consistency, checkpointing operations must be performed at secure locations in the code. When the application is restarted on the target platform, variable values required for the application are loaded from the checkpointing file. To reconfigure the overall state of the process, some parts of the code need to be re-executed.

Examples of variable level checkpointing are shown in Figures 5.15 and 5.16. Figure 5.15 shows the factorial code, and in Figure 5.16, checkpointing marks are inserted into the source code, that is, checkpointing-related calls in the code are prefixed with VLC. First, checkpointing is initialized. Then, variable values that need to be tracked are recorded. In this example, values of fact, curr, and i variables need to be recorded. Record operations of the actual variable values are performed after each iteration. When the loop ends, there is no need to track variable values, thus freeing up the space to record variable values. Finally, the whole checkpointing process is completed before the program returns results. It is worth noting that, for transparency and scalability, inserting checkpointing marks into code is done automatically before compilation.

```
int main (int argc, char **argv)
{
        int fact;
        double curr;
        int i;

        fact=20;
        curr=1;
        for (i=1; i<=fact; i++)
        {
                curr=curr * i;
        }
        printf ("%d factorial is %f", fact, curr);
        return 0;
}
```

Figure 5.15.   Code for Calculating Factorial

```
int main (int argc, char **argv)
{
        int fact;
        double curr;
        int i;
        VLC_INITIALIZE ();
        fact=20;
        curr=1;
        VLC_REGISTER_VARIABLES (fact, curr, i);
        for (i=1; i<=fact; i++)
        {
                VLC_PERFORM_CHECKPOINT ();
                curr=curr * i;
        }
        VLC_UNREGISTER_VARIABLES (fact, curr, i);
        printf ("%d factorial is %f", fact, curr);
        VLC_TEAR_DOWN ();
        return 0;
}
```

Figure 5.16.   Variable Level Checkpointing for Factorial Code

The checkpointing file format must be able to support heterogeneous platforms. If the target platform has different processing bits (32-bit, 64-bit) or big-endian and little-endian, simply saving data into a binary file may cause incompatibility. This technology employs HDF5 format, which can not only represent complex data forms, such as various processing bits, big-endian and little-endian, but also be an open, universal data model.

(3) Variable level checkpointing method

Controller/Precompiler for Portable Checkpointing (CPPC) is an effective variable level checkpointing method that can meet the flexibility, transparency, and scalability requirements. CPPC can save state of the running application into a format independent of the hardware platform and operating system (such as HDF5), and use the saved file to restore operating state of the application on heterogeneous platforms.

CPPC contains four execution processes [17].

(a) Compile code: Code is compiled independently for each platform to generate the executable file for each platform. CPPC can compile traditional C and Fortran 77 code. During compilation, the code does not need to be modified, and the application does not need to obtain the prior knowledge about checkpointing. CPPC automatically determines how and where to perform checkpointing on the application. CPPC interacts directly with user code through a precompiler and uses Cetus compilation architecture to determine where to insert checkpointing instructions in the code. After determining where to insert checkpointing instructions, insert checkpointing functions into the corresponding positions in the code and then compile the modified code using a traditional compiler such as cc or gcc.

(b) Run configuration: configure specific parameters of checkpointing. CPPC uses a configuration file to specify checkpointing parameters, including frequency of performing checkpointing, the number of stored checkpoints, and the storage location. Although there is a default configuration file, users usually expect to determine the configuration file according to the expected behavior of the program. For example, for important applications, frequency of performing checkpointing needs to be increased in order to obtain the latest operating state; for applications with slower updates, frequency of performing checkpointing can be reduced to avoid frequent file writing. Configuration parameters can be modified either by modifying the corresponding parameters in the configuration file or by using the command line during runtime. Usually, there is a specified configuration for a certain application in the configuration file. However, in order to obtain different effects, the user changes the configuration parameter by entering a new parameter value on the command line. The configuration file can be stored in either text or XML format.

(c) Checkpointing: Run the application, and the system automatically performs checkpointing operations on the application state. Because HDF5 format supports heterogeneous platforms, CPPC uses HDF5 as the checkpointing file format. CPPC supports to verify integrity of the checkpointing file based on CRC-32 algorithm. Checkpointing can be automatically performed, and the user can change frequency of performing checkpointing through the configuration file or command line. In addition, the compiler option allows programmers to manually specify the position of checkpointing execution by adding #pragma instruction into the source code. Because some initialization data is not stored in the storage, some code needs to be re-executed during application restart. The code can also be indicated by inserting instructions.

(d) Application restart: After the operating environment is migrated, the application operating state is restored on a new platform. After the application is started and the checkpointing is recorded, the application can be restarted based on the latest checkpointing record, which can be done on the same platform or on different platforms. The checkpointing file records variable value information about the application. This information needs to be loaded when the application is restarted to ensure that the application is restored to the same state where the checkpointing is performed.

CPPC method is used to analyze the factorial code shown in Figure 5.15. First, the code is automatically converted to the marked code. Converted code uses #pragma instructions to indicate where the CPPC mark needs to be inserted, as shown in Figure 5.17. Then, CPPC uses the marks in Figure 5.17 to create the code version that C compiler can understand. For each checkpointing operation, insert row identity indicates the checkpointing position. When CPPC is initialized, these identities are tracked in an array. An ID number is assigned to each identity according to its position in the array.

```
int main (int arge, char ** argv)
{
        int fact;
        double curr;
        int i;
        #pragma cppc init
        fact=20;
        curr=1;
        #pragma cppc register
        for (i=1; i<=fact; i++)
        {
                #pragma cppc checkpoint
                curr=curr *i;
        }
        #pragma cppc unregister
        printf ("%d factorial is %f", fact, curr);
        #pragma cppc shutdown
}       return 0;
```

Figure 5.17.   Factorial Code Added with CPPC Mark

When checkpointing is performed, the corresponding ID number is also stored in the checkpointing file.

When the application is restarted, the initialization process loads variable values from the storage to the register, and then the code goes to the corresponding checkpointing mark position. This procedure can use goto command to jump to the corresponding line identified by the ID number in the checkpointing file. Next, the program runs correctly and continues to perform checkpointing operation based on the position marked in the program.

5.3.3   *Basic Effectiveness and Existing Deficiencies*

Application live migration based on heterogeneous platforms increases randomness, diversity, and uncertainty of the system through dynamic live migration of applications across heterogeneous platforms, and overcomes the weakness that a single platform can be easily detected and attacked by attackers due to its long-term unchanged state. Attackers may not be able to predict when the application migrates and which platform the application is currently running on. Random migration of the application makes the passive scanning, information collection, and other operations meaningless, breaking the attack chain in reconnaissance phase. Because different platforms adopt different processors and operating systems, the attack behavior against a certain processor and operating system vulnerability will be invalid. This technology will be able to prevent binary code injection attacks related to processor instructions and kernel attacks related to operating systems.

If platform migration is not fast enough, attackers may find a way to attack the current system platform. If the number of heterogeneous platforms is not enough, or the randomness of application live migration is insufficient, the probability of successful attacks will be increased. However, increasing the number of heterogeneous platforms not only improves security, but also increases complexity, causing extra costs of construction and maintenance.

5.4 Dynamic Diversification of Web Services

The traditional Web service system is designed with a single architecture which remains unchanged for a long time after deployment, and this allows attackers to have enough time to implement reconnaissance and detection on the system. Once a vulnerability is discovered, attackers can exploit the vulnerability for a relatively long time. Other systems with the same architecture will also face similar threats. In order to eliminate the defects caused by the single architecture design of traditional Web services, this technology introduces diversity and uncertainty of Web service systems to build a dynamically changing service platform, thereby increasing difficulty for malicious attackers to detect and attack the system, and improving the system defense capability.

5.4.1 *Overview*

Currently, most Web services have the same composition architecture, usually consisting of Web server programs, Web applications, operating systems, and virtual layers [18]. Among the components that make up the Web service, as long as one component has a vulnerability, the entire system will be exposed to intrusion threat. The attack may only use a single vulnerability (such as a server buffer overflow vulnerability) to gain full control of the Web service system.

This technology employs diversification of the Web service to improve its defense capability. Its basic idea is to create multiple virtual servers with different software architectures, and make some virtual servers switch dynamically between offline and online states. The scheduler chooses which virtual server will handle the received requests. This technology adopts two kinds of diversification technologies. One is that the virtual server has a diversified software architecture, and for the service request at a different time, the virtual server randomly selects an online virtual server to provide services for it. The second is to switch some virtual servers to an online or offline state at fixed intervals or based on events. When the virtual server is switched to an offline state, it should be restored to the initial security state.

5.4.2 *Technical Principles*

(1) Dynamic diversification design architecture of Web services

Figure 5.18 shows the dynamic diversification architecture of Web services. This architecture puts potentially defective network software in a virtual server pool which can run on one or multiple hosts. The virtual servers are dynamically changing. At some time, some virtual servers provide services online, while the other virtual servers

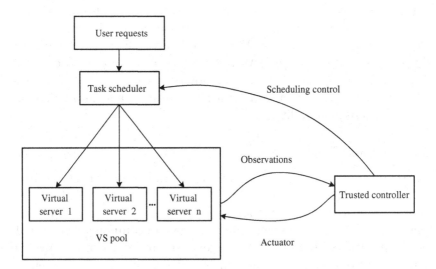

Figure 5.18.   Architecture of Web Service Diversification

stay offline and are restored to an initial security state. The service request from each client is assigned by the scheduler to a virtual server for processing. The trusted controller uses outputs of intrusion detection and exception sensors as observations. Intrusion detection and exception sensors are deployed in network, servers, and each virtual server to report states and events. Observations obtained by the trusted controller include response results of the processing system, effectiveness of the service, exposure time of the virtual server, and attack alarms. By obtaining these observations, the trusted controller invokes the actuator to locate and deal with the potential threats or suspicious services. Processing methods of the actuator include restarting services in the virtual server, shutting down suspicious processes, and restoring the virtual server to an initial security state. By observations and actuators, a closed control loop can be formed to automatically detect and manage the virtual server without manual intervention.

In Figure 5.18, each virtual server has three modes: online, shutdown, and offline. In online mode, it can provide services for client requests. When the trusted controller makes the virtual server offline, the virtual server enters a shutdown mode, in which it completes existing service requests, but will not accept new service requests. Shutdown mode is the intermediate state between online and offline modes. It ensures that the system completes the tasks currently being processed without interrupting them. When all requests are completed, the virtual server enters an offline mode and is restored to its initial security state. The virtual server switches cyclically among the three modes during the working process.

There are three trigger conditions for the virtual server to switch from online to offline. (a) Event-driven: When an exceptional event is detected or an integrity check fails, the virtual server in question is switched to an offline state. (b) Random selection: If there are no exceptional events and integrity check failures, select some virtual servers and switch them to an offline state. This can increase uncertainty of the system without affecting availability of the system. (c) Maximum time cycle: In order to restrict exposure time of the virtual server, it is necessary to limit its maximum online time. This can narrow the time window in which the system is exposed to intrusion attacks.

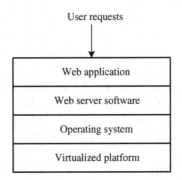

User requests

| Web application |
| Web server software |
| Operating system |
| Virtualized platform |

Figure 5.19.   Software Architecture of Web Service System

(2) Diversification design methods for virtual servers

Figure 5.19 shows the composition of the Web service [19]. There are too many design methods for the components of Web services to enumerate. Diversification design methods for each component of the system are described in the following, only with regard to the commonly used technologies.

(a) Web application

There are many methods to construct Web applications. CGI, ASP, PHP, J2EE, and .NET are mainstream methods to construct Web applications currently. Among them, ASP and .NET can only be used in IIS+Windows platforms, while the other methods can be used in a variety of platforms. It should be noted that CGI program written in C language has a certain platform dependence on the operating system. If used in different operating systems, it may need to be ported and new errors are easily introduced. PHP and J2EE have very good portability. In particular, J2EE applications use Java language, which itself is platform independent. J2EE is very suitable for distributed enterprise computing environments, and JDBC technology in J2EE can also transparently implement operations on multiple databases.

(b) Web server software

Apache and IIS are the most widely used Web servers. Apache can work not only in Unix-like systems but also in Windows systems, while IIS can only work in Windows systems. Web servers also attract close attention of intruders. If the intruder knows exactly the type and version of the Web server, he can attack it by searching for the vulnerable database and trying to exploit known vulnerabilities. In order to increase difficulty for attacks, IIS can usually be used as the Web server in Windows systems, and Apache can be used as the Web server in UNIX-like systems.

(c) Operating system

The operating system provides access interface to the computer for a variety of software. These operating systems mainly include two major series – Windows and Unix. There are fewer Windows versions, and there is little difference between them, while Unix is divided into many different versions such as Linux, AIX, and Frebsd. Information about the operating system draws close attention from intruders, and different operating systems have different command modes. Attackers have entirely different intrusion methods for the operating systems with different security policies. Generally, if intruders master much information about the operating system, the risk of system being intruded is greatly increased. Therefore, it is best to choose different operating systems, especially to choose two entirely different operating systems at the same time – Windows and Unix.

(d) Virtualization technology

Virtualization mainly includes technologies such as hypervisor-based virtualization and operating system-level virtualization. Hypervisor-based virtualization products include VMware, Xen, KVM, etc. This virtualization technology is more secure because it enables a highly isolated virtual machine environment. Operating system-level virtualization products include OpenVZ, Jail, etc. Compared with hardware-level virtualization products, they are more lightweight, start faster, and have less memory and scheduling overhead. However, the operating system kernel defects may threaten the applications running on it, due to the kernel supports multiple independent user space instances.

By selecting different design methods for Web applications, Web servers, operating systems, and virtualization technologies, respectively, the various combinations can generate many Web service systems with different architectures. During the selection process, it is necessary to pay attention to compatibility issues between the various components. For example, IIS can only work in Windows systems and does not support Linux systems.

(3) Process migration method

The correct operation of a Web service system plays an important role in the effectiveness of a large number of services and applications. Any unexpected service interruption or critical data loss will directly bring huge losses to users. So, the Web service system should provide a process migration mechanism to ensure continuous operation of critical services.

Process migration refers to migrating a process from the service system at the current node to the service system at the specified node. Similar to the process migration to idle nodes in a load balancing cluster to improve system performance, process migration in a Web dynamic diversity system is mainly used to improve system survivability and ensure the survival of services even if their service system is attacked. For example, when a Web service system is about to stop working due to a denial of service attack, the system can ensure that the critical business resumes running in another Web service system by process migration, and transparently provide services for users.

In general, a process migration procedure is divided into four steps [20]. (a) Select the migration process and target node. The system first extracts the process identifier to lock the pre-migrated process, and then selects the appropriate Web server as the target node according to the security state and idle time. (b) Send a migration request to the target node and negotiate. The source node first makes a request to the migration daemon of the target node, which receives the request and spawns a new process to deal with the migration request. (c) Extract and transfer the process state. The source node obtains state information of the migration process, including data of the control structure, code segment, data segment, or user stack segment, etc., and transfers it to the target node. According to this process state information, the target node modifies the newly generated process state information. (d) Resume process execution. The process in source node is in a dormant or dead state after the process migration is completed. The source node is converted to an offline state, and the new process on the target node is changed to a ready state to continue to provide external services.

(4) Management complexity

While improving security, introducing the diversity of Web service systems will increase the complexity of system management. There are two main problems: One is deployment of the complex system, and the other is management and maintenance of the system. Building multiple different virtual servers requires more resources than a single system. This problem can be solved by incremental deployment. When the system is built, it is not necessary to establish all virtual servers simultaneously, but to deploy some virtual servers first. After the running is stable, new virtual servers will be added gradually. This method can effectively shorten the time of system deployment.

There are two ways to reduce complexity of routine management and maintenance. The first way is to use a virtual server as a template that is always offline to ensure its security. When you need to patch or update some components of a certain type of virtual server, you can patch or update the virtual server as a template, and then clone the updated components to other virtual servers. The second way is to use automated tools and software that can automatically patch or update virtual servers. For example, the current asset lifecycle management tools have been able to identify the list of software that needs to be updated and automatically update the software.

In conclusion, making use of standard management and maintenance tools can greatly reduce complexity of virtual server management and maintenance. Therefore, complexity of the system is mainly reflected in development of multiple Web service versions that can adapt to multiple platforms.

5.4.3 *Basic Effectiveness and Existing Deficiencies*

Because services run on various systems consisting of different operating systems, server software, and virtualized platforms, it is difficult to develop attack methods that can be applied to all platforms. It is difficult for attackers to predict which system the task scheduler will choose to process user requests, and when the system will go online or offline. Constant changes of the system will make some process such as passive scan and information collection meaningless.

In addition, utilization of multiple operating systems enables systems to effectively defend against kernel attacks (such as Rootkit).

This technology cannot prevent logical defects of Web services, nor can it ensure the validity of input. So, attacks such as SQL injection may still work. Both the scheduler and the trusted controller are static and may be attacked. If attackers break the trusted controller, they can control or stop system rotation. If system rotation is not fast enough, attackers can still achieve the purpose of attack. Attackers may also master the attack method that can be used in a certain configuration, and system rotation may happen to have this configuration. In addition, this technology improves security at the cost of increasing redundancy and complexity of the system, lead to a higher cost of system deployment and management.

5.5 Platform Dynamization Based on Intrusion Tolerance

Intrusion tolerance refers to taking some necessary measures to ensure the continuous and correct operation of critical applications and services when an intrusion behavior is discovered or even some components have been damaged. Intrusion tolerance usually uses technical means such as redundancy and diversification.

Platform dynamization technology based on intrusion tolerance employs the technical principle of intrusion tolerance, adopts multiple heterogeneous service systems, and uses the dynamic change mechanism to process user service requests. For response results of each online service system, it returns the correct processing results to users through voting.

5.5.1 *Overview*

At present, the system is becoming more and more complex due to function integration. It is impossible to find all security vulnerabilities at once while they will be discovered constantly. Once attackers find a vulnerability, the problem becomes serious. Attackers can exploit this vulnerability to attack the system without being detected by general intrusion detection systems. Because it is impossible to determine all security vulnerabilities, it becomes very difficult to accurately determine whether it is an attack by analyzing the data flow.

When the system is intruded into, and the general security defense technologies fail or cannot entirely eliminate impact of the intrusion, intrusion tolerance becomes the last line of defense for the system. The purpose of intrusion tolerance is to enable the entire system to provide full or degraded services even if some components of the system are damaged by attackers. It is a fault-tolerant technology in cyber security and a tolerance mechanism proposed for network services. Intrusion tolerance uses the hardware or software fault-tolerant technology to shield impact of any intrusion or attack on system functions, to ensure security of the key system components and business continuity, so that the network system can still provide users with high-quality application services when it is under attack.

Platform dynamization based on intrusion tolerance uses redundancy and diversification design methods of intrusion tolerance technology, and makes the service system present characteristic of random and dynamic change. This makes it difficult for attackers to carry out effective reconnaissance and detection on the system, thereby improving the system defense capability.

5.5.2 *Technical Principles*

In the following, the concept of intrusion tolerance, commonly used methods and mechanisms are first introduced. Then the design structure of platform dynamization based on intrusion tolerance is discussed, and finally key technologies related to the design structure is described.

(1) Concept of intrusion tolerance

The concept of intrusion tolerance was first proposed by Fraga in 1985 [21], and its purpose was to ensure that the system can operate correctly or stop in a harmless, non-catastrophic way in the event of a system failure. It can be seen that the purpose of intrusion tolerance and fault tolerance is the same, and they both study how to ensure availability of system services. The difference between them is that the fault-tolerant technology focuses on random natural failures, most of which are non-human, while intrusion tolerance

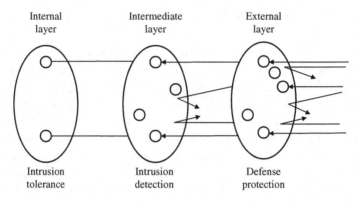

Figure 5.20.   Diagram of Intrusion Tolerance

focuses on malicious, man-made attacks, which are intelligent and uncontrollable.

Figure 5.20 illustrates the relationship between defense protection, intrusion detection, and intrusion tolerance [22]. When a system is threatened by an intrusion, the system's protective measures (such as vulnerability detection) will resist partial intrusion. In addition, some intrusions are detected by the system intrusion detection mechanism and reported to the system administrator for processing. However, there are still a small number of intrusions that cannot be detected and excluded, and in this situation, the intrusion tolerance technology is required to ensure security and availability of the system.

It can be seen from the concept of intrusion tolerance technology that intrusion tolerance mainly considers survivability, self-diagnosis, repair, and reconfiguration capabilities of the system when it is intruded into. It provides a certain resiliency for the system, so that the system can still provide uninterrupted services for legitimate users under the circumstance of being attacked. Platform dynamization technology based on intrusion tolerance uses diversification and redundancy design methods of intrusion tolerance technology, but their purposes are different. Intrusion tolerance focuses on how the system shields or contains an intrusion so that the system can continue to operate safely when it has already been intruded into. The purpose of platform dynamization is to build a dynamically changing platform, so that the system architecture observed by attackers

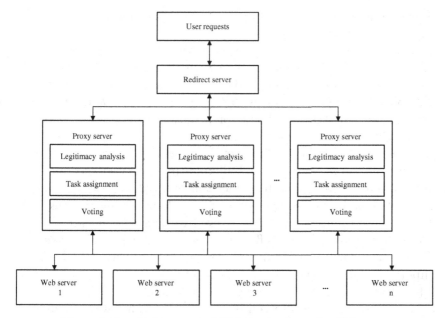

Figure 5.21. Architecture of Web Service Intrusion Tolerance

is uncertain and random, which breaks the attack chain in reconnaissance phase. In this sense, platform dynamization based on intrusion tolerance not only uses redundancy and diversification methods, but also uses randomization and dynamization mechanisms.

(2) Platform dynamization design architecture based on intrusion tolerance

Figure 5.21 is a platform dynamization design architecture based on intrusion tolerance for Web services. The entire system consists of three types of servers: redirect servers, proxy server group, and Web server group. Proxy servers and Web servers adopt redundancy and diversification designs to eliminate the vulnerability of a single design.

The system workflow is as follows: When the redirect server receives a service request from a user, it randomly forwards the user request to a proxy server. The proxy server first analyzes legitimacy of the request, then broadcasts the legitimate request to the Web server group for processing, votes on the result returned by the server, and finally returns the trusted result to the user. At the same time, the possible exceptional Web server is detected and restored to the initial security state.

The redirect server sends the user request to a proxy server, which then invokes the Web server. The redirect server should choose a proxy server as randomly as possible, so that attackers cannot predict the corresponding relationship between the request and the proxy server, which makes it difficult for attackers to carry out effective reconnaissance on the system.

The platform dynamization method shown in Figure 5.21 not only uses the redundancy method to build multiple proxy servers and Web servers, but also uses the diversification method. Because the intrusion behavior has a certain degree of randomness and intelligence, if only the redundancy method is used to deal with network intrusion, the expected defense effect may not be achieved. For example, if the same hardware redundant components are used to back up important data in the system, when intruders are able to successfully break into one of the components, it often implied that they can intrude into other backup components in the same way. Therefore, platform dynamization also needs to use diversified technical means. Here, diversification means that different redundant components in the same redundant method use different implementation methods. For example, the system can choose different hardware platforms to implement hardware redundancy, while software redundancy chooses different operating systems and server programs. Because vulnerabilities of different systems or programs are different, the successful intrusion into a server cannot quickly penetrate into other servers, which can effectively increase difficulty for attackers to intrude.

During the system running, when the response result of a Web server is found to be inconsistent with the expected result by voting, the system will instruct the failed server to quit from the server group to perform recovery operation. At this time, the proxy server will update the scheduling list and no longer assign tasks to it.

(3) Diversification design of Web server and proxy server

Web services usually consist of Web applications, Web servers, operating systems, and so on. In order to enhance capability of the system to defend against attacks, each Web server adopts a different design architecture under the premise of ensuring consistency of system functions. Web applications can use methods such as CGI, ASP,

PHP, J2EE, and .NET. Web servers can use Apache, IIS, etc. Operating systems include Windows, Linux, AIX, Frebsd, etc. Different versions can be used for each operating system. In the design, the compatibility between components should be considered comprehensively. In this way, by increasing redundancy and diversity of Web services, difficulty for attackers to carry out attacks can be increased.

Similarly, a proxy server can also adopt the diversification design methods similar to those of a Web server.

(4) Resource redistribution algorithm

Resource redistribution algorithm is suitable for Web server design. By dynamically adjusting the resources allocated to each service, it can ensure correct operation of critical services even if they are intruded into, and can defend against DoS attacks to a certain extent [23].

The services running on the server fall into two categories according to their importance: critical services and non-critical services. To improve the overall performance of the server, in addition to critical services, non-critical services are also allowed to run on the server. Resource redistribution algorithm focuses on the running state of critical services, and allows non-critical services to be terminated to ensure the correct operation of critical services.

Services require a certain number of resources to operate, such as CPU, storage, bandwidth, and so on. It is often difficult to determine whether there are sufficient resources to support the operation of critical services, and it is also difficult to decide which non-critical services should be terminated first during resource redistribution. In order to solve these two problems, two indicators – baseline and occupied time – are introduced. Baseline refers to the minimum number of resources required to provide a service with the lowest acceptable service quality, which can be described by the resources required for the service (such as CPU, storage, bandwidth, etc.). Occupied time refers to the total time in which a service takes up more resources than the baseline in a fixed time period. Occupied time must be greater than the threshold for the service to operate correctly. When the occupied time of a critical service is lower than the threshold, the system preferentially sacrifices non-critical services that occupy more resources to redistribute resources.

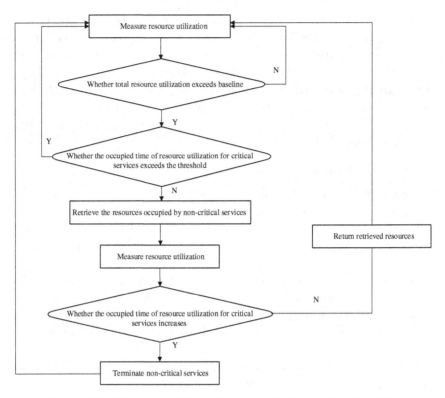

Figure 5.22.   Processing Flow of Resource Redistribution Algorithm

The detailed process of the algorithm is shown in Figure 5.22, which is described as follows.

(a) Establish the baseline of total resource utilization to measure resource utilization.
(b) If the total resource utilization is below the baseline, it indicates that there are many unoccupied resources. The algorithm continues to monitor resource utilization. If the occupied time of total resource utilization is above the threshold, resource utilization of each critical service needs to be measured.
(c) The algorithm continues to monitor resource utilization if the occupied time of resource utilization for critical services is higher than the threshold. Otherwise, the algorithm ensures correct operation of critical services by terminating non-critical services.

(d) In order to ensure operation of critical services, the algorithm retrieves the resources occupied by non-critical services according to the service priority.

(e) When redundant resources are available, and the occupied time of resource utilization for critical services does not increase, it indicates that the critical services do not need more resources. The retrieved resources will be returned to non-critical services, and the algorithm returns to the monitoring phase.

(f) If the occupied time of resource utilization for critical services increases after the resources occupied by non-critical services are retrieved, the algorithm will interrupt the operation of non-critical services.

Resource redistribution algorithm dynamically adjusts resource distribution to ensure the resources required for the operation of critical services, which can resist DoS attacks to a certain extent. When the operation of a critical service depends on other services, other services should also be protected as critical services. This algorithm assumes that there is no threat against critical services. If a critical service is attacked and consumes more resources, the algorithm will not be able to allocate sufficient resources to other critical services, which is also the limitation of this algorithm.

(5) Quantitative analysis of diversified Web servers

Intuitively, the more the Web servers that adopt diversification design methods, the more the difficulty for attackers to successfully intrude into the system, and the higher the system security. But the increasing number of Web servers has led to higher construction and maintenance costs. Therefore, we should consider how many Web servers need to be deployed to meet security requirements of the system. Byzantine Agreement is an effective method to solve this problem [24].

Byzantine Agreement technology originated from the Byzantine generals problem. It can be described as: Several Byzantine generals besieged a city, and the generals must negotiate together to decide whether to attack or retreat. If some attacked and some retreated, they might be defeated. But there were traitors among the generals, and they might expect the patriotic generals to lose the battle. The Byzantine generals problem is to clarify how to make the patriotic generals finally reach an agreement under such circumstances.

Although the treasonous generals could pass false information, it would not affect the patriotic generals to make a right decision. Scholars have proved that if n traitorous generals are to be tolerated, the total number of generals must be at least 3n + 1.

In a system using diversification and redundancy technologies, some servers may have been controlled by intruders and may not work properly. At this time, correct servers need to reach an agreement, which is obviously very similar to the Byzantine generals problem. Byzantine Agreement technology is based on the traditional Byzantine generals problem. It manages individual server members in the server group, maintains state information consistency between the servers, and can tolerate malicious servers spreading false information in the server group. According to Byzantine Agreement, to provide right services when n servers are intruded into, there are at least 3n + 1 servers required.

(6) Analysis of voting function

The voting part mainly includes three functional modules: response receiver, summary calculator, and voting machine [24]. The response receiver is used to receive response results returned by individual heterogeneous Web servers and cache them in the specified memory area for calculating the summary. The summary calculator calculates the summary value of each response result as input of voting machine. The voting machine compares summary values of individual response results. If the number of consistent responses exceeds the preset threshold value, the consistent response is considered to be the correct result and is returned to users as the final result. If the number of consistent responses does not exceed the threshold value, the service is not available.

The existing voting methods mainly include majority voting, dynamic voting, weighted voting, etc. [25]. Majority voting is the most widely used method with high efficiency and good adaptability. Before this method is described, the principle of consensus negotiation needs to be introduced, as it is the basis of this method.

(a) Principle of consensus negotiation

Suppose that input to the voting machine is the sequence of messages $\{x_1, x_2, \ldots, x_n\}$ sent by the Web server, the values input to the voting machine by any two Web servers i and j are x_i and x_j, respectively, and the threshold value is a. If $|x_i - x_j| \leq a$, then Web servers i and j are considered to meet the consensus negotiation, otherwise they are not. Threshold value of the voting machine is the basis for judging whether input values of any two replicas meet the consensus negotiation during voting process. The threshold value is predetermined prior to voting, but it can be changed through the system's reconfiguration policy.

(b) Majority voting

The basic idea of majority voting is that when response results of n Web servers are output to the voting machine, if response results of at least $(n+1)/2$ Web servers meet the principle of consensus negotiation, an output can be produced. At this time, one of the results that meet the consensus negotiation will be arbitrarily selected as output of the voting machine. Otherwise, if the consensus negotiation is not met, the majority voting machine will generate exception code indicating that the majority consensus is not achieved. In each round of voting, majority voting can solve the single point of failure.

(7) Analysis of service redirection function

Service redirection function isolates the entire system from the external network [26, 27]. After the redirect server receives a user request, it randomly directs the request to a proxy server according to availability of each agent. The proxy server processes the user request. When damage degree of the proxy server reaches a threshold and it is considered that there may be an attack against the proxy, migration of the entire system service can be completed by simply notifying the redirect server to switch requests of legitimate users to the IP address of another agent. For example, when the system receives a request from a user, it will randomly deliver this request to a proxy server according to the load balancing algorithm. If it is detected that TCP connection utilization rate of the proxy server exceeds 90%, it means that the proxy may be under attack. The redirect server can redirect IP address of the user to another proxy server with better performance to ensure that the user request will not be interrupted unexpectedly.

After receiving a request from a user, the redirect server returns the address of the proxy chosen to provide service to the user's browser, and notifies the proxy that a request will arrive and it needs to be ready to receive this request. The user browser will be automatically redirected to the proxy server. If the proxy does not receive notification from the redirect server, it will not process the incoming request. This can prevent the user from bypassing the redirection service to establish a connection with the proxy directly, thus preventing attacks on the proxy server.

5.5.3 *Basic Effectiveness and Existing Deficiencies*

Platform dynamization based on intrusion tolerance adopts diversification and redundancy technologies, which can avoid the risks caused by the same security vulnerabilities in different redundant components to a great extent, and prevent intruders from using the same method to intrude multiple redundant components. Because the proxy server and the Web server use multiple operating systems, this technology can defend against attacks to the vulnerabilities in the kernel and application layers of a certain operating system. At the same time, this technology randomly selects a proxy server through the redirect server, which increases uncertainty and dynamics of the system to a certain extent. The Web server uses the resource redistribution algorithm to prevent DoS attacks to a certain extent by dynamically adjusting the resources occupied by services to ensure operation of critical services. The proxy server has an input validity check function which can prevent attacks such as SQL injection attacks. In addition, because this technology uses a voting mechanism, the system has certain intrusion tolerance, and can still provide services reliably even when a few Web servers are attacked.

The redirect server is the single point source of failure of this system. If the redirect server is attacked, the entire system will fail. At the same time, security of the system is improved at the cost of complexity. Redundancy and diversification increase the costs and make it difficult to deploy, manage, and maintain the system.

5.6 Summary

This chapter made an in-depth study on one aspect of dynamic enablement – platform dynamization, and mainly introduced four platform dynamization technologies: platform dynamization based on reconfigurable computing, application live migration based on heterogeneous platforms, dynamic diversification of Web services,

Table 5.1. Comparison of Platform Dynamization Technologies

Serial Number	Dynamization Technology	Technical Principle	Effective Phase	Defense Effectiveness
1	Platform dynamization based on reconfigurable computing	Programmable hardware reconfiguration	Reconnaissance phase, loading phase	Buffer overflow attacks, bypass attacks
2	Application live migration based on heterogeneous platforms	Operating system-level virtualization, checkpointing	Reconnaissance phase, compilation phase	Binary code injection attacks, kernel attacks
3	Dynamic diversification of Web services	Diversified virtual servers	Reconnaissance phase, loading phase	Kernel attacks
4	Platform dynamization based on intrusion tolerance	Diversified servers, voting	Reconnaissance phase, loading phase	SQL injection attacks, DoS attacks

and platform dynamization based on intrusion tolerance. The comparison of these four technologies is shown in Table 5.1.

It can be seen from Table 5.1 that the starting points of these four platform dynamization technologies are identical. They all build a diversified operating platform, and randomly change the application operating environment in a way that the manager can control, so that the operating environment of the application presents diversity, uncertainty, randomness, and dynamics characteristics. The time window in which applications are exposed on a platform is narrowed, making it difficult for internal and external attackers to carry out effective reconnaissance and detection on the system, thereby breaking the attack chain in reconnaissance phase.

The four platform dynamization technologies use different technical principles, and their specific implementation methods and defense efficiency are also different.

Platform dynamization based on reconfigurable computing takes advantage of the characteristic that the reconfigurable system supports reconfiguration. Through diversified software/hardware task partitioning and differentiated logic circuit design, it obtains multiple configuration data variants running on general-purpose processors and programmable logic devices, and randomly changes the configuration data variants loaded in the system to realize the application operating platform dynamization during system operation. Each configuration data variant involves different software and programmable hardware design methods, so this technology can defend against attacks to specific software vulnerabilities and buffer overflow attacks, as well as bypass attacks to programmable hardware. If the number of configuration data variants is small and the randomness of change is not enough, attackers may find an attack method to attack the system.

Application live migration based on heterogeneous platforms uses operating system-level virtualization and checkpointing compilation technologies to realize migration of application operating environments and operating states, which is implemented across heterogeneous platforms while saving application operating states. Because heterogeneous platforms use different processors and operating systems, this technology can defend against binary code injection attacks and kernel attacks. If platform migration is not fast enough, attackers may find a way to attack the running system platform.

Diversification of Web services builds diversified virtual servers and uses two randomization methods: One is to randomly select virtual servers to process user requests. The second is to randomly switch some virtual servers to offline or online state to increase uncertainty and dynamics of the system. This technology can defend against attacks to specific software vulnerabilities and kernel attacks to operating system vulnerabilities, but it cannot prevent logical defects of Web services or cannot ensure the validity of input. At the same time, the scheduler and the trusted controller use a single architecture, so attackers may successfully attack them and control the entire system.

Platform dynamization based on intrusion tolerance uses the technical principle of intrusion tolerance and the ideas of redundancy and diversification, adopts multiple heterogeneous service systems, and randomly selects a proxy server to process user service requests. For the response result of each online service system, it returns the correct processing result to the user through voting. Due to the use of service redirection and validity check methods, this technology can defend against DoS attacks and SQL injection attacks to some extent. However, the redirect server is static, which may be a vulnerability exploited by attackers to intrude into the entire system.

The above four platform dynamization technologies can improve difficulty for attackers to detect and attack the system to some extent. However, the security of system is improved at the cost of increased complexity. These four technologies all face the problems of complex structure, difficult management and maintenance, and high construction costs. In practice, factors such as security, reliability, real-time performance, and cost should be considered comprehensively, and reasonable tradeoff should be made between security and complexity to maximize the benefits.

References

[1] Cardoso, J. M. P., Diniz, P. C., and Weinhardt, M. Compiling for reconfigurable computing: A survey. *ACM Computing Surveys (CSUR)*, 2010, 42(4): 13–27.

[2] Casola, V., Benedictis, A. D., and Albanese, M. A multi-layer moving target defense approach for protecting resource-constrained distributed devices. *Springer International Publishing*, 2014, 263: 299–324.

[3] Bstrin, G., Bussell, B., Turn, R., *et al.* Parallel processing in a restructurable computer system. *IEEE Transactions on Electronic Computers*, 1963, 12(6): 747–755.

[4] Todman, T. F., Constantinides, G. A., Wilton, S., *et al.* Reconfigurable computing: architectures and design methods. *IEEE Proceedings-Computers and Digital Techniques*, 2005, 152(2): 193–207.

[5] Jidin, R., Andrews, D. Z., Peck, W., *et al.* Evaluation of the hybrid multithreading programming model using image processing transforms. *19th Parallel and Distributed Processing Symposium, Denver, Colorado, USA*, 2005, (4–8): 153b.

[6] Huang, M., Narayana, V. K., Simmler, H., *et al.* Reconfiguration and communication-aware task scheduling for high performance reconfigurable computing. *ACM Transaction on Reconfigurable Technology and Systems*, 2010, 1(3).

[7] Wu, J. O., Fan, Y. H., Wang, S. F., *et al.* Using grey relation to FPGA multi-objective task scheduling on dynamic reconfigurable system. *Proceedings of the International Conference of Engineers and Computer Scientists*, 2014.

[8] Compton, K. and Hauck, S. Reconfigurable computing: A survey of systems and software. *ACM Computing Surveys*, 2002, 34(2): 171–210.

[9] Goldstein, S., Budiu, M., Mishn, M., *et al.* Reconfigurable computing and electronic nano technology. *Proceedings of IEEE International Conference on Application-Specific Systems, Architectures and Processors*, 2003, 132–142.

[10] Mu, J. and Lysecky, R. Autonomous hardware/software partitioning and voltage/frequency scaling for low-power embedded systems. *ACM Transactions on Design Automation of Electronic Systems (TODAES)*, 2009, 15(1): 2–11.

[11] Okhravi, H., Comella, A., Robinson, E., *et al.* Creating a cyber moving target for critical infrastructure applications using platform diversity. *Elsevier International Journal of Critical Infrastructure Protection*, 2012, 5(1): 30–39.

[12] Yu, Y., Guo, F., Nanda, S., *et al.* A feather-weight virtual machine for windows applications. *Proceedings of the 2nd International Conference on Virtual Execution Environments*, 2006, 24–34.

[13] Keahey, K., Doeringand, K., and Foster, I. From sandbox to playground: Dynamic virtual environments in the grid. *Proceedings of 5th IEEE/ACM International Workshop on Grid Computing*, 2004, 34–42.

[14] Kolyshkin, K. Virtualization in Linux, OpenVZ (ftp.openvz.org/doc/openvz-intro.pdf)[Z], 2006.

[15] Lee, S., Johnson, T. A., and Eigenmann, R. Cetus-an extensible compiler infrastructure for source-to-source transformation. *Proceedings of the Sixteenth International Workshop on Languages and Compilers for Parallel Computing*, 2003, 539–553.

[16] Rodriguez, G., Martin, M., Gonzalez, P., *et al.* CPPC: A compiler-assisted tool for portable check pointing of message-passing applications. *Concurrency and Computation: Practice and Experience*, 2010, 22(6): 749–766.

[17] Stellner, G. CoCheck: Check pointing and process migration for MPI. *Proceedings of the Tenth International Parallel Processing Symposium*, 1996, 526–531.

[18] Jajodia, S., Ghosh, A. K., Swarup, V., *et al.* Moving target defense: Creating asymmetric uncertainty for cyber threats. *Springer New York*, 2011, 131–151.

[19] Yin, L. and He, S. Research and implementation of an intrusion tolerance system. *Journal on Communications*, 2006, 27(2): 131–136.

[20] Reynolds, J., Just, J., Lawson, E., *et al.* The design and implementation of intrusion tolerant system. *Proceedings of the 2002 International Conference on Dependable Systems and Network*. USA, 2002, 285–292.

[21] Fraga, J. S. and Powell, D. A fault and intrusion-tolerant file system. *Proceedings of the 3rd International Conference on Computer Security, Ireland*, 1985, 203–218.

[22] Deswarte, Y. and Powell, D. Internet security: An intrusion-tolerant approach. *Proceeding of the IEEE*, 2006, 94(2): 432–441.

[23] Byoung, J. M. and Joong, S. C. An approach to intrusion tolerance for mission-critical service using adaptability and diverse replication. *Elsevier Computer Science*, 2003.

[24] Qin, H. Research on the theory and applied technology of network intrusion tolerance. Nanjing University of Science and Technology, 2009.

[25] Huang, Y. and Ghosh, A. K. Automating intrusion response via virtualization for realizing uninterruptible web services. *Eighth IEEE International Symposium on Network Computing and Applications*, 2009, 114–117.

[26] Arsenault, D., Sood, A., and Huang, Y. Secure, resilient computing clusters: Self-cleansing intrusion tolerance with hardware enforced security (SCIT/HES). *Proceedings of the Second International Conference on Availability, Reliability and Security, IEEE Computer Society*, Washington, D. C., 2007, 343–350.

[27] Huang, Y., Arsenault, D., and Sood, A. Incorruptible self-cleansing intrusion tolerance and its application to DNS security. *Journal of Networks*, 2006, 1(5): 21–30.

Chapter 6

Dynamic Data Defense

In previous chapters, we introduced the related technologies of dynamic software defense and dynamic network defense. According to the attack surface model, in addition to probing and attack implementation from the two aspects of software and network, attackers can also launch attacks from the perspective of data, because data is also one of the main system resources that attackers rely on or use to launch attacks against the system. In order to effectively prevent such attacks, it is necessary to explore system defense methods based on data dynamization technology.

Dynamic data defense mainly refers to the ability to dynamically change format, syntax, coding, or expression of relevant data in accordance with defense requirements of the system, thereby increasing attackers' attack surface and enhancing attack difficulty. In the currently known studies, data dynamization technologies mainly refer to the randomization and diversification technologies for in-memory data [1–3]. However, in some studies, diversification technologies for protocol syntax and configuration information data [4] in applications are also classified into the research field of data dynamization technology. In order to maintain unity of the concept, this book collectively refers to the above two related technologies based on dynamic data change to achieve system defense effects as dynamic data defense technologies.

6.1   Essence of Dynamic Data Defense

We have seen many dynamization technologies in previous chapters of this book, such as the classic technologies of Instruction Set Randomization (ISR) [5–9], Address Space Layout Randomization (ASLR) [10, 11], network configuration randomization [12], and so on. These technologies achieve defense effect by dynamically changing instruction set, memory address space, and network configuration information. In theory, the methods of dynamization technology can learn from each other. Instruction set randomization technology can be easily used for data randomization, and software diversification can also be extended to data diversification. However, in practice, data dynamization technology is both similar to and different from other technologies such as ISR and ALSR. The most important point is that, whether in ISR technology or ALSR technology, the changing resource object is relatively fixed in the original system: instruction set of a system may be different from that of similar systems, but it is relatively stable for user input. After the memory address distribution of an application has changed, it may not be what the attacker imagines, but it is still fixed at a certain stage. Data is different. When users use a system, input data is ever-changing and unpredictable. That is to say, the data itself has the characteristic of change, and compared with the data interacting with users, static data is in the minority. Then the question arises: Since the data itself is changing and diverse, what kind of data is data dynamization technology aimed at? And how does it dynamize the data? To explain these issues, we will explore the related concepts of dynamic data defense from multiple dimensions.

(1) What kind of data should be dynamized

The concept of data is complex and vague. Under the classic von Neumann computer architecture, instructions and data are all stored in binary form, and there is no obvious difference between them in address space. Macroscopically, applications, drivers, and database data stored in the computer are all binary data, and the byte streams transmitted on the network are also data. In this interpretation, it is impossible to distinguish between data dynamization technology and other dynamization technologies.

From the day the Pandora's box of buffer overflow attacks was opened, Trojan horses, worms, and zombies that are active on the global Internet have been eager to use this weapon to expand their territory. Today, most large-scale and high-severity cyber attacks around the world rely on the use of buffer overflow. The root cause of buffer overflow is that there is no essential distinction between instructions and data in the von Neumann computer architecture. If instructions are not executed, they are ordinary data; if ordinary data are misjudged as instructions by CPU, they may become authentic instructions, and the static execution becomes active execution, thereby resulting in malicious behaviors. Therefore, in this book the "data" in the data dynamization technology mainly refers to the ordinary data as opposed to the instruction data. At the level of programming language, the data here refers to operands, not instruction opcode or operators defined in the programming syntax. Most data involved in dynamization technology [1–3] in this chapter refer to the data in memory, but the last section "Data Diversification for Web Application Security" also involves the users' data information [4] used to configure the application environment.

(2) Goals and technical characteristics of dynamic data defense

Data dynamization is the means, not the purpose. Earlier, we analyzed the basic category of the concept of data in data dynamization, but this scope is still too large. In practice, what kind of data is dynamically processed is completely determined by its defense target. Relevant researches have shown that the defense effect of data dynamization technology can be reflected in the following three aspects: (a) to prevent unintentional design errors in the system; (b) to prevent attackers from maliciously injecting code and carrying out buffer overflow attacks; and (c) to prevent SQL injection and cross-site scripting attacks in Web applications. So, what kind of dynamization operations should be performed on what kind of data to achieve the above defense goals? In brief, the dynamic data defense technology does not dynamize, randomize, and diversify all data, but adopts dynamization technologies to specific data for specific purposes. The common points of these technologies are: (a) to find a policy to keep data semantics unchanged, so that data dynamization behaviors do not affect the data semantics itself; (b) to avoid vulnerabilities or effectively discover attacks by dynamizing the selected data. The specific implementation technologies will be described in detail in what follows.

(3) Data encryption technology belongs to dynamic data defense technology

A controversial issue is whether the conventional data encryption technology is counted as a data dynamization technology. We think that data encryption technology randomizes data, can realize dynamic change of data and achieve the system defense effect with the help of the key change. Therefore, according to the previous definition of dynamic data defense technology, data encryption technology should belong to the semantic category of data dynamization technology. However, both technological implementation and theoretical integrity of the general data encryption technology have been described in detail earlier in the research literature because it has been widely used in many fields such as secure data storage and confidential communication. Therefore, this book will not separately describe the general implementation of data encryption technology in detail. It should be noted that in the following we will still use data encryption technology as the basis to implement some data dynamization technologies.

6.2   Data Randomization

6.2.1   *Overview*

As mentioned above, Instruction Set Randomization technology (ISR) [5, 6, 8, 13] can encrypt content of instructions in the program, thereby preventing the attacker from injecting code. ALSR [11] can randomize the data and code positions in memory so that the overflow program cannot jump to a specified address, thereby preventing attacks. However, both methods have disadvantages in specific practice. ISR technology needs hardware support to run efficiently. ALSR technology also faces many problems, for example, an attacker can try to rewrite memory data by rewriting the memory address or using heap spray [5] technology that places multiple copies of data in the address space selected by the program.

Microsoft's Cadar *et al.* [1] noticed that ISR and ALSR technologies had obvious defects in solving the problem of non-control-data attacks [14]. ISR technology cannot work because such attacks do not inject code. At the same time, ASLR technology only randomizes the stack, the base address of static data, etc., and has no effect on data overflow in non-control-data attacks. In order to solve this problem, Cadar *et al.* proposed a method called data randomization [1], which classifies and encrypts the data that is written into memory in the program and avoids the possibility that one type of data can overflow to the address space of another, so that original values of the parameters cannot be modified. Any function that attempts to perform a write operation will write randomized data into memory, and any function that attempts to perform a read operation will also read the randomized data that has been encrypted. As long as the overflow attack is processed in different types of data, the data that has been randomized by this type of key will inevitably fail to be decrypted correctly in another type.

The data randomization method is a classic case of data dynamization. Considering the popularity of Windows system, if this method can be reflected in implementation of Windows system, it will effectively improve security of Internet hosts in preventing buffer overflow. In order to better understand this technology, its implementation principle and process will be further described in what follows.

6.2.2   *Technical Principles*

Before explaining data randomization technology, it is necessary to understand its enemy, i.e. the attack method of non-control-data attack. Non-control-data attack is a real attack against SSH service proposed by Chen *et al.* [14] at the USENIX Security Conference in 2005. Figure 6.1 shows the vulnerable code in SSH service.

In Figure 6.1, in the 8th to 10th lines of the code, if the length of Connection object c is a little longer, attackers can cause the message array to overflow, thereby rewriting the user variable. If attackers write an explicit UserID value in the overflowed data, such as the UserID corresponding to the root user, then the SSH Server will use privileges of the root user to execute commands. The reason why this attack is called non-control-data attack is that the attack does not forcefully change any control flow in the program, but raises control permission of the program.

```
1:      void ProcessConnection (connection *c) {
2:          cred_t user;
3:          char message [1024];
4:          int i=0;
5:
6:          auth_user (&user , c);
7:          while (!end_of_message (c))  {
8:              message [i]=get_next_char (c);
9:              i++;
10:
11:     }
12:         seteuid (user.user_id);
13:         ExecuteRequest (message);
14:  }
```

Figure 6.1.   Simplified Vulnerable Code in Remote SSH Service

In order to resist this kind of attack, data randomization technology classifies pointer objects in the program by statically analyzing the program code. It divides the data objects that can be accessed through the same pointer into the same class, otherwise they are reclassified. In Figure 6.1, two data objects, message and user, are divided into different classes. After static analysis, a random mask is assigned to each class when the system is loaded, through which all pointer objects in the same class are randomized. In order to realize this randomization, the program needs to be modified so that processing code is written at the required stage.

In order to describe the process of data randomization more clearly, we will describe it in five steps as follows.

(1) Step 1: Compute the equivalence classes in data objects

Computing equivalence classes is the foundation and difficulty of data randomization. Cadar used the Phoenix compilation tool [1] to assist in analysis of the source code. The main process is as follows: First, the Phoenix tool is used to convert the code into intermediate language code, as shown in Figure 6.2; then, conservative algorithm is used to globally scan all pointed data objects in the program code, collect subset constraints, and perform iterative processing according to the references of instruction operands until none of the data objects are referenced by any pointers. Data objects that can be directly accessed, such as the constant i in Figure 6.1, are divided into one separate class. The classification result of generated data objects is in the form of {i}, {[t277], message}. Combined with Figure 6.2, we can see that [t277] is the only pointer operand in the figure. It can

```
        _i =ASSIGN 0
        CALL &_auth_user, &_user, _c
$L6:    t274=CALL&_end_of_message, _c
        t275=COMPARE (NE) t274, 0
        CONDITIONALBRANCH (True) t275, $L7, $L8
$L8:    t278=CALL&_get_next_char, _c
        t277=ADD &_message, _i
        [t277]=ASSIGN t278
        _i=ADD _i, 1
        GOTO $L6
$L7:    CALL &_seteuid, _user+4
        CALL &_ExecuteRequest, &_message
```

Figure 6.2.   Representation of MIR with Intermediate Language

be concluded from the analysis of pointer reference that [t277] points to the message array, so these two data objects should be grouped into the same equivalence class.

(2) Step 2: Optimize the set of equivalence classes through security analysis

If the amount of program code is relatively large, static analysis will obtain a huge set of equivalence classes according to the method to obtain equivalence classes in step 1. Randomizing data based on large-scale equivalence classes obviously consumes a lot of system resources. Therefore, it is necessary to conduct further screening and analysis on these equivalence classes, discard most of the equivalence classes that do not have security threats, and only keep a small set of classes that may have potential security risks.

Cadar put forward the following analytical principles.

Principle 1: If memory security will not be affected when the operand is accessed at runtime, the operand is considered secure. In general, the analysis system will mark all temporary variables, local variables, and global operands in the MIR as secure operands, because these operands always point to registers or fixed-length bytes starting at a fixed offset between the frame pointer and the data segment.

Principle 2: For pointer operands, it is necessary to determine whether read and write operations performed by the pointer are within the length range. If accessing length does not exceed the limit, the pointer operand is considered secure. In actual operation, the lengths of pointed collection objects (such as structures, classes) and static arrays, etc. are first collected, and then the minimum and maximum lengths of the objects pointed to by the pointer are calculated through symbolic computation. If the length cannot be calculated, the minimum value is conservatively assumed to be 0. Given the maximum and minimum lengths of the pointed object by the pointer and the current target length of read and write access, you can determine whether the pointer can access across the boundary. If not, the pointer operand is considered secure.

Based on the above-mentioned two principles, a large number of secure sets of equivalence classes can be filtered out, avoiding insertion of a lot of redundant code in the subsequent randomization. For example, in Figure 6.2, only the equivalence class which [t277] belongs to is unsecure.

(3) Step 3: Assign masks to equivalence classes

In order to randomize the operands in equivalence classes, it is necessary to assign a mask to each equivalence class, and perform encryption and decryption operations on each operand by means of XOR. In the process of assigning masks, the length of operands between equivalence classes and within equivalence classes may be inconsistent, and even the same operand may be accessed differently at runtime. For example, an array of int type may be accessed by char *. Therefore, it is necessary to adopt an effective policy when assigning a mask to each equivalence class to ensure that each byte of the operand in the equivalence class is XOR-processed by the same mask.

To solve this problem, Cadar proposed two solutions.

Solution 1: Determine length of the mask based on the minimum length of operands in the equivalence class. If the equivalence class has two operands, one with 4 bytes, and the other with 2 bytes, then the mask of the equivalence class is 2 bytes long. If length of the encrypted operand exceeds 2 bytes, length of the mask needs to be extended.

Solution 2: Assign a mask of 4 bytes to all equivalence classes. All operands in the equivalence class can align the class mask according to their own length and dynamically obtain the mask suitable for themselves. This solution is more secure than solution 1 because it ensures that all bits of the operand are XOR-operated by

```
t2=BITXOR o2, m2
t3=BITXOR o3, m3
t1=OPERATION t2, t3
o1=BITXOR t1, m1
```

Figure 6.3.   Example of Memory Code Instrumentation

independent and non-repetitive masks, but this method will cause more performance costs under some conditions of usage.

(4) Step 4: Encrypt/decrypt memory access through code instrumentation

After the equivalence class and the corresponding mask are computed, the data randomization compiler needs to add code to encrypt/decrypt memory access. Code instrumentation also needs to convert the code into MIR language, because the previous equivalence class acquisition is based on the intermediate language MIR. In implementation, the compiler needs to insert code to encrypt operands before executing memory write operations, and insert code to decrypt operands before executing memory read operations. Figure 6.3 shows transformation of the MIR instruction "o1=OPERATION o2, o3", in which o1, o2, and o3 are unsecure original operands, and m1, m2, and m3 are masks. It can be seen that when the operands o2 and o3 are read, it is necessary to first perform XOR operations with the corresponding masks to decrypt and read the operands; after the result t1 of the real instruction is obtained, it is also necessary to use the mask to XOR t1 to complete encrypted writing of the operands.

In the actual code instrumentation process, it is only necessary to perform code instrumentation on unsecure operands, which will effectively reduce its workload and complexity. In his research, Cadar also discussed how to perform code instrumentation during function calls and how to use the method of code instrumentation with fixed-length masks.

(5) Step 5: Update the mask when the program is loaded

Generation and security of masks are also an important part of data randomization. During compilation, the compiler generates a mask file that contains the mask for each equivalence class and the mask used before. Each time the program is loaded, the loader will read the previous mask based on the mask file, query the corresponding new mask value according to the mask, and update it to the binary file. However, there is no mention in the research literature about how this mask file is securely saved.

6.2.3 *Basic Effectiveness and Existing Deficiencies*

Data randomization technology randomizes the reading and writing of unsecure data in memory, which effectively increases difficulty of attacking protected applications. Even if the attacker knows the principle, he must obtain or guess the key used to randomize data in some way to crack the method. If length of the key is 4 bytes, the attacker using brute force methods must face a guess space of 2^{32} bits. Even in the worst case where the mask is only 8 bits, the attacker must guess from 2^8 possibilities. However, brute force attack may lead to a large number of program failures, so it is more likely to be detected.

This technology also has some defects. Operands in the same group use the same key, so the attacker may exploit this vulnerability to obtain the desired memory object. In order to make this technology effective, all link libraries should be protected by encapsulation. If a link library is neglected, the attacker may bypass protection of this technology.

6.3 Data Diversification of N-Variant

6.3.1 *Overview*

Randomization technology is one of the most commonly used technologies in dynamic defense technologies. This book has introduced Instruction Set Randomization (ISR) technology, Address Space Layout Randomization technology (ALSR) [10, 11], and Data Randomization (DR) technology [1]. These technologies comprehensively use encryption/decryption methods to randomize specific elements in the information system, which can effectively resist attacks such as buffer overflow attacks. Feasibility of these technologies is based on the fact that the attacker cannot guess the randomized key. However, Nguyen-Euong *et al.* [2, 15] of University of Virginia, United States, believe that it is very difficult to ensure security of these randomized keys in practice, and there have been studies proving that the finite entropy problem of randomization can be used to counter ISR and ALSR technologies, so Nguyen-Euong *et al.* proposed a new method of data diversification to counter attacks against data [2].

The adversarial object assumed by this technology is still the non-control-data attack problem introduced in Section 6.2 [14], in which attackers can use data overflow to write specific data to obtain privileged access. Different from the way of data randomization, this technology mainly applies the idea of N-variant technology to the field of data confrontation. Through diversifying data of a specific data type, a variant program consistent with semantics of the original program is constructed, and in the envisaged effect of diversification processing, it is impossible for an attacker to successfully attack two variants at the same time with one input. Therefore, the system administrator can set a monitor to compare behaviors of the input value after being executed by various variants, thereby judging rationality of the input value. If there is a difference in behaviors, it is considered that an attack behavior has been detected.

6.3.2 *Technical Principles*

The three core points of this technology are: constructing variants based on re-expression function; ensuring semantic consistency of the variants; the way to conduct behavior detections.

(1) Construct variants based on re-expression function

Each application is composed of a series of interpreters. For example, a Web application needs to use multiple interpreters to process network protocols, HTTP, the interpretive scripts that implement application logic, executable database queries, access services of the operating system, and execution of machine instructions. In order to implement an effective supply, the attacker needs to break through a series of interpreter levels, and finally control the input into the designated interpreter to obtain required resources. For example, the payload of malicious code contains x86 machine instructions, and the target interpreter is the machine hardware itself. If a Shell needs to be opened in the payload, then one of the interpreters is the file system. It can be said that a simple attack that exploits vulnerabilities may involve multiple different interpreters.

The reason why the attacker can send malicious data to the target interpreter is that the high-level interpreter contains vulnerabilities. Human negligence is often involved in software development and deployment, and the unintentional negligence is likely to turn into security vulnerabilities.

Figure 6.3 shows an N-variant system with two variants. These two variants execute the same program, but use different interpreters when dealing with certain data types. The attacker can accurately construct external input to attack the system, but only one communication channel can be used because the system interface that the attacker faces is external. The same type of input data containing malicious payloads may be parsed by a series of interpreters in the application. This series of parsers is simply referred to as the APP interpreter in Figure 6.3. By exploiting vulnerabilities in it, the embedded malicious data will reach the target interpreter.

The general diversification technology attempts to defeat the attack by changing the interface between interpreters. If the attacker does not know representation of the interface, it is difficult to guess what kind of input will have an effect on the target interpreter. Data diversification technology constructs new variants by using data re-expression function (R function for short). If possibility space of data re-expressing function is relatively large, it means that the security is high. The reason is that if the attacker wants to inject specific malicious data to cheat the target interpreter, he must first know the specific inverse data R function.

In general, N-variant data diversification technology avoids the high security requirements for keys in randomization algorithms, and the design of its R function meets the following principles: For a variant, the specific data legal for it will not be legal for other variants. The design goal of the target compiler is not to be able to directly distinguish between malicious data and normal data, but it needs to guarantee that only normal application data will be re-expressed by R function and be correctly parsed after being sent to the target interpreter; and that malicious data will be directly sent to multiple target interpreters without being interpreted by R function.

Taking Figure 6.4 as an example, the two variants contain different R functions, namely R_0 and R_1. Legal data in the same group are respectively converted based on R function in multiple variants. In order to maintain data semantics, the target interpreter will add the

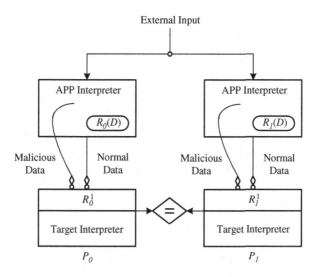

Figure 6.4. *N*-Variant Based on Data Diversification

inverse R function R_0^{-1} and R_1^{-1} before interpretation, which establishes a different data interpretation between the APP interpreter and the target interpreter. But malicious data are violently injected, so they will bypass R function directly, that is, they will be sent directly to the target interpreter without re-expression.

2. Ensure semantic consistency of variants

For the target type T and the known program P, in order to establish a normal equivalence property for each variant P_i, the following steps need to be performed.

(a) All legal data about type T in P will use R function R_i.
(b) All instructions that directly operate T value in P_i will be converted to save the original semantics when operating the data processed by R function.
(c) The inverse R function should satisfy the reciprocal property, namely

$$\forall x : T, R_i^{-1}(R_i(T)) \equiv T \qquad (6.1)$$

Program conversion is required in the first two steps. To convert legal program data, it is necessary to identify the constant value of the target type in P, and apply R_i function to generate variant P_i.

This operation can be carried out directly if it is easy to determine the target type, but how to maintain semantic equivalence is a difficult problem, which needs to be analyzed according to the actual situation.

3. How to conduct behavior detections

The ideal detection effect requires that if a variant is successfully attacked, then other variants must be able to indicate the attack. This requires the target interpreter, when comparing input data, to be able to detect any injected data into the target type. To achieve this goal, the inverse R function must satisfy the following disjoint property, namely

$$\forall x : T, R_0^{-1}(x) \neq R_1^{-1}(x) \tag{6.2}$$

Based on this property, a warning will be generated when any equivalent data are sent to the target interpreter. The reason is that their different inverse functions will produce different analytical results.

Case analysis: Design idea of the N-variant system based on data diversification technology was introduced above. The following illustrates this technology with the example of constructing N-variant based on the UID data type given by David *et al*. At this point, R function is as shown in Table 6.1.

By adopting data diversification technology for UID data types, attacks against user ID data can be defeated. As in Section 6.2, one of

Table 6.1. R Function

Variant	Target Type	R Function	Inverse R Function
Address space partition [16]	Address	$R_0(\alpha) = \alpha$ $R_1(\alpha) = \alpha + 0\text{x}80000000$	$R_0^{-1}(\alpha) = \alpha$ $R_1^{-1}(\alpha) = \alpha - 0\text{x}80000000$
Extended address space partition [9]	Address	$R_0(\alpha) = \alpha$ $R_1(\alpha) = \alpha + 0\text{x}80000000$ $+ \text{ } offset$	$R_0^{-1}(\alpha) = \alpha$ $R_1^{-1}(\alpha) = \alpha - 0\text{x}80000000$ $- \text{ } offset$
Instruction set label [16]	Instruction	$R_0(inst) = 0 \,\|inst$ $R_1(inst) = 0 \,\|inst$	$R_0^{-1}(0 \,\|inst\,) = inst$ $R_1^{-1}(0 \,\|inst\,) = inst$
UID variant	UID	$R_0(u) = u$ $R_1(u) = u \oplus 0\text{x}7\text{FFFFFFF}$	$R_0^{-1}(u) = u$ $R_1^{-1}(u) = u \oplus 0\text{x}7\text{FFFFFFF}$

the attack types defended by this technology is also the non-control-data attack proposed by Chen *et al.* [14]. The specific attack method is shown in Section 6.2, which will not be described in detail here.

In the specific implementation process, in order to achieve data diversification, not only construction of the variant itself, but also cooperation and support of the operating system are required. The variant designed in this chapter needs to modify the Linux kernel to synchronize the relevant system calls when the variant is executed, and to monitor operating results of each variant. Such design is beneficial in the following two aspects.

(a) When multiple variants call the system, it will first determine whether the calls of multiple variants are consistent. If so,the real system call function interface will be called by the encapsulated function. This ensures that the real system call will only be called once without affecting the availability of the program.

(b) The purpose of attack detections: According to the design idea of basic N-variant data diversification, if differences in variant behaviors are detected, malicious attacks are considered to have occurred.

In short, the following problems need to be solved in the specific implementation process: defining R function; applying R function; modifying relevant system calls.

(1) Defining R function

R function is the basic condition for constructing variants. Two variants will be defined here.

The first variant P_0 is the original program itself. R function and the inverse R function are original values of UID.

$$R_1(u) = u \qquad (6.3)$$

$$R_1^{-1}(u) = u \qquad (6.4)$$

The second variant P_1 defines R function $R_1(u)$ and the inverse R function $R_1^{-1}(u)$ as

$$R_1(u) = u \oplus 0 \times 7\text{FFFFFFF} \qquad (6.5)$$

$$R_1^{-1}(u) = u \oplus 0 \times 7\text{FFFFFFF} \qquad (6.6)$$

The analysis shows that both R function and the inverse R function of each variant satisfy the reciprocal property, and inverse functions of the two variants satisfy disjointness.

For R function of P_1, the ideal object is that XORs with the UID value should be $0 \times 7\text{FFFFFFF}$, because it can protect all bits from being attacked. However, the UID value is generally unsigned type. In the Linux system kernel, the negative value of UID has special meanings. Therefore, it is difficult to filter the highest bit, while in the actual attack environment, single-bit attacks are meaningless, so such a situation is not considered here.

(2) Applying R function

In practical use of R function, not only the source code of the original program but also the relevant system call function needs to be modified. According to the definition of R function as mentioned, the first variant P_0 is the original program itself, and the second variant P_1 needs internal application of R function in the original program. Taking a program written in C language as an example, after locating the variable of type uid_t, the following operations should be performed.

(a) All UID values must be converted with $R_1(u)$ function. For example, in order to maintain semantics, first convert if (! getuid ()) into getuid()==0, and then synchronously convert the constant value 0 according to the definition of $R_1(u)$ function.

(b) All operation functions that operate the UID value in the program must be converted in order to maintain the original semantics of the UID value. However, in the actual application environment, the program operations on UID are generally value assignment and comparison operation, and the UID data itself has been converted, so these two operations do not need to be converted. But if it is any other operation, additional conversion is required.

(3) Modifying system call

In order to detect attacks by comparing operation behaviors of multiple variants, it's necessary to supplement system call functions to implement the detection. There are three categories of new system call functions as given in Table 6.2.

Table 6.2. Supplemental System Calls

	Function	Description
1	Uid_t uid_value (uid_t)	Pass the current UID value into the kernel, and compare the UID values among several variants through the kernel, return if they are the same (after applying the inverse R function), or trigger an attack alarm if they are not.
2	bool cond_chk (bool)	Check if condition values are the same among variants.
3	cc_eq (uid_t, uid_t) cc_neq (uid_t, uid_t) cc_lt (uid_t, uid_t) cc_reg (uid_t, uid_t) cc_gt (uid_t, uid_t) cc_geq (uid_t, uid_t)	Compare UID parameters and return the comparison result.

The first category is used to obtain the UID value, but true size of the value relies on the current values of multiple variants compared by the system kernel. If the values are consistent (the variant needs to execute the inverse R function), a result is returned; if inconsistent, the variant behavior is considered abnormal, and an attack warning can be triggered. For example, getpwnname (uid) needs to be modified to getpwnname (uid_value (uid)).

The second category of function is suitable for the case where the variant compares UID variables with UID constant values, for example, pw=Null needs to be modified to cond_chk (pw==Null).

The third category of function is suitable for the case where the variant compares UID variables with UID variables. In Table 6.2, the functions that start with cc respectively represent the following operations: $=$, $\neq$, $<$, $\leqslant$, $>$, $\geqslant$. For example, uid==variant_ROOT needs to be modified to cc_eq (uid, variant_ROOT).

David *et al.* implemented the above-mentioned data diversification technology for the UID data type on Apache Web Server. There are a total of 73 changes in source code: 15 applications of R function to UID constant values; 16 references of new system calls to expose UID value to the monitor; 22 UID value comparison operations; 20 condition status inspections.

6.3.3　Basic Effectiveness and Existing Deficiencies

David *et al.* [2] verified feasibility of such technology by experiment, and analyzed performance loss caused by the technology. The result shows that for different servers, performance loss is within the range of 1%–4.5%. Considering significant improvement of the security brought about by the technology, the loss ratio is acceptable.

Compared with the general data randomization algorithm, the greatest advantage of this technology is that it can achieve data diversification with no need to ensure security of the key, and effectively prevent non-control-data attacks. However, the protection scope of this technology is relatively limited. Only a small amount of data (UID value) is randomized in the method mentioned in the system, and it is difficult to implement. To achieve the purpose of attack detection, it is often necessary to modify or add system calls, and modify the operating system source code and program source code. At the current research stage, costs of development and maintenance are relatively high because of the reliance on manual code development.

6.4　N-Copy Data Diversification for Fault Tolerance

6.4.1　Overview

N-version programming and Recovery Block model are two methods for building fault-tolerant software [16,17]. Both of these technologies rely on the diversification of design, that is, multiple implementations are designed for one method.

The N-version model requires that a plurality of independently developed programs of different versions receive the same input, respectively, and output of each program is checked by voting to determine whether the input is acceptable. In general, a multi-vote result is regarded as the correct output result. The Recovery Block model submits algorithm results to the test set, and if the results fail test, the system restores machine state to the state before running the algorithm, and executes other candidate algorithms, which loops until a satisfactory result is produced or all candidate algorithms are tested. It can be seen that both models require multiple implementations of programs, as well as overcoming the problem of semantic equivalence, which is very difficult to implement. It should be noted that the N-version programming and N-variant described above are different expressions of the same concept, and the concept here is mainly derived from the literature [16, 17].

Paul *et al.* [3] believe that in order to improve fault tolerance of software, we can not only adopt the design diversification technology, that is, constructing multiple equivalent program bodies to run the same data, but also adopt the data diversification technology whereby one program body runs multiple equivalent datasets. One thing to be noted is that data diversification does not always have the same meaning in each specific technology. They are all called data diversification in English, but their meanings vary with different researches. For example, the data diversification introduced in Section 6.3 is obviously different from the data diversification for fault tolerance in this section. Paul thinks that software always fails due to the special circumstances in data space. In practice, a program can survive large-scale testing and works well in many conditions, but it fails in some special circumstances. The special circumstances here can be seen as the output generated for a particular dataset input. The reason why large-scale frequent testing does not accurately reveal software failures caused by special circumstances is that these tests do not produce the required accurate environment. He also observed that some software malfunctioned under a series of special conditions, but if the execution conditions are slightly changed, it is possible to make the software function again. For example, some fixed errors that lead to failures of asynchronous business systems do not necessarily cause failures when submitted for execution again.

Based on the above-mentioned observations, Paul believes that it is possible to start with the input data and construct equivalent datasets or approximately equivalent datasets to test the system multiple times. The system may produce two results: One is that test results are the same and all inputs cause system failures; the other is that the system functions normally after partially equivalent datasets are used as inputs. Therefore, this method may improve the operation success rate of defective systems, and results are within the acceptable range.

6.4.2 *Technical Principles*

Data diversification is an orthogonal approach to design diversification. A set of diverse algorithms generates a set of associated data points. Execute these data points in the same software (running on multiple copies of a piece of software in parallel, so it is called N-copy data diversification), and then use a decision algorithm to determine the system output. From the analysis above, Paul's thought is very enlightening. If it can be put into practice, it can improve reliability of software and reduce probability of software failure to a certain extent. However, there are still many difficulties in implementing this idea in a real software environment. First of all, the form of data input is ever-changing, in face of fixed program, some data have equivalent input, while some are not necessarily found; secondly, there is no accurate answer to the question whether equivalent datasets can make the system function normally when the original input data causes system failure. The answer may be yes or no. In his research, Paul used probability theory to describe, but he did not give the factors that could affect probability, which shows the obscurity of this problem. Considering innovativeness of this idea, here we will further explore the research ideas and design concept of Paul *et al.*

(1) Fault Region

Paul describes the set and distribution of all input points that may cause the system failure as Fault Region (FR), and thinks that the reason why a system fails is that the current input data value is located in the fault region of the system. Some input points can make the system work normally because these data points are not in the fault region.

Therefore, the ability of data diversification is, given a certain input data point in the fault region, to generate data points outside of FR through the data diversification interpreter. Such an algorithm for generating a diversified dataset is regarded as R algorithm. We can say that one of the main problems in realization of data diversification in this section is how to design the R algorithm.

(2) R algorithm: Data diversification interpretation algorithm

R algorithm (shown in Figure 6.5) aims to generate datasets that are not in the fault region but enable the system to run normally. In fact, design of R algorithm can have two goals: One is the so-called precise R algorithm, which ensures that the generated dataset and original dataset can produce completely equivalent system output results (the equivalent output set as shown in Figure 6.6). The other

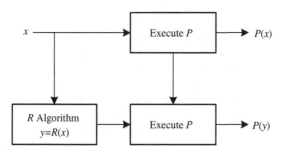

Figure 6.5. *R* Algorithm

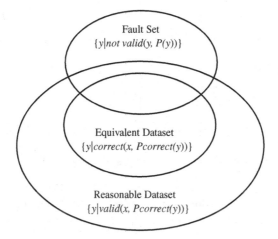

Figure 6.6. Distribution of Output Results Corresponding to Input Data Generated by Different Algorithms

is the so-called approximate R algorithm, and system output corresponding to the dataset which it produces is within the acceptable range (the reasonable output set as shown in Figure 6.6). Based on practical experience, Paul gives the following multiple R algorithm design ideas.

(a) When input data are numeric, the numerical value is adjusted to a certain threshold range, for example, increasing the latter and decreasing by a certain percentage. The specific ratio needs to be determined according to inherent design of the system, and for some hardware systems, it can be determined by sensitivity of the sensor.

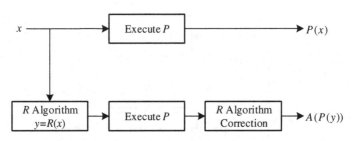

Figure 6.7. R Algorithm with Execution Result Correction

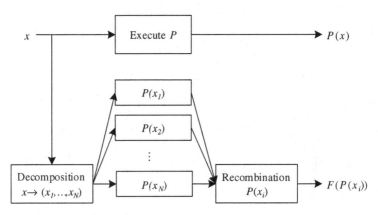

Figure 6.8. R Algorithm for Decomposing and Recombining Inputs

(b) When input data are numeric, adjust the storage order of the data.

(c) When input data are numeric, adjust the operation order of the data.

(d) When input data are non-numeric, adjust the data structure of the data, for example, adjusting the data stored as string to a tree structure, etc.

(e) On the basis of the input data generated previously by R algorithm, make targeted corrections to the results of this input after the system is running, as shown in Figure 6.7.

(f) Decompose input data, and merge them after the output results are obtained, as shown in Figure 6.8.

The design of R algorithm is a very challenging task. After a comprehensive analysis, Paul believes that there is no universal R

algorithm, and the R algorithm should be customized with specific problems; R algorithm should be simple and easy in design; R algorithm may bring more design defects.

(3) Decision-making of output results

Different R algorithms may produce different forms of input data, which in turn may produce different output results. The system can determine these output results in the following two ways.

(a) For the output results generated by precise R algorithm, most output results will be taken as good output results during voting.
(b) For the output results of approximate R algorithm, voting will be more subjective, because at this time it is possible to generate many different but still acceptable results.

6.4.3 *Basic Effectiveness and Existing Deficiencies*

Unlike the data diversification technology described in other sections of this chapter, this technology is not designed to directly counter malicious input, but rather to address unintended system defects. Since input data are regenerated and a better result is selected by voting on output results of the system, this technology helps to cope with some of the coding defects that exist in the system itself, and also make it more difficult for the attacker to break or maliciously manipulate program output. However, in the specific implementation, if interpretation algorithms used to generate diversified input data are not sufficiently different, the attacker may still achieve his goal; if the attacker can achieve the goal without need for program output, the technology may lose its effect.

In the meantime, this technology relies on a voting mechanism, so the attacker may still destroy all or most processes in order to bypass more protection. The attacker may also find output that appears to be valid during output inspection, thus no longer uses different algorithms to perform calculations. Another possibility is that for the same malicious input, the results obtained by using different algorithms are not different. For the program or service whose output is constantly changing dynamically, it may be difficult to create a component that can accurately detect validity of the output.

6.5   Data Diversification for Web Application Security

6.5.1   *Overview*

When attackers use SQL injection, Cross-Site Scripting (XSS), and other means of attack, they must have a prior understanding of the background system used by the vulnerable program. For almost all SQL injection attacks, the attacker must know (or be able to learn) the name of the database table and the types and names of the columns in the table; for command injection attacks, the attacker must know names of the available executable files in the system; for cross-site scripting attacks, the attacker must be clear about the structure of the HTML document object model and the node identifier of the concerned document object model. However, it is impossible for an attacker to easily obtain such information. When the program uses a table in the database, there is no need for the program user to know its name. Polymorphism technology can use such information asymmetry to increase difficulty of attacks with help of embedded subroutines (SQL query statements, Shell commands, HTML text with JavaScript code). If combining transformations on subroutines (such as SQL queries) with transformations on executable environments (such as databases), each instance of the program may use the subroutines that have significantly different syntax and semantics. Therefore, after the software is polymorphized, proportion of successful attacks will be greatly reduced.

Mihai *et al.* [4] believe that Internet services are characterized by externally visible interfaces. The syntax and semantics of these interfaces are fixed, and their internal implementation can be changed arbitrarily, as long as the external interface constraints are satisfied. Therefore, polymorphism can be applied to any part of these implementations, and to any degree that achieves the desired security assurance. In other words, as long as the interface provided to the user can be maintained, the specific implementation can adopt any composition and can change dynamically at runtime. In a typical multi-layer network application, there are many aspects that can be polymorphic: the HTML document provided to the client browser and its communication with the Web server, the application running on the Web server and communication between it and the middle ware, the middle ware itself, communication between the middle ware and the database server, etc. This ensures that the service is protected from multiple types of attacks instead of just one specific type.

Some polymorphism technologies discussed in other chapters of this book, such as diversification of SQL keywords, can also fall into the category of instruction set randomization or dynamic software defense. However, this section continues the discussion here, mainly to illustrate that not only can the instruction set be polymorphic and diversified, there are many elements (such as data types, data interfaces, and data encoding. etc.) that can also adopt polymorphism technology to further improve the ability to cope with attacks through technology combinations.

6.5.2 *Technical Principles*

The core idea of this technology is that in dynamic defense, not only can a certain dynamization technology be used, but a variety of different dynamization technologies can also be combined and applied to all levels of services without affecting functions of the program. Taking diversification of Internet services as an example, Mihai *et al.* [4] proposed implementation schemes, technical combinations, and general design principles of related diversification technologies. In order to clearly show the technical implementation, here are some examples.

Figure 6.9 shows a complex Web service: Facebook. The core functions of this service include continuous data input by users in different ways, third-party script interaction, and direct data retrieval by users. Implementation of this service must be complex and error-prone. Each of its features may provide the attacker with another method, thus sending the data that will cause vulnerabilities to the background program. Here are two diversification schemes related to the system.

Figure 6.9.   Facebook Network Service

```
1   string userName=request.getQueryString ();
2   string query="SELECT*FROM profiles WHERE
        name='"+userName+"'"
3
4   statement stmt=conn.createStatement ();
5   stmt. executeQuery (query);
```

Figure 6.10.   SQL Injection Vulnerability in Java Programs

(1) Use SQL keywords/syntax diversification to cope with SQL injection attacks

Imagine that a user is searching for a variety of corresponding information in the profile table according to a given name. Assume that the background stores all data of a given user in a relational database and responds to the search request by building appropriate SQL statements. In this case, part of the background code may look like Figure 6.10.

However, because developers have made very common mistakes and failed to clean up the input provided by users, the code is vulnerable to SQL injection attacks. For example, by initiating a query and setting the user name as "'123'; DELETE * FROM profiles;", an attacker can force the program to initiate the following SQL query to the database.

```
SELECT * FROM profiles WHERE name = "123";
DELETE * FROM profiles;
```

This is obviously not the effect expected by developers, since the search program that is open to users should not delete content of the configuration database. To solve this problem, SQL key data diversification technology can be introduced.

First, various identifiers of the database interface can be randomized to reduce the losses caused by SQL injection attacks, and this method will not affect semantics of the program. In the example, this policy is simplified to create a new database structure for this query, as shown in Table 6.3.

To reflect this change, we must also change the interface between this program and the database.

```
String query = "SELECT * FROM fc11 WHERE bbd6 =
    '"" + userName + """;
```

Table 6.3.   New and Old Database Names

Old Names	New Names
table profiles	table fc11
column name	column bbd6

Table 6.4.   Modify Table Names

Old Names	New Names
table profiles	table ae76e015705
column name	column beb38f0f750

The above attack will require execution of the following query, which will be rejected by the database server as an illegal operation because the tables and columns it specifies do not exist.

```
SELECT * FROM profiles WHERE name = "123";
DELETE * FROM profiles;
```

In fact, the DELETE part of this SQL query will also be considered invalid, thus defeating the attack.

Of course, changing the database structure only once is unlikely to provide sufficient security, because the attacker may eventually obtain a new name of the object in the database. Therefore, when another user accesses the same network application, this database structure can be used, as shown in Table 6.4.

In this way, details of the database have been randomized, and it becomes very difficult for an attacker to build code that is legal to use for injection attacks.

(2) Diversify JavaScript scripts to cope with XSS attacks

Another type of attack that user-driven websites are vulnerable to is XSS. There are dozens of ways for users to send content to Web applications, and this content is then extracted and placed in the context of the HTML document. Currently, the best way to prevent users from sending JavaScript content is to correctly place string cleanup identifiers in all code that generates HTML text based on untrusted input, and the JavaScript content will then run in the Web

```
 1  <input name="status">
 2  <input type="submit" value="Share">
 3
 4  <!-- User-provided data starts here-->
 5  <script>
 6  //Find the status input box
 7  statusBox=document.getElementById ("input");
 8  statusBox.innerHTML="skipping work";
 9  btns=document.getElementsByTagName ("input");
10  //Submit the form
11  foreach (var btn in btns) {
12              if (btn.getAttribute ("value")=="Share")
13                  btn.onclick ();
14  }
15  </script>
```

Figure 6.11.   HTML Page with Injection Code (Lines 5–15)

application environment. This is usually considered an error-prone process. The automatic handler that places cleanup identifiers must be able to understand the information flow at the program level, as well as understand the subtle interactions between different HTML environments and semantics of string cleanup identifiers. Due to these factors, string cleanup operations are far from solving the problem completely. The HTML page with injection code (lines 5–15) is shown in Figure 6.11.

A feasible solution is to polymorphize the JavaScript runtime environment to avoid these types of attacks. Firstly, make a plan to turn some unimportant features of the environment into random elements. In this case, the unimportant features are API method function names. Next, analyze all JavaScript source code files sent to the client to see if they refer to the polymorphized API method function names, and then rewrite source code files to call the real method functions.

Figure 6.12 shows the results of polymorphizing operating environment in this case. The JavaScript code on this page creates a new environment at the forefront and deletes the default environment. The loose nature of JavaScript in the browser allows one to do this without having to modify implementation of the interpreter or browser, simply swapping a few references to the necessary document object model methods. It should be noted that API method function names in each document object model used in the attack must be

```
1   <input name="status">
2   <input type="submit" value="Share">
3
4   <!--User-provided data starts here-->
5   <script>
6   <document. getelbyid10239=document.getElementById;
7   document.getElementById=Null;
8   document.getatt90254=document.getAttribute;
9   document.getAttribute=Null;
10  //...Additional diversification setup
11  </script>
12
13  <!-- User-provided data starts here -->
14  </script>
15  statusBox=documet.getElementById ("input");
16  statusBox.innerHTML="skipping work";
17  btns=document.getElementsByTagName ("input");
18  foreach (var btn in btns) {
19      if (btn.getAttribute("value")="Share")
20          btn.onclick ();
21  }
22  </script>
```

Figure 6.12. HTML Page Under Protection of Polymorphism (Lines 5–11) with Injected Code (Lines 14–22)

polymorphized, and the default reference of each application program interface must be set to Null. Most importantly, because function calls in the document object model all point to Null references, code of the cross-site scripting attack cannot run successfully.

In addition to the data types in SQL and JavaScript keywords that can be diversified, Mohai also lists other alternative elements that can be used for polymorphism, see Table 6.5.

It should be noted that there may be other parts not mentioned that can also be diversified. In general, the number and types of items that can be diversified depend on the expected service and software used to provide this service. However, each diversification method has its own negative impact and performance overhead. In practice, the appropriate technology combination should be selected according to the characteristics of each polymorphism technology.

6.5.3 *Basic Effectiveness and Existing Deficiencies*

This technology can effectively resist code injection attacks at different levels and certain authentication attacks. Among them,

Table 6.5. Alternative Elements Used for Polymorphism in Network Application System

JavaScript API	SQL Keywords
JavaScript variables	SQL syntax
HTML document object model structure	Database table name
HTML document object model identifier	Database column name
HTTP keywords	SQL return format
HTTP syntax	Database server IP address and port number
HTTP header information	ISA database server
HTTP content encoding	Local files used by the Web server
Web server memory layout	Local files used by the database server
Web server	ISA data server memory layout

instruction set randomization, script API randomization, stored data reference name randomization, and code component randomization all help resist high-level code injection attacks (such as SQL injection attacks) and low-level code injection attacks against internal applications. At the same time, these technologies also help prevent attacks aimed at disrupting authentication, such as cross-site scripting attacks that attempt to inject code at high levels. Other diversification methods used in conjunction with this technology help prevent injection attacks at other levels.

However, this idea of combinations also has some uncertainties. For instance, according to the specific implementation, if randomization of the memory layout is allowed, system overhead may increase. The combination of two seemingly unrelated policies may lead to undesirable results (such as multiplied performance overhead), so the composition is not necessarily simple.

6.6 Summary

As the name suggests, dynamic data defense technology improves the system's protection capabilities by dynamizing data. Table 6.6 introduces data randomization, N-variant data diversification, N-copy data diversification for fault tolerance, and data diversification for

Table 6.6.   Comparative Analysis of Multiple Data Dynamization Technologies

Serial Number	Technology	Data Object	Defense Effectiveness
1	Data randomization	Memory data	Code injection, control injection
2	N-variant data diversification	Memory data	Control injection
3	N-copy data diversification	Memory data	System defects
4	Data diversification for Web applications	Script syntax, data encoding, application data	SQL injection, XSS attack, code injection

Web application technologies. The common point of these technologies is that they change the existing form of data in different space and different dimensions, preventing attackers' conventional attack methods from being implemented effectively, but each technology has its own characteristics and application scope.

Data randomization technology classifies and encrypts the unsecure operands in memory data to ensure that the data that have overflowed from one data type to another cannot be effectively identified. This method has obvious defensive effects on most buffer overflow attacks. However, this technology relies on encryption keys, so it also faces the problem of brute force.

Since randomization technology has the problem of brute-force attack on the keys, no strong encryption is required in N-variant data diversification technology, and only variants for specific data types need to be constructed. As long as the variants can cause differences in the system behavior while defending against an attack, the attack behavior can be detected. However, this technology cannot directly defend against attacks like data randomization technology, it can only detect attack behaviors.

The main design purpose of N-copy data diversification technology for fault tolerance is not to resist external attacks, but to provide an automatic fault tolerance processing capability for key data application handlers (such as missile launching programs, aircraft trajectory planning programs). The core idea is that a kind of data input may cause the system to malfunction, but the equivalent form of this data input or the quasi-equivalent input form can circumvent defects of the system, thereby realizing the proper system output capability. This technology relies on a voting mechanism, so many decision-making methods are subjective and cannot be used universally to improve software reliability.

In the end of this chapter, we introduced data diversification for Web application security. What is introduced here is not a simple data diversification technology, but a concept of technology combination. In the process of preventing Web attacks, many data elements can confuse opponents through diversification technologies. The defense scope of one diversification technology may be limited, but the combined diversification matrix may produce multiplied defense capabilities. This technology also faces the problem of performance loss caused by combination selection and diversification technology combination.

In general, the data diversification technologies proposed above have effectively improved defense capabilities of the system from different perspectives. However, considering the individual characteristics and usage scopes of various technologies, we should make targeted selections based on development language, system environment, and main prevention targets of the system in practice.

References

[1] Cadar, C., Akritidis, P., Costa, M., *et al.* Data randomization. *Microsoft Research*, 2008.

[2] Nguyen-Tuong, A., Evans, D., Knight, J. C., *et al.* Security through redundant data diversity. *IEEE International Conference on Dependable Systems and Networks with FTCS and DCC*, 2008.

[3] Ammann, P. E. and Knigh, T. J. C. Data diversity: An approach to software fault tolerance. *IEEE Transactions on Computers*, 1988, 37(4): 418–425.

[4] Christodorescu, M., Fredrikson, M., Jha, S., *et al.* End-to-end software diversification of internet services. *Springer New York*, 2011, 117–130.

[5] Barrantes, E. G., Ackley, D. H., Palmer, T. S., *et al.* Randomized instruction set emulation to disrupt binary code injection attacks. *Proceedings of the 10th ACM Conference on Computer and Communications Security*, 2003.

[6] Jackson, T., Homescu, A., Crane, S., *et al.* Diversifying the software stack using randomized NOP insertion. *Springer New York*, 2013, 151–173.

[7] Kc, G. S., Keromytis, A. D., and Prevelakis, V. Countering code-injection attacks with instruction-set randomization. *Proceedings of the 10th ACM Conference on Computer and Communications Security*, 2003.

[8] Boyd, S. W., Kc, G. S., Locasto, M. E., *et al.* On the general applicability of instruction-set randomization. *IEEE Transactions on Dependable and Secure Computing*, 2010, 7(3): 255–270.

[9] Xu, J., Kalbarczyk, Z., and Iyer, R. K. Transparent runtime randomization for security. *Proceedings of 22nd International Symposium on Reliable Distributed Systems*, 2003.

[10] Shacham, H., Page, M., Pfaff, B., *et al.* On the effectiveness of address-space randomization. *Proceedings of the 11th ACM Conference on Computer and Communications Security*, 2004.

[11] Bhatkar, S., Duvarney, D. C., and Sekar, R. Address obfuscation: An efficient approach to combat a broad range of memory error exploits. *USENIX Security*, 2003.

[12] Al-Shaer, E. Toward network configuration randomization for moving target defense. *Springer New York*, 2011, 153–159.

[13] Pappas, V., Polychronakis, M., and Keromytis, A. D. Practical software diversification using in-place code randomization. *Springer New York*, 2013, 175–202.

[14] Chen, S., Xu, J., Sezer, E. C., *et al.* Non-control-data attacks are realistic threats. *USENIX Security*, 2005.

[15] Evans, D., Nguyen-Tuong, A., and Knight, J. Effectiveness of moving target defenses. *Springer New York*, 2011, 29–48.

[16] Avizienis, A. The N-version approach to fault-tolerant software. *IEEE Transactions on Software Engineering*, 1985, 11(12): 1491–1501.

[17] Chen, L. and Avizienis, A. N-version programming: A fault-tolerance approach to reliability of software operation. *Digest of Papers FTCS-8: Eighth Annual International Conference on Fault Tolerant Computing*, 1978.

Chapter 7

Dynamic Defense Effectiveness Evaluation Technology

7.1 Introduction

System security is realized through network configuration random-ization, instruction set randomization, software polymorphism, and other dynamic change technologies [1–3]. It needs comprehensive analysis and evaluation to determine its defense effectiveness and whether it can change game rules in the actual network attack–defense game. Evaluation refers to assessment and estimation of relevant performance or effectiveness of an object made by the evaluation subject according to the specific purpose, following certain criteria and standards, and using scientific methods.

At present, there are no formal evaluation theories and methods for the overall security evaluation of network information systems. The existing security evaluation methods can be roughly classified into the following four categories: security audit, risk analysis, System Security Engineering Capability Maturity Model (SSE-CMM), and security evaluation. The corresponding international standards include TCSEC, ITSEC, CTCPEC, ISO 17799, and CC criteria (ISO 15408), etc. Various evaluation methods inevitably involve empirical judgment of evaluation subject, and the dynamic enable-ment technology has not been widely used in engineering practice. Therefore, there are still some difficulties in objectively and rea-sonably evaluating defense effectiveness of the dynamic enablement technology.

In essence, the evaluation method is nothing more than qualitative evaluation and quantitative evaluation. Qualitative evaluation describes defense effectiveness of the dynamic enablement technology through physical concepts and meanings. This method is clear and simple in concept, but poor in objectivity. Quantitative evaluation evaluates defense effectiveness of the dynamic enablement technology through quantitative calculation, which has strong objectivity, but needs to establish complete physical and mathematical models. This chapter will comprehensively use qualitative evaluation and quantitative evaluation methods to explore how to evaluate defense effectiveness of the dynamic enablement technology.

Selecting a reasonable evaluation index system is a prerequisite for carrying out defense effectiveness evaluation of the dynamic enablement technology. When selecting evaluation indexes, the key factor is the contribution of indexes in the evaluation. If there are too many evaluation indexes, it will increase complexity of the evaluation process and even affect objectivity of the evaluation results. The essence of dynamic enablement technology is to realize random changes of system state based on the randomization of software, networks, platforms, data, etc. Therefore, the reasonable idea is to select evaluation indexes based on their capabilities to describe randomization of software, networks, platforms, data, etc. The preliminary set of evaluation indexes is shown in Table 7.1.

In the selection of evaluation criteria, we believe that a comprehensive evaluation based on the above indexes can certainly measure the overall defense effectiveness of dynamic enablement technology, but due to the lack of accurate and objective measurements of evaluation indexes, the credibility and application value of evaluation results may be reduced. On the other hand, adopting a single criterion such as vulnerability assessment may also intuitively and concisely embody the dynamic enablement effect. In addition, if attacker elements are introduced to directly evaluate dynamic changes of system attack surface in the network attack–defense game, it may be possible to actually verify effectiveness and rationality of the dynamic enablement technology. Therefore, this chapter intends to comprehensively evaluate defense effectiveness of the dynamic enablement technology from different dimensions by adopting overall evaluation, vulnerability evaluation, dynamic evaluation of the attack surface and other technologies, respectively.

Table 7.1.   Evaluation Index and Measurement Method of Dynamic Enablement Technology

Evaluation Dimension	Randomization Index	Index Description	Measurement Method	Property
Software	Instruction (S_1)	The difficulty of instruction randomization being analyzed	Analyze randomization methods to judge the difficulty of being cracked	Qualitative
	Memory address (S_2)	Memory address space location and change range of process components and objects	Calculate memory address change space according to system characteristics	Quantitative
	Number of variants (S_3)	The number of variants that can be compiled from the same program source code	Generate software entities with the same function and different internal structures for the same source code based on the compiler, distribute them to different users, and calculate the number of variants that can be obtained by compiling the same source code	Quantitative
Network	IP address (N_1)	Change range and average change rate of IP address	Frequency of change within a given observation window (minute/hour/ day/week/month)	Quantitative
	Network port number (N_2)	Average change rate of network ports	Frequency of change within a given observation window (minute/hour/day/ week/month)	Quantitative
	Protocol (N_3)	Hopping types of a certain protocol (such as data encryption protocol)	Number of hops for a given link (hour/minute/ second)	Quantitative
	Data packet path (N_4)	Dynamic change response rate of routing in overlay networks	The successful routing ratio for a given source and destination link	Quantitative

(*Continued*)

Table 7.1.   (*Continued*)

Evaluation Dimension	Randomization Index	Index Description	Measurement Method	Property
Platform	Basic computing platform (P_1)	The rate and randomness of application migration on the hardware and operating system hosting its operation	Frequency of change within a given observation window (day/week/ month) and heterogeneity degree of the platform	Quantitative
	Programmable logic device configuration file (P_2)	The rate and randomness of switching and loading configuration files in programmable logic devices	Frequency and degree of change within a given observation window (day/week/ month)	Quantitative
	Web server (P_3)	Heterogeneity degree, quantity, and randomness of choice of Web servers	Heterogeneity degree of Web servers and change frequency of the system within a given observation window (day/week/ month)	Quantitative
Data	Memory data (D_1)	The difficulty of memory data randomization being analyzed	Analyze data randomization methods (obfuscation, encryption, etc.) to judge the difficulty of being cracked	Qualitative
	N-variant data (D_2)	The capability to build variants consistent with semantics of the original program after a specific data type is diversified	Number of data variants for a given data type	Quantitative
	Web application data (D_3)	Diversification capability of Web application data (SQL query statements, Shell commands, HTML text with JavaScript code, etc.)	Web application data type, data interface, data encoding, and other polymorphism representation degree	Qualitative

7.2 Overall Evaluation of Defense Effectiveness of Dynamic Enablement Technology

In this chapter, 13 metrics are initially selected to comprehensively evaluate dynamic enablement effect of the system. Obviously, different information systems have different network structures, computing environments, application architectures, and randomization methods, and each metric contributes differently to the overall evaluation of dynamic enablement. To this end, it is necessary to sort the above metrics in terms of importance while excluding relatively minor metrics to simplify the calculation. In addition, there are complex causal relationships between the selected metrics, which makes the comprehensive evaluation of dynamic enablement equip the character of uncertainty. The fuzzy comprehensive evaluation method provides a powerful tool for dealing with this uncertainty.

In view of this, the basic idea of the overall evaluation of dynamic enablement technology is as follows. First, use Analytical Hierarchy Process (AHP) [4, 5] (that is, judge the maximum eigenvalue of the matrix and perform an index consistency test by calculating the importance) to obtain the weight of each metric, and then remove the relatively unimportant metrics according to the importance constant to simplify calculation. Second, establish the fuzzy relation matrixes at each observation time of the system, and use the fuzzy evaluation method to find the comprehensive evaluation grade of randomization after dynamic change of the system. In addition, when there are enough observation data in the system, the comprehensive evaluation grade of system randomization at the next observation time can be estimated by using the Markov chain evaluation method based on accumulated prior data.

7.2.1 *Analytical Hierarchy Process*

Analytical Hierarchy Process (AHP) was proposed by American operations researcher T. L. Satty in the 1970s. It is a multi-objective decision analysis method combining qualitative and quantitative analysis. The main idea is to analyze the relevant elements of complex systems and their interrelations, merge these elements into different levels, establish a judgment matrix at each level, obtain the relative weight of the elements at each level, and finally calculate the combined weight of multi-level elements to the overall goal, providing a basis for decision-making and selection.

The basic steps of AHP are as follows.

(1) Analyze the practical problems and construct a hierarchy model (hierarchy chart)

Classify the factors involved in the problem, and then construct a hierarchy model in which all factors are connected with each other. The factors can generally be divided into three categories.

Target category, refers to the object to be evaluated.

Criteria category, refers to the criteria for measuring whether the goal can be achieved.

Measure category, refers to the plans, methods, and means to achieve the goal.

From target to criteria, and then to measure, the direct impact relationships between various factors are arranged at different levels from top to bottom to form a hierarchy chart.

(2) Make pairwise comparisons layer by layer to obtain a number of positive-inverse square matrices

While considering several factors, the pairwise comparison method is used to determine the order of advantages and disadvantages of several factors in some aspects by comparing all possible combinations in pairs.

In order to obtain a quantified judgment matrix through pairwise comparison among various factors, a 9-level score system is introduced, as shown in Table 7.2.

According to the above table, the values obtained by comparing various factors can be used to construct matrix J as follows:

$$J = \begin{pmatrix} a_{11} & a_{12} & \cdots & a_{1n} \\ a_{21} & a_{22} & \cdots & a_{2n} \\ \vdots & \vdots & \cdots & \vdots \\ a_{n1} & a_{n2} & \cdots & a_{nn} \end{pmatrix} \tag{7.1}$$

The element $a_{ij}(i, j = 1, 2, \ldots, n)$ is importance ratio of the i-th factor to the j-th factor, and the above matrix is called pairwise judgment matrix.

Table 7.2. 9-Level Score System

Metric A is Compared with B	Absolutely More Important	Very Much More Important	Much More Important	Somewhat More Important	Equal Importance	Somewhat More Unimportant	Much More Unimportant	Very Much More Unimportant	Absolutely More Unimportant
Evaluation value	9	7	5	3	1	1/3	1/5	1/7	1/9

Notes: Take 8, 6, 4, 2, 1/2, 1/4, 1/6, 1/8 as medians of the above evaluation values.

In this way, the hierarchy model can give a judgment matrix between factors of the layers through the pairwise comparison method.

(3) Find the principal eigenvalues and corresponding principal eigenvectors of positive-inverse square matrices, and check the compatibility of these matrices.

When all positive-inverse square matrices satisfy the compatibility condition, the combination weight coefficient can be obtained according to the principle of hierarchical compound. Steps for calculating the eigenvector using the sum-product algorithm are as follows.

(a) Normalize each column element of the judgment matrix, and the general items of its elements are shown as the following formula:

$$\overline{a_{ij}} = \frac{a_{ij}}{\sum_{k=1}^{n} a_{kj}}, \quad i, j = 1, 2, \ldots, n \tag{7.2}$$

(b) Add the judgment matrix of which each column has been normalized by row.

$$\overline{\omega_i} = \sum_{j=1}^{n} \overline{a_{ij}}, \quad i = 1, 2, \ldots, n \tag{7.3}$$

(c) Normalize the added vectors again to obtain the required eigenvector $\boldsymbol{\omega}$.

$$\omega_i = \frac{\overline{\omega_i}}{\sum_{j=1}^{n} \overline{\omega_j}}, \quad i = 1, 2, \ldots, n \tag{7.4}$$

(d) Calculate the maximum eigenvalue $\lambda_{\max}$ of the judgment matrix by judgment matrix $\boldsymbol{J}$ and eigenvector ω.

$$\lambda_{\max} = \sum_{i=1}^{n} \frac{(\boldsymbol{J}\omega)_i}{n\omega_i} \tag{7.5}$$

$(\boldsymbol{J}\omega)_i$ represents the i-th element of vector $\boldsymbol{J}\omega$.

The steps of consistency check are as follows:

(a) Calculate the consistency index $CI, CI = (\lambda_{\max} - n)/(n - 1)$, where n is the order of the judgment matrix.
(b) Select the random consistency index RI. For the matrix of order 1–9, the consistency index is shown in Table 7.3. When

Table 7.3. Consistency Index

Order	3	4	5	6	7	8	9
RI	0.58	0.90	1.12	1.24	1.32	1.41	1.45

the order is less than 3, the judgment matrix always has complete consistency.

(c) Calculate CR, $CR = CI/RI$. If $CR < 0.10$, the judgment matrix is considered to have satisfactory consistency. Otherwise, the judgment matrix must be adjusted.

7.2.2 *Fuzzy Comprehensive Evaluation*

Fuzzy comprehensive evaluation is to make a comprehensive evaluation and decision on a certain thing for a certain purpose in an uncertain environment, considering the influence of various factors [6–8].

The mathematical model of fuzzy comprehensive evaluation is as follows.

Suppose $I = \{I_1, I_2, \cdots, I_n\}$ is the set of all evaluation items, and $I_k (k = 1, 2, \cdots, n)$ represents the k-th evaluation item.

$L = \{L_1, L_2, \cdots, L_m\}$ represents various possible qualitative evaluation results of each evaluation item I_k $(k = 1, 2, \cdots, n)$, then a fuzzy subset l_i can be established for each L_i $(i = 1, 2, \cdots, m)$.

Suppose that $d_{ki} = l_i|I_k$ represents the membership degree of I_k to l_i, that is, the degree to which the k-th evaluation item can be specified as the evaluation result L_i. There are several ways to determine the value of d_{ki}. When evaluation item I_k is qualitative, it can be determined by a fuzzy statistical experiment. In order to make the evaluation result assert that the proportion of L_i tends to the membership degree d_{ki}, the fuzzy statistical experiment method requires enough evaluation experts. When evaluation item I_k is quantitative, d_{ki} can be calculated using the membership function $\mu_{ki}(x)$, where x is the measured value of I_k.

When all $d_{ki}(i = 1, 2, \cdots, n, k = 1, 2, \cdots, m)$ are evaluated and determined, a fuzzy relation matrix can be established.

$$R = (d_{ki}) = \begin{bmatrix} d_{11} & d_{12} & \cdots & d_{1m} \\ d_{21} & d_{22} & \cdots & d_{2m} \\ \vdots & \vdots & \cdots & \vdots \\ d_{n1} & d_{n2} & \cdots & d_{nm} \end{bmatrix} \qquad (7.6)$$

Generally speaking, n evaluation items $I_1, I_2, \cdots, I_n$ are not equally important. They have different impacts on comprehensive evaluation results, so the fuzzy weight vector must be determined before comprehensive evaluation. Suppose that $\boldsymbol{W} = (w_1, w_2, \cdots, w_n)$ represents the fuzzy weight vector, and $\boldsymbol{P} = \{$evaluation items that are meaningful to evaluation$\}$ is a fuzzy subset, then $w_j (j = 1, 2, \cdots, n)$ represents the membership degree of evaluation item I_j to $\boldsymbol{P}$.

The fuzzy weight vector can be determined by expert estimation. The estimation values given by experts need to be averaged and normalized. In other words, assuming that W_j' is the average membership degree of evaluation item I_j to $\boldsymbol{P}$, the normalized fuzzy weight vector is

$$W_j = W_j' / \sum_{i=1}^{n} W_j' \tag{7.7}$$

Once the fuzzy weight vector $\boldsymbol{W}$ is determined, the fuzzy comprehensive evaluation result $\boldsymbol{E}$ can be obtained.

$$\boldsymbol{E} = \boldsymbol{W} \circ \boldsymbol{R} = (w_1, w_2, \cdots, w_n) \circ \begin{bmatrix} d_{11} & d_{12} & \cdots & d_{1m} \\ d_{21} & d_{22} & \cdots & d_{2m} \\ \vdots & \vdots & \cdots & \vdots \\ d_{n1} & d_{n2} & \cdots & d_{nm} \end{bmatrix}$$

$$= (a_1, a_2, \cdots, a_m) \tag{7.8}$$

"$\circ$" is the fuzzy comprehensive operator. And $a_i \ (i = 1, 2, \cdots, m)$ is a value obtained through operation of the ith column element of $\boldsymbol{W}$ and $\boldsymbol{R}$, which means the membership degree of the overall evaluation result to the fuzzy subset l_i, i.e. the degree to which L_i can be specified as the overall evaluation result.

The result of fuzzy evaluation is a vector $\boldsymbol{E}$. In order to compare the overall evaluation results of multiple systems, $\boldsymbol{E}$ should be analyzed and uniformized. This can be achieved by maximum membership principle or weighted average method. For example, the weighted average algorithm is as follows:

$$Q = \sum_{i=1}^{m} i a_i^k \Big/ \sum_{i=1}^{m} a_i^k \tag{7.9}$$

Q represents the overall comprehensive evaluation result, and the constant k has an effect on the larger a_i. When $k \to \infty$, the value of Q will be the same as that obtained through the maximum membership principle.

7.2.3 Markov Chain Evaluation

Consider a system that may have m states, and state changes only occur at time $t_1, t_2, \ldots, t_n$. X_{n+1} represents the system state at time t_{n+1}. In general, the probability that the system will be in state i in the future is related to its entire history, which is expressed by the conditional probability $P(X_{n+1} = i \,|\, X_0 = x_0, \; X_1 = x_1, \ldots, X_n = x_n)$, where $X_0 = x_0, X_1 = x_1, \ldots, X_n = x_n$ represent the state that the system has previously experienced. If the future state of the system is only related to the current state, it can be changed to

$$P(X_{n+1} = i \mid X_0 = x_0, X_1 = x_1, \ldots, X_n = x_n)$$
$$= P(X_{n+1} = i \mid X_n = x_n) \tag{7.10}$$

Such discrete random processes are called Markov chains [9, 10].

For Markov chains, the conditional probability of changing from state i (at time t_m) to state j (at time t_n) can be expressed as

$$P_{ij}(m, n) = P(X_n = j \mid X_m = x_i), n > m \tag{7.11}$$

If $P_{ij}(m, n)$ is only related to the time interval $t_n - t_m$, but not to the time starting point t_m, the Markov chain is said to be homogeneous. In this case, $P_{ij}(k) = P(X_k = j \,|\, X_0 = i) = P(X_{s+k} = j \,|\, X_s = i) \, (s \geqslant 0)$ is defined as k-step transition probability.

When $k = 1, P_{ij}(1)$ is a one-step transition probability, which is abbreviated as P_{ij}. And P_{ij} has the following properties:

(a) $0 \leqslant P_{ij} \leqslant 1, i, j = 1, 2, \ldots, m$;
(b) $\sum_{j=1}^{m} P_{ij} = 1, i = 1, 2, \ldots, m$.

For finite state space $\boldsymbol{E} = \{1, 2, \cdots, m\}$, there is the following one-step state transition probability matrix, namely

$$\boldsymbol{P} = \begin{bmatrix} P_{11} & P_{12} & \cdots & P_{1m} \\ P_{21} & P_{22} & \cdots & P_{2m} \\ \vdots & \vdots & \cdots & \vdots \\ P_{m1} & P_{m2} & \cdots & P_{mm} \end{bmatrix} \tag{7.12}$$

$P_{ij} = n_{ij}/n_i$, and n_{ij} represents the number of samples of the transition from state i to state j and from time n to time $n + 1$; $n_i = \sum_{j=1}^{m} n_{ij}$ represents the total number of samples in state i.

Suppose that $P(0) = (p_1(0), p_2(0), \cdots, p_m(0))$ is the initial state probability. After one-step transition, probability $p_j(1)$ in state j is obtained from the full probability expression: $p_j(1) = P(X_1 = j) = \sum_i P(X_0 = i)P(X_1 = j \,|\, X_0 = i)$, that is, $p_j(1) = \sum_i p_i(0)p_{ij}$, and the matrix is expressed as $P(1) = P(0)\boldsymbol{P}$.

In this way, after n steps of transition, the system state probability is

$$P(n) = P(n-1)\boldsymbol{P} = P(n-2)\boldsymbol{P} \cdot \boldsymbol{P} = \cdots = P(0)\boldsymbol{P}^n \tag{7.13}$$

$\boldsymbol{P}$ is a one-step probability transfer matrix, and the equation (7.13) is the Markov prediction model. According to the above model, the overall effectiveness of the system defense at a certain moment in the future can be predicted.

In the efficiency analysis based on Markov chain described above, if the probability transition matrix of system state change trend remains unchanged, the system state will tend to be stable. The so-called steady state refers to the overall efficiency when the system reaches a steady state (balanced state). Mathematically this is described as, if there is a probability distribution $\{\pi_k, k \geqslant 0\}$ such that there is $\lim_{n \to \infty} P_{jk}(n) = \pi_k$ for any state j, k of the Markov chain, then $\{\pi_k, k \geq 0\}$ is called the limit distribution of Markov chain. At this time, for any state k, $\pi_k = \sum_{j=0}^{\infty} \pi_j p_{jk}, k \geq 0$, that is,

$$\pi = \pi \cdot \boldsymbol{P} \tag{7.14}$$

$\pi = (\pi_0, \pi_1, \pi_2, \cdots)$, the equation (7.14) is called stationary equation.

There are two important categories for all the states in the state space of Markov chain. One is the nonreturn state, and once you leave this state, it will never return. The other is the absorption state (also known as the ergodic state). Once you enter this state, you will not go out again. The following is an important theorem about limit distribution of Markov chains.

Theorem 7.1: *The aperiodic irreducible Markov chain with normal returns has a unique stationary distribution, that is, the limit distribution.*

7.2.4 *Comprehensive Evaluation Example*

As mentioned before, the evaluation index set C of the dynamic enablement technology is composed of 13 metrics, namely $C = \{S_1, S_2, S_3, N_1, N_2, N_3, N_4, P_1, P_2, P_3, D_1, D_2, D_3\}$. These 13 metrics have different contributions to randomization comprehensive evaluation. Therefore, it is necessary to calculate the importance of each metric, and at the same time, remove the relatively less important performance metrics to simplify the calculation process. Section 7.2.1 has given in detail the calculation process of each metric weight. First, the importance judgment matrix is established according to expert scoring results. Then weights are obtained by solving the maximum eigenvalue of the judgment matrix and performing a consistency test. The whole calculation process can be completed by Matlab or other AHP special software. For an information system, three relatively unimportant metrics, namely $\{N_4, P_2, D_3\}$, are removed by calculation. And weights of the remaining 10 metrics are $w_{s_1} = 0.30$, $w_{s_2} = 0.05$, $w_{s_3} = 0.08$, $w_{N_1} = 0.12, w_{N_2} = 0.07, w_{N_3} = 0.02, w_{P_1} = 0.11, w_{P_3} = 0.12$, $w_{D_1} = 0.03$, and $w_{D_2} = 0.10$, respectively.

Through the above AHP-based index set simplification method, 10 key indexes $\{S_1, S_2, S_3, N_1, N_2, N_3, P_1, P_3, D_1, D_2\}$ for comprehensive evaluation of dynamic enablement are obtained, which include both qualitative and quantitative indexes. In actual evaluation, some metrics may not be easy to collect. For convenience of processing, the hierarchical processing is carried out as shown in Table 7.4.

Suppose that according to the historical experience of observing system random change, the comprehensive evaluation results of randomization are divided into four levels of L1, L2, L3, and L4, corresponding to the excellent, good, medium, and poor states of the comprehensive randomization evaluation, respectively. The basis for division is shown in Table 7.5.

The meaning of Table 7.5 is obvious. For example, the first line indicates that if following conditions are met, comprehensive randomization evaluation of the system is considered excellent: Instruction randomization intensity of the information system reaches level 4, randomization degree of the memory address is level 4, software source code is compiled to obtain more than 10 types of variants, IP address change capability reaches level 4, network port change rate is more than 200 times per month, the number of hopping types for the given protocol is more than 10, heterogeneity degree of basic computing platform changes is greater than 90%, heterogeneity degree of Web server changes is more than 90%, analysis difficulty of memory data randomization is level 4, and the number of data variants for the given data type is more than 10.

The fuzzy relationship matrix is established as follows. The single factor evaluation matrix takes the membership degree of each factor on the evaluation set, so it is necessary to determine the membership degree of each single factor on the evaluation set. For qualitative evaluation indexes S_1, S_2, N_1, D_1, the membership degree is determined by the fuzzy statistical test method. For the convenience of calculation, each membership function is taken as a linear function for the remaining quantitative indexes. According to the classification standard table, the membership functions of S_3 belonging to various types are established as follows:

$$\mu_{L_4}^{S_3}(x) = \begin{cases} 1, x \geqslant 10 \\ (x-6)/4,\ 6 \leqslant x < 10 \\ 0, x < 6 \end{cases} \quad \mu_{L_3}^{S_3}(x) = \begin{cases} 0, x \geqslant 10, \quad x \leqslant 3 \\ (10-x)/4,\ 6 \leqslant x < 10 \\ (x-3)/3, \quad 3 < x < 6 \end{cases}$$

Table 7.4. Simplified Evaluation Indexes of Dynamic Enablement Technology

Evaluation Dimension	Randomization Index	Index Description	Measurement Method	Property	Hierarchical Method (Level L1–L4)
Software	Number of variants (S_3)	The number of variants that can be compiled from the same program source code	Generate software entities with the same function and different internal structure for the same source code based on the compiler, distribute them to different users, and calculate the number of variants that can be obtained by compiling the same source code	Quantitative	L1: There are less than 3 variants that can be obtained by compiling the same source code. L2: There are 3 to 6 variants that can be obtained by compiling the same source code. L3: There are 6–10 variants that can be obtained by compiling the same source code. L4: There are more than 10 variants that can be obtained by compiling the same source code.
Software	Instruction (S_1)	The difficulty of instruction randomization being analyzed	Analyze randomization methods to judge the difficulty of being cracked	Qualitative	L1: Instruction randomization is easy to analyze. L2: Under given constraints, instruction randomization can be analyzed. L3: Under given constraints, instruction randomization is difficult to analyze. L4: Under given constraints, instruction randomization is almost impossible to analyze.

(*Continued*)

Table 7.4. (Continued)

Evaluation Dimension	Randomization Index	Index Description	Measurement Method	Property	Hierarchical Method (Level L1–L4)
	Memory address (S_2)	Memory address space location and change range of process components and objects	Calculate memory address change space according to system characteristics	Quantitative	L1: Randomization granularity of heap address, stack base address, executable file image base address, PEB and TEB addresses, dynamic link library address, etc. is relatively low (for example, the memory address space distribution of process components and objects is 8 bits). L2: Randomization granularity of heap address, stack base address, executable file image base address, PEB and TEB addresses, dynamic link library address, etc. is medium. (for example, the memory address space distribution of process components and objects is 16 bits). L3: Randomization granularity of heap address, stack base address, executable file image base address, PEB and TEB addresses, dynamic link library address, etc. is relatively high (for example, the memory address space distribution of process components and objects is 24 bits).

					L4: Randomization granularity of heap address, stack base address, executable file image base address, PEB and TEB addresses, dynamic link library address, etc. is very high (for example, the memory address space distribution of process components and objects is 32 bits).
Network	IP address (N_1)	Change range and average change rate of IP address	Frequency of change within a given observation window (minute/hour/day/week/month)	Quantitative	L1: C network segment changes at a rate less than 50 times per month. L2: C network segment changes at a rate of more than 50 times per month. L3: B network segment changes at a rate less than 50 times per month. L4: B network segment changes at a rate of more than 50 times per month.
	Network port number (N_2)	Average change rate of network ports	Frequency of change within a given observation window (minute/hour/day/week/month)	Quantitative	L1: The port change rate is less than 50 times per month. L2: The port change rate is 50 to 100 times per month. L3: The port change rate is 100 to 200 times per month. L4: The port change rate is more than 200 times per month.

(Continued)

Table 7.4. (Continued)

Evaluation Dimension	Randomization Index	Index Description	Measurement Method	Property	Hierarchical Method (Level L1–L4)
	Protocol (N_3)	Hopping types of a certain type of protocol (such as data encryption protocol)	Number of hops for a given link (hour/minute/second)	Quantitative	L1: The number of hopping types for a given protocol are less than 3. L2: The number of hopping types for a given protocol are 3 to 6. L3: The number of hopping types for a given protocol are 6 to 10. L4: The number of hopping types for a given protocol is more than 10.
Platform	Basic computing platform (P_1)	The rate and randomness of application migration on the hardware and operating system hosting its operation	Change frequency and heterogeneity degree of the platform within a given observation window (day/week/month)	Quantitative	L1: Change frequency of the basic computing platform changes is low, and the degree of heterogeneity is less than 30%. L2: Change frequency of the basic computing platform is medium, and the degree of heterogeneity is 30% to 60%. L3: Change frequency of the basic computing platform is high, and the degree of heterogeneity of 60% to 90%. L4: Change frequency of the basic computing platform is very high, and the degree of heterogeneity is greater than 90%.

Platform	Web server (P_3)	Heterogeneity degree, quantity and randomness of choice of the Web server	Heterogeneity degree of the Web server and frequency of system changes within a given observation window (day/week/month)	Quantitative	L1: Change frequency of the Web server is low, and the heterogeneity degree is less than 30%. L2: Change frequency of the Web server is medium, and the heterogeneity degree is 30% to 60%. L3: Change frequency of the Web server is relatively high, and the heterogeneity degree is 60% to 90%. L4: Change frequency of the Web server is very high, and the heterogeneity degree is greater than 90%.
Data	Memory data (D_1)	The difficulty of memory data randomization being analyzed	Analyze data randomization methods (confusion, encryption, etc.) to judge the difficulty of being cracked	Qualitative	L1: Data randomization is easy to analyze. L2: Under the given constraints, data randomization can be analyzed. L3: Under the given constraints, data randomization is difficult to analyze. L4: Under the given constraints, data randomization is almost impossible to analyze.

(Continued)

Table 7.4. (*Continued*)

Evaluation Dimension	Randomization Index	Index Description	Measurement Method	Property	Hierarchical Method (Level L1–L4)
	N-variant data (D_2)	Capability to build variants consistent with the semantics of the original program after a specific data type is diversified	The number of data variants for a given data type	Quantitative	L1: The number of data variants for a given data type is less than 3. L2: The number of data variants for a given data type is 3 to 6. L3: The number of data variants for a given data type is 6 to 10. L4: The number of data variants for a given data type is more than 10.

Table 7.5. Comprehensive Grading Standard of Randomization

Grade	S_1	S_2	S_3	N_1	N_2	N_3	P_1	P_3	D_1	D_2
L4	4	4	≥ 10	4	≥ 200	≥ 10	$\geq 90\%$	$\geq 90\%$	4	≥ 10
L3	3	3	[6,10)	3	(100,200]	[6,10)	(60%,90%]	(60%,90%]	3	[6,10)
L2	2	2	[3,6)	2	(50,100]	[3,6)	(30%,60%)	(30%,60%]	2	[3,6)
L1	1	1	[0,3)	1	[0,50)	[0,3)	(0,30%)	(0,30%]	1	[0,3)

$$\mu_{L_2}^{S_3}(x) = \begin{cases} 0, x \geq 6, & x \leq 0 \\ (6-x)/3, & 3 \leq x < 6 \\ x/3, & 0 < x < 3 \end{cases} \quad \mu_{L_1}^{S_3}(x) = \begin{cases} 0, & x \geq 3, & x \leq 0 \\ (3-x)/3, & 0 < x < 3 \end{cases}$$

Similarly, membership functions of other evaluation indexes belonging to various types can be established, respectively.

(1) N_2

$$\mu_{L_4}^{N_2}(x) = \begin{cases} 1, x \geq 200 \\ (x-100)/100, & 100 \leq x < 200 \\ 0, x < 100 \end{cases}$$

$$\mu_{L_3}^{N_2}(x) = \begin{cases} 0, x \geq 200, & x \leq 50 \\ (200-x)/100, & 100 \leq x < 200 \\ (x-50)/50, & 50 < x < 100 \end{cases}$$

$$\mu_{L_2}^{N_2}(x) = \begin{cases} 0, x \geq 100, & x \leq 0 \\ (100-x)/50, & 50 \leq x < 100 \\ x/50, & 0 < x < 50 \end{cases}$$

$$\mu_{L_1}^{N_2}(x) = \begin{cases} 0, x \geq 50, & x \leq 0 \\ (50-x)/50, & 0 < x < 50 \end{cases}$$

(2) N_3

$$\mu_{L_4}^{N_3}(x) = \begin{cases} 1, x \geqslant 10 \\ (x-6)/4, & 6 \leqslant x < 10 \\ 0, x < 6 \end{cases}$$

$$\mu_{L_3}^{N_3}(x) = \begin{cases} 0, x \geqslant 10, & x \leqslant 3 \\ (10-x)/4, & 6 \leqslant x < 10 \\ (x-3)/3, & 3 < x < 6 \end{cases}$$

$$\mu_{L_2}^{N_3}(x) = \begin{cases} 0, x \geqslant 6, & x \leqslant 0 \\ (6-x)/3, & 3 \leq x < 6 \\ x/3, & 0 < x < 3 \end{cases}$$

$$\mu_{L_1}^{N_3}(x) = \begin{cases} 0, x \geqslant 3, & x \leqslant 0 \\ \\ (3-x)/3, & 0 < x < 3 \end{cases}$$

(3) P_1

$$\mu_{L_4}^{P_1}(x) = \begin{cases} 1, x \geqslant 90\% \\ (x-0.6)/0.3, & 60\% \leqslant x < 90\% \\ 0, x < 60\% \end{cases}$$

$$\mu_{L_3}^{P_1}(x) = \begin{cases} 0, x \geqslant 90\%, & x \leqslant 30\% \\ (0.9-x)/0.3, & 60\% \leqslant x < 90\% \\ (x-0.3)/0.3, & 30\% < x < 60\% \end{cases}$$

$$\mu_{L_2}^{P_1}(x) = \begin{cases} 0, x \geqslant 60\%, & x \leqslant 0 \\ (0.6-x)/0.3, & 30\% \leq x < 60\% \\ x/0.3, & 0 < x < 30\% \end{cases}$$

$$\mu_{L_1}^{P_1}(x) = \begin{cases} 0, x \geqslant 30\%, & x \leqslant 0 \\ \\ (0.3-x)/0.3, & 0 < x < 30\% \end{cases}$$

(4) P_3

$$\mu_{L_4}^{P_3}(x) = \begin{cases} 1, x \geqslant 90\% \\ (x-0.6)/0.3, & 60\% \leqslant x < 90\% \\ 0, x < 60\% \end{cases}$$

$$\mu_{L_3}^{P_3}(x) = \begin{cases} 0, x \geqslant 90\%, & x \leqslant 30\% \\ (0.9-x)/0.3, & 60\% \leqslant x < 90\% \\ (x-0.3)/0.3, & 30\% < x < 60\% \end{cases}$$

$$\mu_{L_2}^{P_3}(x) = \begin{cases} 0, x \geqslant 60\%, & x \leqslant 0 \\ (0.6-x)/0.3, & 30\% \leqslant x < 60\% \\ x/0.3, & 0 < x < 30\% \end{cases}$$

$$\mu_{L_1}^{P_3}(x) = \begin{cases} 0, x \geqslant 30\%, & x \leqslant 0 \\ \\ (0.3-x)/0.3, & 0 < x < 30\% \end{cases}$$

(5) D_2

$$\mu_{L_4}^{D_2}(x) = \begin{cases} 1, x \geqslant 10 \\ (x-6)/4, & 6 \leqslant x < 10 \\ 0, x < 6 \end{cases}$$

$$\mu_{L_3}^{D_2}(x) = \begin{cases} 0, x \geqslant 10, & x \leqslant 3 \\ (10-x)/4, & 6 \leqslant x < 10 \\ (x-3)/3, & 3 < x < 6 \end{cases}$$

$$\mu_{L_2}^{D_2}(x) = \begin{cases} 0, x \geqslant 6, & x \leqslant 0 \\ (6-x)/3, & 3 \leqslant x < 6 \\ x/3, & 0 < x < 3 \end{cases}$$

$$\mu_{L_1}^{D_2}(x) = \begin{cases} 0, x \geq 3, & x \leq 0 \\ \\ (3-x)/3, & 0 < x < 3 \end{cases}$$

Suppose that the evaluation index set of an information system has values of $\{S_1, S_2, 8, N_1, 70, 2, 75\%, 50\%, D_1, 9\}$, where the membership degrees of S_1, S_2, N_1, and D_1 are $\{1, 0, 0, 0, 0\}$, $\{0, 1/2, 1/2, 0\}$, $\{0, 0, 3/4, 1/4\}$, and $\{0, 2/3, 1/3, 0\}$, respectively.

Then according to the above membership degree calculation formulas, the fuzzy relation matrix can be obtained as

$$R = \begin{bmatrix} 1 & 0 & 0 & 0 \\ 0 & \frac{1}{2} & \frac{1}{2} & 0 \\ \frac{1}{2} & \frac{1}{2} & 0 & 0 \\ 0 & 0 & \frac{3}{4} & \frac{1}{4} \\ 0 & \frac{2}{5} & \frac{3}{5} & 0 \\ 0 & 0 & \frac{2}{3} & \frac{1}{3} \\ \frac{1}{2} & \frac{1}{2} & 0 & 0 \\ 0 & \frac{2}{3} & \frac{1}{3} & 0 \\ 0 & \frac{2}{3} & \frac{1}{3} & 0 \\ \frac{3}{4} & \frac{1}{4} & 0 & 0 \end{bmatrix} \tag{7.15}$$

According to the fuzzy comprehensive evaluation method, since the weight vector is $W = (0.30, 0.05, 0.08, 0.12, 0.07, 0.02, 0.11, 0.12, 0.03, 0.10)$, it is calculated as follows:

$$W \cdot R = (0.470, 0.273, 0.220, 0.037) \tag{7.16}$$

Therefore, according to the maximum membership principle, it is determined that the overall effectiveness evaluation level of the system's dynamic enablement is L4, that is, the comprehensive evaluation of randomization is excellent.

7.3 Defense Effectiveness Evaluation of Dynamic Enablement Technology Based on Vulnerability Analysis

7.3.1 *Vulnerability Evaluation Idea*

When randomization metrics such as software, network, platform, and data can be obtained or there exists more prior data accumulation, it is more effective to adopt the system's overall defense effectiveness evaluation. However, sometimes the above metric data is not easy to collect. Here, using a single criterion such as vulnerability evaluation may also intuitively and concisely embody the dynamic enablement effect. The reason is that the core idea of dynamically enabled defense is that the random changes in the system state are caused by random changes in software, network, platform, data, and other elements, which makes it difficult for attackers to directly use the accumulated "outdated" system vulnerabilities. The essence is that inherent changes in the system make attackers' carefully prepared attacking techniques and methods fail on the spot. However, this is only an ideal cyber defense scenario. The reality is that once the configuration and debugging of a complex information system are completed, the random change of its state always has a short or long interval period. During this period, a skilled attacker may analyze potential weaknesses of the system and implement a successful cyber attack. Theoretically, after the system randomly changes its state, this random change is meaningful only when the system's new state has decreased in both the number and severity of vulnerabilities and has increased in the difficulty of exploiting compared with the old state. Therefore, analyzing and evaluating the distribution of vulnerabilities after random changes in the system have a positive significance for evaluating dynamic defense effectiveness of the system.

7.3.2 *Vulnerability Analysis Methods*

Diversification of information systems makes the vulnerability analysis methods present a complicated situation. But through induction, it can be found that there are not many types of common vulnerability analysis technologies, and many have common features. System vulnerability analysis technologies are diverse, and the boundaries between each of them are not clear. In terms of analysis objects, vulnerability patterns, and other factors, software vulnerability analysis can be divided into four categories: software architecture security analysis technology, source code analysis technology, binary vulnerability analysis technology, and operating system vulnerability analysis technology. The characteristics and application scope of each type of technology are described in [11–13]. According to the software description model, black box or white box analysis, and other factors, each type of technology can be further divided into several subcategories. The vulnerability analysis technology system is shown in Figure 7.1.

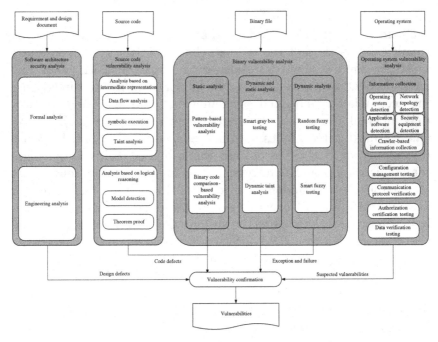

Figure 7.1.   Vulnerability Analysis Technology System

Software architecture security analysis technologies can be divided into formal analysis methods and engineering analysis methods. Source code vulnerability analysis technology can be divided into analysis technology based on intermediate representations and analysis technology based on logical reasoning. Among them, analysis methods based on intermediate representations include data flow analysis, symbolic execution, and taint analysis, etc. Methods based on logical reasoning include model detection and theorem proof, etc. Binary vulnerability analysis technology can be divided into static analysis technology, dynamic analysis technology, and dynamic and static analysis technology. Among them, static analysis technology includes pattern-based vulnerability analysis, binary code comparison, etc.; dynamic analysis technology includes vulnerability fuzzy testing, dynamic taint analysis, etc.; dynamic and static analysis technology includes smart gray box testing, etc. Operating system vulnerability analysis technology can be divided into information collection and vulnerability detection, etc. Among them, information collection includes operating system detection, network topology detection, application software detection, security equipment detection, crawler-based information collection, etc.; vulnerability detection includes configuration management testing, communication protocol verification, authorization certification testing, data verification testing, etc. The problems found in the four types of technical analysis will eventually be verified by vulnerability confirmation and confirmed as real vulnerabilities. Table 7.6 summarizes four types of specific technologies, and compares and explains them in terms of basic principles, analysis phase, pros/cons, etc.

7.3.3 Vulnerability Classification Methods

Vulnerabilities are widespread in various information systems with increasing numbers and different types. In order to better understand the specific information of security vulnerabilities and manage security vulnerability resources in a unified manner, it is necessary to classify security vulnerabilities reasonably. Classification of security vulnerabilities refers to the classification and storage of a large number of vulnerabilities according to the factors such as causes, representation, and consequences, so that they are easy to index, search, and use. This book divides security vulnerabilities into SQL injection, trust boundary violation, operating system command injection, code injection, format string, buffer overflow, integer overflow, denial of service, encryption issues, race conditions, cross-site scripting, cross-site request forgery, path traversal, configuration errors, file permission manipulation, memory leak, resource injection, file upload, open redirection, reuse after release, system information leak, etc. The meanings of vulnerabilities are shown in Table 7.7.

7.3.4 Vulnerability Scoring Methods

Vulnerabilities are usually divided into different levels according to the severity of their impact. This classification helps people to pay different degrees of attention to a large number of security vulnerabilities and take different levels of measures. It also helps to assess whether the security has changed after system state changes

Table 7.6.   Comparison of Vulnerability Analysis Technology

Technology Category	Fundamental Principle	Analysis Phase	Advantages	Disadvantages
Software architecture security analysis	Model the software architecture and describe the security requirements or security mechanisms of the software, then check the architecture model until all security requirements are met	Software design	Considering the overall security of the software, carried out in the software design phase, with a high level of abstraction	Lack of practical and highly automated technology
Source code vulnerability analysis	Through model extraction of the program code and extraction of the program inspection rules, the static vulnerability analysis technology is used to analyze the results	Software development	High code coverage, able to analyze deep hidden vulnerabilities, with low underreporting rate	Requires manual assistance, high technical difficulty, more dependent on prior knowledge, and high false alarm rate
Binary vulnerability analysis	Through the analysis of binary executable code at multiple levels (instruction level, structured, formalized, etc.) and multiple angles (external interface testing, internal structure testing, etc.), security flaws and security vulnerabilities in software programs are discovered	Software design, testing, and maintenance	No source code required, high accuracy of vulnerability analysis, and wide practicality	Lack of upper-level structural information and type information makes analysis difficult

(*Continued*)

Table 7.6. (*Continued*)

Technology Category	Fundamental Principle	Analysis Phase	Advantages	Disadvantages
Operating system vulnerability analysis	Check security of the operating system by inputting data of a specific construction into the operating system, and then analyzing and verifying the output	Operation and maintenance	Considering the overall security of the operating system composed of multiple software, with comprehensive detection items and high accuracy	More dependent on analyst experience

randomly. Therefore, it is necessary to establish a flexible and coordinated vulnerability level evaluation mechanism. Initially, the vulnerabilities were divided into three levels: high, medium, and low. Most remote and local administrator permission vulnerabilities correspond to high levels; general user permissions, privilege escalation, reading restricted files, and remote and local denial of service generally correspond to medium levels; remote unauthorized file access, password recovery, spoofing, and server information disclosure roughly correspond to low levels. Currently, the mainstream vulnerability rating method is to use the popular Common Vulnerability Scoring System (CVSS) for classification [14]. This book mainly conducts a comprehensive evaluation of system vulnerabilities based on the improved CVSS.

7.3.4.1 *CVSS method*

CVSS is an open evaluation system developed by the National Infrastructure Advisory Council (NIAC) and maintained by the Forum of Incident Response and Security Teams (FIRST) that can be adopted by product manufacturers free of charge. The system can be used to score vulnerabilities, and helps to determine the priority of fixing different vulnerabilities.

CVSS is mainly composed of three parts: base metrics, temporal metrics, and environmental metrics. Among them, base metrics

Table 7.7.   Vulnerability Description

Name	Description
SQL injection	By constructing dynamic SQL commands that users can input, attackers can modify meanings of the commands or execute arbitrary SQL commands.
Trust boundary violation	In the same data structure, mixing trusted and untrusted data together causes the program to incorrectly trust unverified data.
Operating system command injection	Executing commands in untrusted resources or executing commands in an untrusted environment causes the program to execute malicious commands in the name of the attacker.
Code injection	When writing code, programmers do not judge legality of the data input by users, which caused applications to have potential security risks. Users can submit database query code to obtain some data that they want.
Format string	Mainly use the security vulnerability mistakenly caused by subtle programming of the formatting function, and pass the carefully prepared text string containing formatting instructions to make the target program execute arbitrary commands.
Buffer overflow	The program writes data outside the allocated memory boundary, which may damage the data, cause the program to crash, or provide an opportunity for malicious code to execute.
Integer overflow	Arithmetic operations will cause the value to be greater than the maximum value of the data type or less than the minimum value of the data type, which may cause logic errors or buffer overflows.
Denial of service	Attackers can cause programs to crash or make programs unavailable to legitimate users.
Encryption issues	Use weak encryption algorithms, shorter encryption keys, clear text storage, empty passwords, hard coding, weak encryption, passwords in comments, keys in files, etc.
Race conditions	When multiple threads or processes read or write the shared data, the result depends on the relative time of their execution. This situation is called race condition. The race condition occurs when multiple processes or threads read and write data, and the final result depends on the execution order of multiple processes.

(*Continued*)

Table 7.7. (*Continued*)

Name	Description
Cross-site scripting	Using shortcomings of the website program in filtering user input, the input can be displayed as HTML code that affects other users on the page, thereby stealing user information, using the user's identity to perform certain actions, or infringing visitors.
Cross-site request forgery	Also known as One-Click Attack or Session Riding, usually abbreviated as CSRF or XSRF, CSRF is an attack method that hijacks the user to perform unintended operations on the currently logged-in Web application.
Path traversal	Through the path used to control operation of the file system input by the user, the attacker can access or modify other protected system resources.
Configuration errors	Allows external control on system settings, which may result in service interruption or unexpected application behaviors.
File permission manipulation	If user input is allowed to directly change file permissions, it may allow attackers to access protected system resources.
Memory leak	The space created dynamically by dynamic storage allocation function is not released after use, resulting in the memory being occupied until the end of the program.
Resource injection	Using the control resource identifiers input by user, an attacker can take this opportunity to access or modify other protected system resources.
File upload	Allowing users to upload files may allow attackers to inject dangerous content or malicious code and run it on the server.
Open redirection	If unauthenticated input is allowed to control the URL used by redirection mechanism, it may be beneficial for attackers to launch phishing attacks.
Reuse after release	Referencing memory after freeing it will cause the program to crash.
System information leakage	Revealing system data or debugging information helps attackers understand the system and make an attack plan.

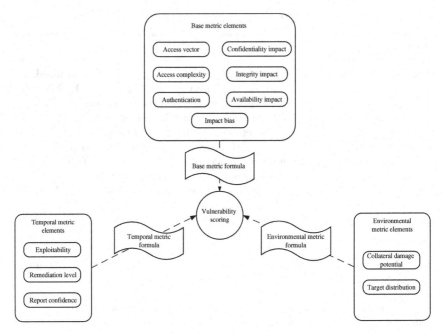

Figure 7.2.   CVSS Metrics

include the factors such as access vector, access complexity, authentication, confidentiality impact, availability impact, integrity impact, and impact bias; temporal metrics include the factors such as exploitability, remediation level, and report confidence; environmental metrics include the factors such as collateral damage potential, host distribution, and so on. CVSS metrics are shown in Figure 7.2.

Elements of base metrics, temporal metrics, environmental metrics, and their value ranges are shown in Tables 7.8–7.10.

CVSS evaluation synthesizes the results obtained by base metrics, temporal metrics, and environmental metrics to obtain a comprehensive score. According to the CVSS mathematical formula, first calculate the base metrics to get a basic score; then, calculate the temporal metrics based on this and get a temporary score; finally, calculate environmental metrics to get the final score. Each metric has its own calculation formula. CVSS has a full score of 10. The higher the score, the more threatening the vulnerability; the lower the score, the lesser the threat.

Table 7.8.   Value Ranges of Base Metric Elements

Element	Symbol	Optional Value	Grading Standard
Access vector	AccessVector	Local/Adjacent/Remote	0.3/0.6/1.0
Access complexity	Access Complexity	High/Medium/Low	0.6/0.8/1.0
Authentication	Authentication	Need/No need	0.6/1.0
Confidentiality impact	ConfImpact	Not affected/Partially affected/ Completely affected	0/0.7/1.0
Integrity impact	IntegImpact	Not affected/Partially affected/Completely affected	0/0.7/1.0
Availability impact	AvailImpact	Not affected/Partially affected/Completely affected	0/0.7/1.0
Impact bias	ImpactBias	Normal/Confidentiality/ Integrity/Availability	0.333/0.25/ 0.25/0.25

Table 7.9.   Value Ranges of Temporal Metric Elements

Element	Symbol	Optional Value	Grading Standard
Exploitability	Exploitability	Not provided/Verification method/ Functional code/Complete code	0.85/0.90/ 0.95/1.0
Remediationlevel	RemediationLevel	Official patch/Temporary patch/ Temporary solution/None	0.85/0.90/ 0.95/1.0
Reportconfidence	ReportConfidence	Rumors/Unconfirmed/ Confirmed	0.90/0.95/ 1.0

The mathematical formula of base metrics is

$$
\begin{aligned}
BaseScore = round\,(&10 \times AccessVector \times AccessComplexity \\
&\times Authentication \times ((ConfImpact \times ConfImpactBias) \\
&+ (IntegImpact \times IntegImpactBias) + (AvailImpact \\
&\times AvailImpactBias))).
\end{aligned}
\tag{7.17}
$$

Table 7.10.   Value Ranges of Environmental Metric Elements

Element	Symbol	Optional Value	Grading Standard
Collateral damage potential	CollateralDamage Potential	None/Low/ Medium/High	0/0.1/0.3/0.5
Target distribution	TargetDistribution	None/Low/ Medium/High	0/0.25/0.5/1.0

Note: When ImpactBias is one of confidentiality impact, availability impact, or integrity impact, the bias value increases by 0.25. For example, when *ImpactBias* is confidentiality, $ConfImpactBias = 0.5$, $IntegImpactBias = 0.25$, $AvailImpactBias = 0.25$.

The formula of temporal metrics is

$$TemporalScore = round\ (BaseScore \times Exploitability$$
$$\times RemediationLevel \times ReportConfidence) \quad (7.18)$$

The mathematical formula of environmental metrics is

$$EnvironmentalScore = round\ ((TemporalScore$$
$$+ ((10 - TemporalScore)$$
$$\times CollateralDamagePotential))$$
$$\times TargetDistribution) \quad (7.19)$$

7.3.4.2   *Improved CVSS method*

The CVSS metrics have shortcomings such as poor repeatability, lack of consideration for attack chains and attacker unreachability. This section will improve on them in three main ways.

(a) Several indexes related to the vulnerability's own characteristics have been added. The privilege index has been added to base metrics, and the technique details and intrusion detection capability indexes have been added to temporal metrics.

Figure 7.3. Improved CVSS Metrics

(b) The environmental metrics with greater arbitrariness are removed, and the report confidence index in temporal metrics is removed.

(c) According to the actual situation of the system, the values of some metric elements have been adjusted, such as the remediation level index in temporal metrics, which increases the difference in whether there is a patch score, because the risk of 0-day vulnerability in actual cyber attack and defense is greater.

The improved CVSS metrics are shown in Figure 7.3.

Evaluation indexes in the improved CVSS metrics are divided into two parts, namely the base metrics and the temporal metrics, which are shown in Tables 7.11 and 7.12, respectively.

The mathematical formulas of the improved CVSS metrics have also changed accordingly. First, the base metrics are calculated according to the new elements to obtain a basic score. Then, based on this, the temporal metrics are calculated according to the new elements to obtain the final score.

The formula of base metrics is

$$
\begin{aligned}
BaseScore = round\,(&10 \times AccessVector \times AccessComplexity \\
&\times Authentication \times Privilege \times ((ConfImpact \\
&\times ConfImpactBias) + (IntegImpact \\
&\times IntegImpactBias + (AvailImpact \\
&\times AvailImpactBias)). \quad\quad (7.20)
\end{aligned}
$$

The formula of temporal metrics is

$$
\begin{aligned}
TemporalScore = round\,(&BaseScore \times Exploitability \\
&\times RemediationLevel \times TechniqueDetail \\
&\times DetectionCapability) \quad\quad (7.21)
\end{aligned}
$$

Table 7.11.   Value Ranges of Base Metric Elements

Element	Symbol	Optional Value	Grading Standard
Access vector	AccessVector	Local/Adjacent/ Remote	0.8/0.9/1.0
Access complexity	AccessComplexity	High/Medium/Low	0.8/0.9/1.0
Authentication privilege	Authentication privilege	Need/No need	0.8/1.0
		Administrator/ Unsure/General user	0.8/0.9/1.0
Confidentiality impact	ConfImpact	Not affected/Partially affected/Completely affected	0/0.7/1.0
Integrity impact	IntegImpact	Not affected/Partially affected/Completely affected	0/0.7/1.0
Availability impact	AvailImpact	Not affected/Partially affected/Completely affected	0/0.7/1.0
Impact bias	ImpactBias	Normal/Confidentiality/ Integrity/Availability	0.333/0.25/ 0.25/0.25

Table 7.12.   Value Ranges of Temporal Metric Elements

Element	Symbol	Optional Value	Grading Standard
Exploitability	Exploitability	Not provided/Verification method/ Functional code/Complete code	0.85/0.90/ 0.95/1.0
Remediation level	RemediationLevel	Official patch/Temporary patch/ Temporary solution/None	0.85/0.90/ 0.95/1.0
Technique detail	TechniqueDetail	Unpublished/Published	0.9/1.0
Detection capability	DetectionCapability	High/Medium/Low	0.8/0.9/1.0

7.3.4.3   *Vulnerability evaluation example*

Regarding the improved CVSS, a calculation example is given as follows. This example is the remote overflow vulnerability of Apache

Web Server Chunked Encoding. The description of this vulnerability can be referred to the TechNet technical resource library. (http:// www.nsfocus.net/vulndb/2975). Assuming that the system provides Web services with Apache at a certain time, Apache has a design vulnerability when processing HTTP requests that transmit data in chunks. A remote attacker may exploit this vulnerability to execute arbitrary instructions or conduct a denial of service attack on some Apache servers with permissions of the Web server process. The chunked encoding transmission is a method for Web users to submit data to the server specified in HTTP 1.1 protocol. When the server receives the chunked encoding data, it will allocate a buffer to store it. If the size of the submitted data is unknown, the client will submit data to the server in a negotiated chunk size. The Apache server provides support for chunked encoding by default. Apache uses a signed variable to store the chunk length, while allocating a fixed-size stack buffer to store the chunked data. For security reasons, before copying chunked data to the buffer, Apache will check the chunk length. If the chunk length is greater than the buffer length, Apache will only copy data of the buffer length at most, otherwise it will copy data according to the chunk length. However, during the above check, the chunk length is not converted to unsigned for comparison, so if the attacker sets the chunk length to a negative value, the above security check will be bypassed and Apache will copy a very long chunked data (at least greater than 0x80000000 bytes) into the buffer, causing a buffer overflow.

Now it has been proven that for Apache 1.3 to 1.3.24 (including 1.3.24), under Win32 systems, remote attackers can use this vulnerability to execute arbitrary code. Under Unix systems, it has also been proven that this vulnerability can be exploited to execute code at least under OpenBSD systems. According to related research reports, the following systems may also be successfully used by attackers: Sun Solaris 6-8 (sparc/x86), FreeBSD 4.3-4.5 (x86), OpenBSD 2.6-3.1 (x86), Linux (GNU) 2.4 (x86).

For Apache 2.0 to 2.0.36 (including 2.0.36), despite the same problem code, it will detect conditions under which the errors occur and make the child process exit. According to different factors (including influence of the thread mode supported by the affected system), this vulnerability can cause the Apache Web server running under various operating systems to deny service.

Table 7.13.   Evaluation Scores of Base Metric Elements

Element	Symbol	Evaluation Value	Score
Access vector	AccessVector	Remote	1.0
Access complexity	AccessComplexity	Medium	0.9
Authentication	Authentication	No need	1.0
Privilege	Privilege	General user	1.0
Confidentiality impact	ConfImpact	Completely affected	1.0
Integrity impact	IntegImpact	Partially affected	0.7
Availability impact	AvailImpact	Partially affected	0.7
Impact bias	ImpactBias	Normal	0.333

Table 7.14.   Evaluation Scores of Temporal Metric Elements

Element	Symbol	Optional Value	Grading Standard
Exploitability	Exploitability	Functional code	0.95
Remediation level	RemediationLevel	Official patch	0.85
Technique detail	TechniqueDetail	Published	1.0
Detection capability	DetectionCapability	Low	1.0

In the improved CVSS evaluation, the values of base metric elements are as shown in Table 7.13, and the values of temporal metric elements are as shown in Table 7.14.

The score of base metrics is

$$BaseScore = round \left(10 \times 1.0 \times 0.9 \times 1.0 \times 1.0. \times ((0.7 \times 0.25) \right.$$
$$\left. + (0.7 \times 0.25) + (1.0. \times 0.5))\right) = 7.65. \quad (7.22)$$

The score of temporal metrics is

$$TemporalScore = round \left(7.65. \times 0.95. \times 0.85. \times 1.0. \times 1.0\right) = 6.18. \quad (7.23)$$

Since the system has the characteristic of random dynamic change, assuming that at the next moment it is switched to provide external Web services with IIS, but there is a MS15-034 remote execution vulnerability, then for the description of the vulnerability one can refer to the TechNet technical resource library (https://tcch

net.microsoft.com/zh-CN/library/security/ms15-034.aspx). IIS is a Web service program provided by Microsoft. It can provide HTTP, HTTPS, FTP, and other related services. At the same time, it supports ASP, JSP, and other Web-side scripts, and has a relatively wide range of applications. According to the level of MS15-034 and related descriptions, an attacker can obtain the execution code and privilege escalation capability of a remote host running IIS service, which aims at driving HTTP.SYS to implement a specially constructed HTTP request, and execute arbitrary code in context of the system account. Versions affected by this vulnerability include: Windows 7 (most versions do not install IIS by default), Windows Server 2008 R2, Windows 8, Windows 8.1, Windows Server 2012, Windows Server 2012 R2.

In the improved CVSS evaluation, the values of base metric elements are as shown in Table 7.15, and the values of temporal metric elements are as shown in Table 7.16.

Table 7.15.   Evaluation Scores of Base Metric Elements

Element	Symbol	Evaluation Value	Score
Access vector	AccessVector	Remote	1.0
Access complexity	AccessComplexity	Low	1.0
Authentication	Authentication	No need	1.0
Privilege	Privilege	General user	1.0
Confidentiality impact	ConfImpact	Completely affected	1.0
Integrity impact	IntegImpact	Partially affected	0.7
Availability impact	AvailImpact	Partially affected	0.7
Impact bias	ImpactBias	Normal	0.333

Table 7.16.   Evaluation Scores of Temporal Metric Elements

Element	Symbol	Optional Value	Grading Standard
Exploitability	Exploitability	Verification method	0.9
Remediation level	RemediationLevel	Official patch	0.85
Technique detail	TechniqueDetail	Published	1.0
Detection capability	DetectionCapability	Low	1.0

The score of base metrics is

$$BaseScore = round\ (10 \times 1.0 \times 1.0 \times 1.0 \times 1.0 \times ((0.7. \times 0.25)$$
$$+ (0.7 \times 0.25) + (1.0 \times 0.5))) = 8.5. \qquad (7.24)$$

The score of temporal metrics is

$$TemporalScore = round\ (8.5. \times 0.9. \times 0.85. \times 1.0. \times 1.0) = 6.50. \tag{7.25}$$

According to the above calculation results, it can be seen that when the system's external Web service is switched from the Apache server to the IIS server, although the status has changed, the Web service vulnerability level has been increased from 6.18 to 6.50. That is, from the perspective of attackers, the vulnerability after status change seems to be easier to exploit. It shows that not every change in system state is effective. If system change fails to fundamentally eliminate the number of security vulnerabilities and reduce their levels, it will instead give attackers a chance. Of course, in the actual network attack–defense game, whether an attacker can seize such an opportunity to successfully invade the system still requires careful modeling of attacker behaviors. The next section will try to measure and comprehensively evaluate the change of the attack surface from the perspective of the network attack–defense game.

7.4   Effectiveness Evaluation of Moving Target Defense Based on Attack Surface Measurement

7.4.1   *Effectiveness Evaluation of Moving Target Defense Against Network Attack–Defense Game*

The overall effectiveness evaluation based on system randomization metric sets and the single criterion evaluation based on vulnerability classification have been introduced earlier. All the above-mentioned evaluation methods are considered from the perspective of "knowing yourself", that is, changes of the attacker's behaviors and policies are not considered for the time being. In the actual network attack–defense games, behaviors and policies of both the attacker and the defender are dynamically changing, and there is a zero-sum game between them. If the attacker elements are introduced, modeling the attacker's behaviors and directly evaluating dynamic changes of the system attack surface during the attack–defense game can effectively verify scientificity and rationality of the dynamic enablement technology.

An attack surface is a series of ways for attackers to enter the information system and possibly cause damage, that is, the operating system, software, data, and network system resources used to attack the system. The larger the attack surface, the less secure the system. System security vulnerabilities are difficult to eradicate completely. In the case of inevitably existing vulnerabilities, the way to reduce security risks is to reduce the system attack surface. The main idea of moving target defense is to present an ever-changing attack surface to attackers, and increase difficulty for attackers to detect and use the attack surface, in order to achieve the effect of reducing the system attack surface. In short, the process of continually improving the security protection system is the process of continually reducing the attack surface.

The idea of achieving security through dynamic changes is mainly based on automatically generating system variables or target programs that can change certain characteristics of the system. At present, the industry's research work focuses on the specific implementation technology of moving target defense. There is still lack of formal analysis and measurement methods for the changing attack surface of the system, so it is difficult to evaluate the actual effectiveness of moving target defense. This section attempts to comprehensively evaluate moving target defense from the perspective of dynamic change of the system attack surface. It should be noted that due to the treacherous and varied behaviors and attack processes of cyber attackers (national level/gangs/individuals, etc.), there is no definite conclusion on objective description and theoretical modeling in the industry at present. Therefore, attack surface measurement methods based on stochastic Petri network and Markov chain described in what follows still need more attack–defense practices to verify.

7.4.2   *Attack Surface Measurement Methods Based on Stochastic Petri Network*

7.4.2.1   *Attack behavior description model*

Compared with the discrete time model at a given time interval, it is easier to use a stochastic model to fully and effectively describe the security of network and system state. accurately characterize the random behavior of the information system and the correlation between attackers, calculate various security indexes, and solve various security properties.

The description model of network attack behavior is shown in Figure 7.4.

The above model consists of the following elements.

(a) System boundary: Defines functions and input/output boundaries of the system.
(b) Function module: The code unit for the system to complete its own functions.

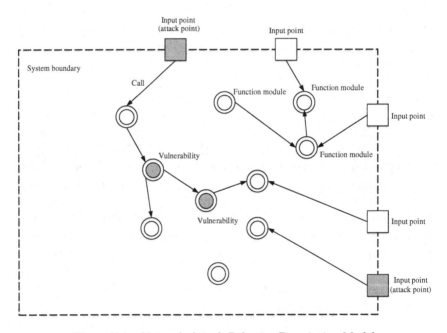

Figure 7.4.   Network Attack Behavior Description Model

(c) Vulnerability: The functional modules that may be used maliciously. They are constant for the system and their number will not change.

(d) Input point: An interface through which the system accepts external information and changes its own operating state. The input data packets include normally called data and maliciously injected data.

(e) Attack point: An input point that can trigger a vulnerability through a call path.

(f) Attack sequence: An input information stream used to trigger a vulnerability at an attack point.

(g) Attack surface: The number of attack points in the system at a certain moment. The size of the attack surface can change due to dynamic characteristics of the system.

(h) Dynamic policy: Makes the system have dynamic characteristics and dynamically change the connection relationship between input points and functional modules according to a predetermined configuration, which may make the input point that was originally an attack point no longer an attack point, and vice versa, thus causing dynamic change of the system attack surface, as shown in Figure 7.5. Change of the dynamic policy is completed within a certain time interval. To simplify the description, the model in this section assumes that the change is in place instantaneously.

It can be seen that under influence of the dynamic change policy, the number of system input points may also change due to the additional influence of the control policy.

7.4.2.2 *Description of attacker capability*

Attackers hope to break through the security defense system of the information system, find and exploit security vulnerabilities, so as to achieve the purpose of destroying the system and stealing data. Attackers can mobilize the three elements of space resources, time resources, and personal skills to accelerate the attack process. For ordinary attackers, they need to traverse each input point of the system to find the attack points that may trigger the vulnerability to take effect. It is assumed that after the attacker finds the attack point, its breakthrough time conforms to probability distribution

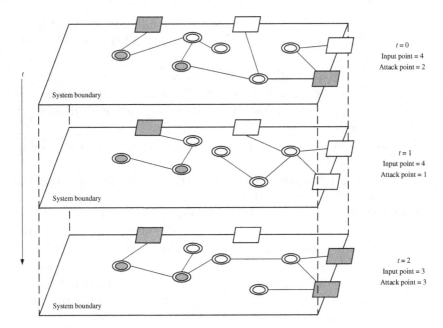

Figure 7.5. Dynamic Change Diagram of System Attack Surface

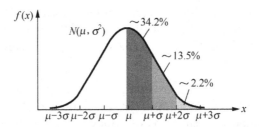

Figure 7.6. Probability Model of Time Consumed by Attackers to Break Through the System

of the position parameter μ and the scale parameter σ, as shown in Figure 7.6, where σ reflects the attacker's space resources and μ reflects the attacker's personal skills. The attacker's time resources cannot play a significant role in the information system with rapid and dynamic changes.

The distribution is described as

$$f(x) = \frac{1}{\sqrt{2\pi}\sigma} \exp\left(-\frac{(x-\mu)^2}{2\sigma^2}\right) \qquad (7.26)$$

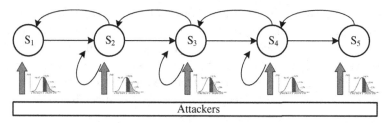

Figure 7.7.   System State Change Model from Attacker's Perspective

It can be seen that the larger the system attack surface, the more likely that the attacker will find the attack point; the stronger the attacker's personal skills, the earlier the attacker is expected to break the vulnerability; the more abundant the space resources available to the attacker, the shorter the overall time consumed to break through the vulnerability.

Combining capabilities of the attacker with random changes in the system, we can get the attacker view as shown in Figure 7.7.

When the system enters each state, the attacker resets the time and generates a corresponding normal probability distribution according to size of the attack surface existing in the system, the attacker's capabilities, and the space resources available to the attacker. Based on this, the threat coefficient that the system is facing can be obtained.

Scenario 1: The system is about to transit to another state, and when state transition is completed, the attacker has not yet made a breakthrough. In this case, the threat that the system faces during this time period is considered to be zero.

Scenario 2: The system is about to transit to another state, and before state transition is completed, the attacker has made a breakthrough. In this case, the threat that the system faces during this time period is considered to be the product of the attacker's personal skills and the time interval (from the time the attacker makes a breakthrough to the time the system completes state transition).

Scenario 3: The next state of the system is still this state. After state transition is completed, the attacker does not reset time, and still runs the probability of normal distribution breakthrough with the original parameters. If a breakthrough is made within this time period, then refer to scenario 2.

Assuming that the attacker does not record all attack points, then within a certain execution interval, the threat value the system is facing can be obtained through emulation. The threat value can be controlled by adjusting parameters of the system's dynamic change random time. It can be expected that reducing the time the system remains in the attack surface state will help reduce threats.

7.4.2.3   *Stochastic Petri network model of system dynamic change*

Stochastic Petri Network (SPN) is an effective method among the state-based stochastic model analysis methods [15]. It has a strong dynamic analysis capability for concurrency, asynchrony, and uncertainty of the system, and has the advantages of fewer module primitives and intuitive graphical representation. It can not only describe the state of the system, but also represent the behavior of the system, which is especially suitable for modeling and analysis of the system. At the same time, various characteristic parameters of the information system can be solved based on the characteristic that the stochastic Petri network and the Markov process are isomorphic. The stochastic Petri network can complete system description, security analysis, and verification and testing in a graphical manner on the framework of a system model, as shown in Figure 7.8.

Stochastic Petri nets can be used to reflect parameters of the system's random dynamic change and the attacker's capabilities in the same system. Given a property of interest to users, it is possible to run the model and solve the problem by means of emulation, giving answers to the following questions. (a) Activity problem: If the threats accumulate to a certain value, it can be considered that the attacker has captured the system. Calculate the average time that attacker can capture the system. (b) Path reachability problem: Given the restriction condition that the system threat does not exceed a certain value within a certain time period, can a system path (change pattern) be found to meet the constraint? (c) Parameter problem: Under the condition that state transition probability of the system is unchanged, given the constraint that the system threat does not exceed a certain value within a certain time period and the system has the minimum change time, optimize the time parameters configured by the system for each transition.

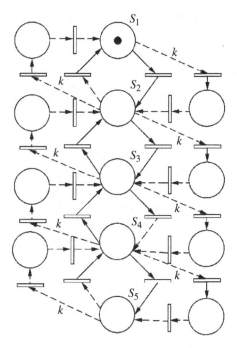

Figure 7.8. Stochastic Petri Network Description Model

7.4.3 *Attack Surface Measurement Method Based on Markov Chain*

In the following, an attack surface modeling measurement method based on Markov chain is proposed. Through the attack detection probability index, it quantitatively measures the changing attack surface, and analyzes and validates effectiveness and implementation policy of the moving target defense method in the network attack–defense game.

7.4.3.1 *Model description*

Three types of security protection methods such as control, detection, and dynamics can act on the attack surface W. It is assumed that each input point of the system may become an attack point, and these attack points are integrated into the attack surface. Therefore, W can be regarded as the number of all input points of the system.

(a) Control method: It is a method to directly reduce state space of the attack surface. After control, the attack surface changes to $W_c = W - \sum C$, where C is the specific control measure.

(b) Detection method: It is a method to indirectly reduce the attack surface state space. Detection can provide auxiliary support for control. After detection, the attack surface changes to $W_m = W_c - \sum M$, where M is the specific detection measure.

(c) Dynamic method: It is state transition of the attack surface between each state with a certain probability. The transition probabilities between various states constitute a transition probability matrix. The state after a certain time is only related to the state at that time, but not to the previous state. This mathematical model conforms to the Markov process condition of time dispersion and state dispersion [10], that is, the Markov chain.

Regardless of the initial state, the system will eventually reach a balanced state after a finite-step transition. Therefore, the probability that the system attack surface will eventually fall into a certain state can be determined, and the mathematical expectation of the attack surface, that is, the desired defense effect of the dynamic changes can be calculated. The relevant calculation model is shown in Figures 7.9 and 7.10.

Definition 7.1: Supposing that system state S is a discrete set $\boldsymbol{A} = \{A_0, A_1, \cdots, A_n\}$, the number of attack points for each state A_i is K_i, the transition probability between states is P_{ti}, and the attack surface detection probability is P_{di}, then the system state transition matrix is an *n+1* order square matrix, which can be defined as

$$\boldsymbol{P} = \begin{bmatrix} p_{0,0} & \cdots & p_{0,n} \\ \vdots & \ddots & \vdots \\ p_{n,0} & \cdots & p_{n,n} \end{bmatrix} \tag{7.27}$$

7.4.3.2 *Measurement method of changing attack surface*

According to whether attackers and defenders know the specific situations of the state attack surface, the model can be refined into the following four situations.

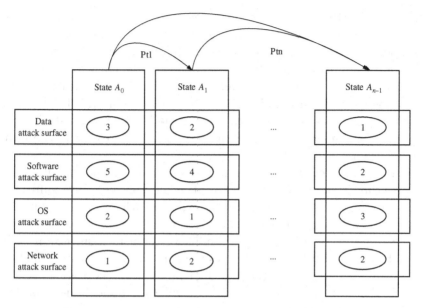

Figure 7.9.   Diagram of Attack Surface State Transition

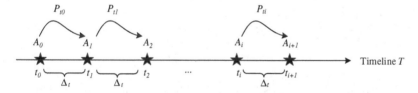

Figure 7.10.   Markov Chain State Transition on Attack Surface

(a) The first case: The defender is not clear about the specific situation of the state attack surface. Shift of the system attack points is random. The attacker has sufficient capabilities to master the attack path at each moment within the time interval, that is $P_{di} = 1$.

(b) The second case: The defender knows the specific situations of the attack surface, and intentionally guides the system to shift in the direction of reduced attack surface, that is $\forall i, k_i \leq k_0$. At the same time, the attacker has sufficient capabilities to master the attack path at each moment within the time interval Δt. This situation is similar to the first situation, except that the system state space is reduced.

(c) The third case: The defender does not know the specific situations of the state attack surface, that is, shift of the system attack points is random, and the attacker may not have sufficient capabilities to master the attack path at each moment within the time interval Δt. Suppose that detection probability of the attack surface in each state is P_d, $P_d \in [0,1]$. This is similar to the first case, which is equivalent to solving the Markov chain stationary state equation in the state space set $\{A_i P_{di}\}$. If $\forall i$, $P_{di=1}$, and it degenerates into the first case.

(d) The fourth case: The defender is aware of the specific situation of the attack surface, and the attacker may not have sufficient capabilities to master the attack path at each moment within the time interval Δt. This situation is most beneficial to the defender. Suppose that detection probability of the attack surface in each state is P_d, $P_d \in [0,1]$. This is similar to the second case, which is equivalent to solving the Markov chain stationary state equation in the state space set $\{A_i P_{di}\}$. If $\forall i$, $P_{di=1}$, and it degenerates into the second case.

If the transition probability matrix between system states is $\boldsymbol{P}_t$, then according to equation (7.28), stationary distribution of the Markov chain X^* can be obtained.

$$X^* = X^* \times P \qquad (7.28)$$

If the attack surface detection probability vector is $\boldsymbol{P}_d$, the expectation of the system state is

$$A^* = X^*(k \times \boldsymbol{P}_d) \qquad (7.29)$$

From the perspective of defenders, we hope to adopt appropriate dynamic methods and system state transition policies, so that

$$X^*(K \times \boldsymbol{P}_d) \leqslant k_0 \qquad (7.30)$$

k_0 is the initial value of the static system attack surface, that is, the trend of the system attack surface is shrinking.

7.4.3.3 *Attack detection probability measurement method*

Attack detection probability P_d is an important index that affects the dynamic system's attack surface and has a great influence on the mathematical expectation of the attack surface. The attack detection probability can be quantified from several dimensions such as state transition rate, randomization degree, and state space size, and the total contribution of state transition rate, randomization degree, state space size, and detection protection capability to attack detection probability can be evaluated.

Definition 7.2: Supposing that the state transition time interval of the dynamic system S is $\Delta t \in [0, T_0]$, the randomization degree is $R \in [0, 1]$, the state space size is the number of states $N \in [0, N_0]$, the detection and protection capability is the detection packet interception rate $L \in [0, 1]$, then the state attack surface detection rate P_d of the dynamic system S is

$$P_d = \frac{\Delta t}{T_0} \times R \times \frac{N}{N_0} \times L \qquad (7.31)$$

T_0 is defined as the maximum time required to detect all attack surfaces, and N_0 is defined as the maximum number of state spaces that the defender can transform.

7.4.3.4 *Example analysis*

Suppose that the initial state attack surface of a cloud center can be transited between 5 states, and the state space of the attack surface S is $\boldsymbol{A} = \{A_0, A_1, A_2, A_3, A_4\}$. Suppose that the transition rule for this state is: If it is in states A_1, A_2, A_3 before transition, it will transition one state forward or backward with the probability of $1/3$, respectively, or stay in place; if it is at the point of A_0 before transition, it will transition to A_1 with the probability of 1; if it is at the point of A_4 before transition, it will transition to A_3 with the probability of 1. Therefore, the system transition probability matrix is

$$\boldsymbol{P} = \begin{bmatrix} 0 & 1 & 0 & 0 & 0 \\ \frac{1}{3} & \frac{1}{3} & \frac{1}{3} & 0 & 0 \\ 0 & \frac{1}{3} & \frac{1}{3} & \frac{1}{3} & 0 \\ 0 & 0 & \frac{1}{3} & \frac{1}{3} & \frac{1}{3} \\ 0 & 0 & 0 & 1 & 0 \end{bmatrix} \qquad (7.32)$$

The stationary state vector $\boldsymbol{X} = (x_1, x_2, x_3, x_4, x_5)$ is calculated by $\boldsymbol{X} = \boldsymbol{X}\boldsymbol{P}$, that is

$$\begin{cases} x_1 = 0 \cdot x_1 + \frac{1}{3}x_2 + 0 \cdot x_3 + 0 \cdot x_4 + 0 \cdot x_5 \\ x_2 = x_1 + \frac{1}{3}x_2 + \frac{1}{3}x_3 + 0 \cdot x_4 + 0 \cdot x_5 \\ x_3 = 0 \cdot x_1 + \frac{1}{3}x_2 + \frac{1}{3}x_3 + \frac{1}{3}x_4 + 0 \cdot x_5 \\ x_4 = 0 \cdot x_1 + 0 \cdot x_2 + \frac{1}{3}x_3 + \frac{1}{3}x_4 + x_5 \\ x_5 = 0 \cdot x_1 + 0 \cdot x_2 + 0 \cdot x_3 + \frac{1}{3}x_4 + 0 \cdot x_5 \\ x_1 + x_2 + x_3 + x_4 + x_5 = 1 \end{cases} \quad (7.33)$$

The above equation is solved to obtain

$$\boldsymbol{X} = \left(\frac{1}{11}, \frac{3}{11}, \frac{3}{11}, \frac{3}{11}, \frac{1}{11} \right) \quad (7.34)$$

Therefore, after the finite-step state transition, the expected value of the system state is

$$A^* = \frac{1}{11}k_0 P_{d0} + \frac{3}{11}k_1 P_{d1} + \frac{3}{11}k_2 P_{d2} + \frac{3}{11}k_3 P_{d3} + \frac{1}{11}k_4 P_{d4} \quad (7.35)$$

(1) Results analysis of changing attack surface

(a) The first case: The defender is not clear about the specific situation of the state attack surface. Shift of the system attack points is random. The attacker has sufficient capabilities to master the attack path at each moment within the time interval.

Supposing that the initial state attack surface $k_0 = 4$, $k_1 = 7$, $k_2 = 3$, $k_3 = 2$, $k_4 = 5$, then the expectation of the attack surface $A^* = 4.09$.

(b) The second case: The defender knows the specific situations of the attack surface, and intentionally guides the system to shift in the direction of reduced attack surface. The attacker has sufficient capabilities to master the attack path at each moment within the time interval.

Supposing that the initial state attack surface $k_0 = 4$, $k_1 = 3$, $k_2 = 2$, $k_3 = 4$, $k_4 = 1$, then the expectation of the attack surface $A^* = 2.90$.

(c) The third case: The defender is not clear about the specific situations of the state attack surface. Shift of the system attack points is random. The attacker may not have sufficient capabilities to master the attack path at each moment within the time interval.

Similar to the first case, supposing that the initial state attack surface $k_0 = 4$, $k_1 = 7$, $k_2 = 9$, $k_3 = 2$, $k_4 = 5$, the attack surface detection probability $P_{d_0} = 0.3$, $P_{d_1} = 0.5$, $P_{d_2} = 0.4$, $P_{d_3} = 0.2$, $P_{d_4} = 0.6$, then the mathematical expectation of the attack surface $A^* = 2.43$.

(d) The fourth case: The defender knows the specific situations of the attack surface, and intentionally guides the system to shift in the direction of reduced attack surface. The attacker may not have sufficient capabilities to master the attack path at each moment within the time interval.

Similar to the second case, supposing that the initial state attack surface $k_0 = 4$, $k_1 = 3$, $k_2 = 2$, $k_3 = 4$, $k_4 = 1$, the attack surface detection probability $P_{d_0} = 0.3$, $P_{d_1} = 0.5$, $P_{d_2} = 0.4$, $P_{d_3} = 0.2$, $P_{d_4} = 0.6$, then the mathematical expectation of the attack surface $A^* = 1.009$.

From the perspective of defenders, we hope to adopt appropriate protection methods and system state transition policies, so that

$$A^* = \frac{1}{11}k_0 P_{d0} + \frac{3}{11}k_1 P_{d1} + \frac{3}{11}k_2 P_{d2} + \frac{3}{11}k_3 P_{d3} + \frac{1}{11}k_4 P_{d4} \le k_0 \tag{7.36}$$

In the third case above, the following constraint is imposed on the attacker detection probability, namely

$$4P_{d0} + 21P_{d1} + 27P_{d2} + 6P_{d3} + 5P_{d4} \le 44 \tag{7.37}$$

Convert to vector multiplication as

$$[4\ 21\ 27\ 6\ 5] \cdot \boldsymbol{P}_d^T \le 44 \tag{7.38}$$

For simplicity, supposing that the detection probability of each attack P_{di} is the same constant, then $P_d^* \le \frac{44}{63} = 0.698$, and this is the inflection point to judge whether the system state adjustment policy is effective, as shown in Figure 7.11.

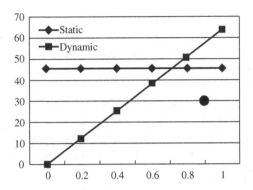

Figure 7.11.   Inflection Point of System Dynamic Adjustment

As can be seen from Figure 7.11, when $P_d^* \geqslant 0.698$, the mathematical expectation of the dynamic system's attack surface is greater than the value of the static system. At this time, dynamic adjustment of the system has no protective effect.

(2) Simplified analysis of attack detection probability

The detection probability is closely related to various factors, such as the attacker's skill level, mastery degree of the system in advance, the number of computing resources, and the length of analysis time. For simplicity, supposing that given the computing resources, and without considering the randomization degree and state space, etc., the detection probability is only linearly related to the time that allows the attacker to analyze the system, and the system state changes periodically, then the equation (7.31) becomes

$$P_d = \Delta t / T_0 \qquad (7.39)$$

Δt is the time interval during which the system state changes, and T_0 is the time period required for the attacker to study all attack points of the system at the current moment.

Suppose that an attacker organization can analyze all attack points in the current state of the system within 12 hours when given certain attack resources. In the third case of the above calculation example, the minimum time period $\Delta^* t_s$ for the system state adjustment policy to take effect can be calculated through $\frac{\Delta t_s}{12} \times 63 \leq 44$ and the result is 8.38 h, that is, the system state adjustment time period is at most 8.38 hours. If the adjustment period is greater than this value, the attacker will be able to capture more attack surfaces than those in the static state, which makes the dynamic adjustment policy of system state meaningless.

7.5 Moving Target Defense and System Availability Evaluation

As mentioned earlier, defenders are not always able to shift and reduce the attack surface. In order to provide the required services to users of the system, defenders may have to enable some new features or modify the original features, thereby increasing the bearing value of the attack surface. For example, users may need to access the system remotely. To meet such requirements, defenders have to open a new communication channel, such as a TCP port. The increase in attack surface may make the system suffer new attacks. Similarly, the reduction of attack surface also has to pay a price, because it will disable or modify features of the system, causing the system to fail to provide some services. Therefore, defenders must make trade-offs between security and availability when implementing moving target defense.

When applying dynamic enablement technology in actual systems, it is necessary to answer questions such as how much the cost (performance, availability, etc.) needs to be paid, how to model and measure these costs, and how dynamic enablement implements optimal deployment based on the above costs. K. A. Farris and G. Cybenko [16] summarized the comprehensive measurement methods for the effectiveness, implementation cost, performance cost, availability, and security priority of the existing dynamically enabled systems, as shown in Table 7.17.

The meanings of the properties in Table 7.17 are as follows.

Effectiveness: Prevent the enemy from succeeding successfully by increasing the burden.

Implementation cost: Cost of deploying defenses in the enterprise system.

Performance cost: Performance loss of the host and the network after defenses are deployed in the enterprise system.

Availability: Efforts made by administrators and end users to manage and apply defensive methods.

Security priority: The importance of solving the attack surface problem.

Table 7.17.   Comprehensive Measurement Methods of Dynamically Enabled System

Dimension \ Method	Analytics (Mathematics or Data)	Testbed Network	Emulation	Red Team Test	Expert Investigation	Actual Operation and Maintenance Network
Effectiveness	√	o	o	√	o	o
Implementation cost	√	o	×	×	o	√
Performance cost	×	√	o	×	o	√
Availability	×	×	×	×	o	√
Security priority	√	×	√	√	o	×

Analytics (mathematics or data): The method of network defense evaluation using mathematical means or data analysis, including parameter adaptation, mathematical modeling, etc. The relevant models may come from operation and maintenance research, game theory, computer performance model, etc.

Testbed network: Evaluate the load and traffic of the system in an isolated network environment by using instrument testing.

Emulation: Run business, load, and traffic on a single computer or a small network to reproduce the defense behavior of the system. The emulation output results give the conclusion of defense means or system reliability.

Red team test: Experts act as penetration testers, perform stress tests on actual networks or testbeds, find and exploit system vulnerabilities, evaluate the effectiveness of defense methods, and point out the security focuses that the system should give priority to.

Expert investigation: Judgments and conclusions of the selected experts, which cannot be used for quantitative measurement.

Actual operation and maintenance network: Use the actual network in the real environment to implement evaluation.

In Table 7.17, the symbol "√" indicates that the property can be reliably measured by the corresponding method, symbol "o" indicates that the property is valid, but there is no guarantee that the corresponding method can always be used for reliable measurement, and symbol "×" indicates that the property cannot be reliably measured by the corresponding method in most cases.

According to the preliminary conclusions of many researchers such as Farris and Cybenko, control and game theory reasoning are better methods to evaluate the moving target defense technology and system availability in the network attack–defense game. The specific evaluation methods are described in detail in what follows.

7.5.1 Game Theory Method

In previous studies, we have not made any assumptions about attack policy changes of attackers. In this section, we will consider the method of reducing and shifting the attack surface in the moving target defense environment, that is, defenders achieve the goal of continuously protecting the system from attack by reducing and shifting the attack surface. In this regard, from the perspective of a two-player game, the relationship between defenders and attackers is modeled, and the optimal defense policy is determined by using game theory. Game theory model is helpful to clearly establish attacker model. Therefore, defenders can choose the optimal defense policy for different targets and their attack methods, such as script kiddies, veteran hackers, organized criminals, and hostile countries.

In the following, the mutual relationship between system defenders and attackers is modeled according to a two-player stochastic extended game [17].

7.5.1.1 Game model

Our model is a seven-tuple $\langle \boldsymbol{S}, \boldsymbol{A}^d, \boldsymbol{A}^a, T, R^d, R^a, \beta \rangle$, where $\boldsymbol{S}$ is a system state set, $\boldsymbol{A}^d$ is a defender action set, $\boldsymbol{A}^a$ is an attacker action set, $T : \boldsymbol{S} \times \boldsymbol{A}^d \times \boldsymbol{A}^a \times \boldsymbol{S} \to [0,1]$ is the state transition function, $R^d : \boldsymbol{S} \times \boldsymbol{A}^d \times \boldsymbol{A}^a \to \boldsymbol{R}$ is the defender's reward function (where $\boldsymbol{R}$ is a real number set), $R^a : \boldsymbol{S} \times \boldsymbol{A}^d \times \boldsymbol{A}^a \to \boldsymbol{R}$ is the attacker's reward function, and $\beta \leq 1$ is a discount factor, which represents discount of the expected reward.

The game between the defender and the attacker is played in the following way: The system is in state $\boldsymbol{s}_i \in \boldsymbol{S}$ at t. The defender makes an action $a^d \in \boldsymbol{A}^d$, and the attacker makes an action $a^a \in \boldsymbol{A}^a$. Subsequently, the system transits to state $s_{t+1} \in \boldsymbol{S}$ with the probability of $T(s_t, a^d, a^a, s_{t+1})$. The defender's reward for this action is $r_t^a = R^d(s_t, a^d, a^a)$, and the attacker's reward is $r_t^a = R^d(s_t, a^d, a^a)$. The purpose of both the defender and the attacker is to maximize their discounted rewards.

7.5.1.2   *State, action, and transition*

When modeling the system, we treat it as a feature set $\boldsymbol{F}$. $\boldsymbol{F}$ includes various features that the system can provide, for example, the login feature of the Web server provides authentication function for users. A feature can be disabled, if enabled, this feature will become one of the series of configurations. Each configuration is a mapping relationship between the state variable and its value. A state $s_i \in \boldsymbol{S}$ of the system is a mapping relationship between the feature and its configuration, that is, $s_t : \boldsymbol{F} \to$ configuration. In a certain system state, the defender can choose to shift and reduce the attack surface through actions on the feature. For example, the defender can enable a disabled feature, disable an enabled feature, modify the configuration of an enabled feature, or leave the configuration of a feature unchanged. Therefore, the defender's action $a^d \in \boldsymbol{A}^d$ is a mapping relationship between the feature and the actions issued by the defender on the feature, that is $a^d : \boldsymbol{F} \to \{$enable, disable, modify, and remain unchanged$\}$. In a certain system state, the defender can select from a certain subset of the action set $\boldsymbol{A}^d$. For example, if a certain feature f is in a configuration enabled by a state s, the defender cannot issue any action that enables f, but can only disable f, modify f, or leave f unchanged. When the defender makes a certain action, the attack surface of the system will change. Subsequently, the attacker will use this change in attack surface to launch a certain action to attack the system; the attacker's action will further enable and disable the system's features. Because actions of the defender and the attacker can enable and/or disable certain system features, the system will transition to a new state according to the probability transition function. The specific value of transition probability is determined by the system and its operating environment.

There are two deficiencies in this model: One is that state space explosion may occur, and the other is that action space explosion may occur. The number of states and operations is directly exponential with the number of features. In order to simplify and facilitate processing, only an important subset of system features will be of concern here, while limiting the number of features enabled, disabled, or modified by actions.

7.5.1.3   *Reward function*

When the defender takes an action, it may bring the following three benefits to the defender. First, the defender can provide convenience for system users by enabling features. Second, the defender can reduce security risks of the system by shifting the attack surface. Third, the defender can reduce security risks of the system by reducing metrics of the attack surface. However, if this action disables some features or improves attack surface metrics of the system, the defender may have to pay a certain price. Therefore, the defender's reward depends on change of the feature value, shift of the attack surface, and change of the attack surface metrics.

Similarly, when an attacker makes an action, the attacker will benefit from improvement of the attack surface metrics. But shift of the attack surface will also cause the attacker to pay a certain price. Therefore, the attacker's reward depends on shift of the attack surface and change of the attack surface metrics.

Let's take a state s of the system as an example. If the defender takes action a^d and the attacker takes action a^a in a state s, change of the system features is represented as ΔF, shift of the attack surface is represented as ΔAS, and change of the attack surface metrics is represented as ΔASM. Therefore, the following model can be established for the defender's reward R^d and the attacker's reward R^a :

$$R^d(s, a^d, a^a) = B_1(\Delta F) + B_2(\Delta AS) - C_1(\Delta ASM) \quad (7.40)$$
$$R^a(s, a^d, a^a) = B_3(\Delta ASM) - C_2(\Delta AS) \quad (7.41)$$

B_i and C_i are functions that map feature changes, attack surface shift changes, and attack surface metrics changes to the real numbers, which reflect the benefits and costs associated with changes. The actual selection of B_i and C_i depends on the specific system and its operating environment. Please note that when selecting the reward function, the general sum game is used.

7.5.1.4   *Optimal defense policy*

The game proposed above is a complete and perfect information game. Both sides know the policy and reward of their opponents, and are familiar with the history of this game, i.e. familiar with various operations taken by both sides in the game [18]. The aim of both sides is to maximize their expected discount reward.

The policy of each side refers to the action plan that each side can make in the game; the policy specifies the actions that one side can take against the policy of the other side in different phases of the game. The optimal policy can maximize the reward of the player involved in the game.

Static policy refers to a policy that has nothing to do with time and history but only relates to the system state. Pure policy refers to a policy in which a state corresponds to an action. Hybrid policy refers to a policy with a certain probability distribution among various possible actions in a state. Nash equilibrium method can be used to obtain the optimal static policy of defenders. Filar and Vrieze established a non-linear program for finding the static equilibrium policy in general sum game [19].

The defender may need an optimal policy that depends on time and history to obtain the optimal defender action for each game history. Therefore, the defender can take the optimal policy against the attacker's actions at any point in the game. The subgame perfect equilibrium concept can be used to determine the optimal policy for defenders [17]. Murray and Gordon established a dynamic programming algorithm for finding the subgame perfect equilibrium in the general sum game [20].

Thus, the defender can use the concepts of Nash equilibrium and subgame perfect equilibrium to determine the optimal policy for shifting and reducing the attack surface. Using the optimal policy, the defender makes a trade-off between security and availability after mastering all kinds of information; and in this way, the system can provide the required services for its users without reducing its security.

7.5.2   *Impact on System Development, Deployment, Operation, and Maintenance*

Dynamic enablement technology aims to realize network configuration randomization, instruction set randomization, software polymorphism, etc. Compared with traditional static technology, it may bring some impacts on the development, deployment, operation, and maintenance of information systems [21, 22].

(1) Software development

Because a large number of vulnerabilities are caused by negligence or poor skills of programmers, they cannot be expected to apply transformations for each polymorphism policy in a reliable and consistent manner. Polymorphism should be applied automatically at the end of the development phase as part of the compilation process. In fact, this cannot be fully automated. Developers must provide information which is needed for functions and must be reserved. This poses another challenge, namely, how to minimize the size and complexity of functional specifications required by the tool chain. However, when designing and developing software components, for many components, developers do not know much about how they will integrate with the entire system in the future. Therefore, it is a challenge to determine the source of each data item that flows through the entire program. One solution is to create a symbol source chart to bind input and output, regardless of whether an input is user-generated. In the system compilation phase, when components are connected and input sources are clearly defined, the system architecture designers or developers may recognize a few inputs sent by users, while the remaining inputs and outputs will be polymorphized.

(2) Performance impact

Polymorphism policy has unusually significant performance impact. For example, the randomized instruction set architecture can effectively counter buffer overflow attacks, but it also causes huge runtime performance overhead because commercial hardware platforms lack built-in support for this function. Therefore, the polymorphism of Internet Security and Acceleration Server (ISA) depends on the system emulator, which converts polymorphism instructions at runtime into real hardware instructions. This kind of emulator is extremely expensive, making ISA polymorphism a costly technology and limiting its use. At present, no general method has been found to optimize the polymorphism policy, but there is still optimism that performance overhead caused by the specific polymorphism policy may be reduced. And compared with other performance bottlenecks in the system, the performance overhead will become irrelevant.

(3) Software deployment

Polymorphism introduces new fault modes, and end-to-end polymorphism doubles the number of fault modes. In a Web application instance, XSS polymorphism may not bring new faults when encountering an attack, because in this case the attack is only unsuccessful, and actually polymorphism has no side effects. However, in the same instance, an attack against an SQL polymorphic application will cause the database to return a "No specified form" error, and the application may be unprepared for this error. The challenge here is to incorporate error handling into the polymorphic part when converting the application.

(4) Operation and maintenance management

There are mainly two different problems: One is the preparation cost of this complex system, and the other is the challenge of continuously managing the system. For example, building N different virtual servers requires more resources and work than building a single system. This problem can be buffered by incremental push-out. Instead of setting up all N virtual servers at once before the system starts to operate, it is better to lower the level of polymorphic program at the beginning, and then introduce some new virtual servers when they are ready. For daily management tasks, the key to reduce complexity is to use a virtual server as a standard template for the software stack management of each virtual server. When a component of a virtual server is patched or updated, the standard template for all virtual servers containing this component should be updated. Next, these K new virtual servers will be cloned with the updated standard virtual servers. To avoid being attacked, standard virtual servers cannot be deployed online.

7.6   Summary

In this chapter, effectiveness evaluation of the dynamic enablement technology is deeply studied, and three evaluation methods are mainly introduced: comprehensive evaluation based on measurable index sets, single criterion evaluation based on system vulnerabilities, and dynamic evaluation of the attack surface in the attack–defense

Table 7.18. Comparison of Evaluation Methods

Serial Number	Evaluation Methods	Technical Principles	Advantages	Disadvantages
1	Comprehensive evaluation based on measurable index sets	Analytical Hierarchy Process (AHP), fuzzy comprehensive evaluation	Comprehensive and systematic	Difficult to collect indexes, need prior data
2	Single criterion evaluation based on system vulnerabilities	Vulnerability analysis and mining	Simple and intuitive, easy to understand	High technical requirements for personnel
3	Dynamic evaluation of the attack surface in attack–defense game	Stochastic Petri network model, Markov chain model	Close to attack and defense practice, easy to understand	Model solving is complicated, and attacker modeling is difficult

game. The comparison of these three technologies is shown in Table 7.18.

As can be seen from Table 7.18, each evaluation method has its own advantages and disadvantages. The comprehensive evaluation based on measurable index sets can comprehensively measure the overall defense effectiveness of dynamic enablement technology, but due to the lack of measurement accuracy and objectivity of evaluation indexes, the credibility and application value of evaluation results may be reduced. On the other hand, the single criterion evaluation based on system vulnerabilities can intuitively and concisely reflect dynamic enablement effects, but it requires vulnerability analysts of high technical level. The attack surface dynamic evaluation in the attack–defense game introduces attacker elements, and directly evaluates dynamic changes of the system attack surface in the attack–defense game, which has good practicality. However, attacker modeling is not easy, and model solving is more complicated.

At present, the theory and application of dynamic enablement technology in the industry are not yet mature, and its comprehensive efficiency evaluation methods are still under exploration. This chapter is only a preliminary analysis on the effectiveness of the dynamic enablement technology. Nevertheless, we can still draw the following conclusions through the research results: (a) Dynamic enablement technology may not necessarily reduce the attack surface, and may be counterproductive. (b) Whether the defender knows the specific situations of the state attack surface has an important impact on the dynamic system's attack surface. If the defender does not know the specific situations, the attack surface of the dynamic system may be larger than that of the static system. (c) Attack detection probability is an important index that affects the attack surface of the dynamic system. The lower the detection probability, the smaller the attack surface. The detection probability value is mainly affected by factors such as state transition rate, randomization degree, state space size, and detection packet interception rate.

To achieve dynamic defense effect, the dynamic enablement technology must equip the following characteristics: (a) Fast and unpredictable state transition. Dynamic state transition must be fast to ensure that attackers do not have enough time and space to scout and detect targets, so as to realize the protection effect of reducing actual attack surface. (b) Sufficient state space to reduce the repetition of attack surfaces between different states and increase difficulty for attackers to master the system. (c) Transparent state transition. In the process of state transition, the protected target must be transparent to ensure that the entire session and service will not be interrupted by state transition.

In addition, when applying the dynamic enablement technology in actual systems, it is necessary to balance system efficiency with implementation cost, performance loss, availability, and security priority. This chapter uses game theory methods to model the relationship between defenders and attackers, makes a comprehensive evaluation of moving target defense and system availability, and points out the impact of dynamic enablement technology on the development, deployment, operation, and maintenance of information systems.

References

[1] Al-Shaer, E., Morrero, W., El-Atawy, A., *et al.* Network configuration in a box: Towards end-to-end verification of network reachability and security. *Proceedings of 17th International Conference Network Communication and Protocol (ICNP'09)*, 2009, 123–132.

[2] Boyd, S., Lucasto, M., Locasto, M. E., *et al.* On the general applicability of instruction-set randomization. *IEEE Transaction on Dependable and Secure Computing*, 2010, 7(3): 255–270.

[3] Salamal, B., Jackson, T., Santa Clara, C. A., *et al.* Run-time defense against code injection attacks using replicated exception. *IEEE Transaction on Dependable and Secure Computing*, 2011.

[4] Satty, T. L. How to make a decision: The analytic hierarchy process. *European Journal of Operational Research*, 1990.

[5] Hou, D. and Wang, Z. Theoretical exploration and application of non-linear evaluation. Hefei: University of Science and Technology of China Press, 2001.

[6] Liu, P. and Wu, M. Fuzzy theory and its applications. Changsha: National Defense Science and Technology University Press, 2000.

[7] Zadeh, L. A. Fuzzy sets. *Information and Control*, 1965, 8(3): 338–353.

[8] Nola, A. D., Sessa, S., Pedrycz, W., *et al.* Fuzzy relation equations and their applications to knowledge engineering. Kluwer Academic Publishers, 1989.

[9] Bolch, G., Greiner, S., Meer, H. D., *et al.* Queuing networks and markov chains-modeling and performance evaluation with computer science applications (2nd Edition). A John Wiley & Sons, Inc., Publication, 2006.

[10] Lu, D. Stochastic process and its application. Beijing: Tsinghua University Press, 1986.

[11] Wu, S., Guo, T., Dong, G., *et al.* Software vulnerability analysis technology. Beijing: Science Press, 2014.

[12] Sutton, M., Greene, A., and Amini, P. Fuzzing: Brute force vulnerability discovery. Translated by Duan, N. and Zhao, Y. Beijing: Publishing House of Electronics Industry, 2013.

[13] Perla, E. and Oldani, M. A guide to kernel exploitation: Attacking the core. Translated by Wu Shizhong. Beijing: China Machine Press, 2012.

[14] The Latest Update of CVSS. https://www.first.org/cvss/specificatio n-document.

[15] Lin, C., Li, Y., and Shan, Z. Performance evaluation of systems using stochastic petri nets. Beijing: Tsinghua University Press, 2005.

[16] Farris, K. A. and Cybenko, G. Quantification of moving target cyber defenses. Edward M. Carapezza (Ed.), *Sensors, and Command, Control, Communications, and Intelligence (C3I) Technologies for Homeland Security, Defense and Law Enforcement XIV*. Baltimore: USA, 2015.

[17] Osborne, M. and Rubinstein, A. A course in game theory . MIT Press, 1994.

[18] Roy, S., Ellis, C., Shiva, S., *et al.* A survey of game theory as applied to network security. *Hawaii International Conference on System Sciences*, 0, 2010, 1–10.

[19] Filar, J. and Vrieze, K. Competitive Markov decision processes. Springer, Berlin, 2012, 36(4): 343–358.

[20] Murray, C. and Gordon, G. Finding correlated equilibria in general sum stochastic games. *Technical Report CMU-ML-07-113*, Carnegie Mellon University, 2007.

[21] Jajodia, S., Ghosh, A. K., and Swarup, V. Moving target defense: Creating asymmetric uncertainty for cyber threats. Translated by Yang, L. Beijing: National Defense Industry Press, 2014.

[22] Yiu, H., Ghosh, A. K., Bracewell, T., *et al.* A security evaluation of a novel resilient web serving architecture: Lessons learned through industry/academia collaboration. *International Conference on Dependable Systems and Networks Workshops (DSN-W)*, 2010.

Index

Printed in the United States
by Baker & Taylor Publisher Services